I MEET
MY CONTEMPORARIES

I MEET MY CONTEMPORARIES

By

MAXIMILIAN HARDEN

Translated from the German by
WILLIAM C. LAWTON

With an Introduction by
the Hon. JAMES W. GERARD

Essay Index Reprint Series

BOOKS FOR LIBRARIES PRESS
FREEPORT, NEW YORK

First Published 1925
Reprinted 1968

LIBRARY OF CONGRESS CATALOG CARD NUMBER:
68-57319

PRINTED IN THE UNITED STATES OF AMERICA

FOREWORD

BEFORE 1914 we knew nothing of the real Germany —today we are still ignorant of the great personalities of Germany.

Among these, Maximilian Harden stands out—a fearless brain-giant. Of course, I do not always agree with him, but this man of mystery who in the Germany of 1916 dared to defend President Wilson, who more than once defied the Kaiser, who was the intimate friend of the great Bismarck, has played a great rôle not only in the political life of Europe but in the intellectual development of the German people.

We, in America, owe it to the world to support the new Germany, the new Republic which has to fight for its existence against the Reds on one side and those who would restore the Hohenzollerns and once more plunge the world in war. We owe it ourselves to search the soul of this new Germany—above all to read the books of this Maximilian Harden whose vision in time of war was so clear and who so ably dissects the motives of nations and of men.

I knew Harden when I was in Berlin—he dined and lunched in our Embassy. His whole personality breathes fearlessness—courage, and it was the courage of no minor quality which carried him through by contests with the most powerfully organized government the world has ever seen.

His power of delineating a personality is more than photographic—his keen mind discovers not only the outstanding traits of men, but their hidden thoughts, their secret motives are as plain to him as if he pierced their being with a mental x-ray.

You must read this book.

                              (Signed)   JAMES W. GERARD.
September 24, 1924.

CONTENTS

I MEET
MY CONTEMPORARIES

I

MAXIMILIAN HARDEN

MAXIMILIAN HARDEN was born in Berlin, in 1862, the son of a merchant. When many years after marriage a separation of his parents became necessary, an imperious craving for freedom drove the boy from the desolated home to the theater, a course then still regarded as a disgraceful one. Much too young, and without proper preparation, he followed this career for a few years, playing youthful hero rôles in German classics, Shakespeare's Romeo and Mark Antony, but also happier lovers in modern dramas. Naturally, in so short a time and at so immature an age, he did not attain to the foremost rank. One of the most eminent German actors, however, Oscar Sauer, who chanced to see him on the stage in a provincial capital, wrote, several decades later, when at the point of death (and so, impartially): "You would have become a Josef Kainz, a foremost man, if you had not turned to a higher calling."

Harden did in fact presently return (an action almost unheard-of) to the Berlin gymnasium, from which his longing for freedom had driven him. The task of interpreting the thoughts and feelings of others, and setting them forth dramatically, did not satisfy him. He wished to be a student, but his father did not put the necessary means at his disposal, and his mother had barely enough for her own needs. His father's wish was that the son should also be a merchant.

So for the second time he left the gymnasium, where he had been by far the youngest member of the second class ("Secunda") at the time of his "first flight." The director gave public expression to his keen regret at losing "the best student in the institution" just before the completion of his course. What knowledge Harden has acquired he owes to his own persistent efforts. As the university career was closed to him, he turned to literature. Characteristically, his first political article was directed, with unheard-of audacity, against William von Hohenzollern, who, then Crown Prince, was endeavoring, by the powerful means of militaristic self-advertising, to displace his father, the dying Emperor Frederic, in the favor of the people. The article was entitled *The Inheritance of Byzantium*. It opened the series of Harden's calls to battle against the "Neo-Byzantinism of Berlin"—the mischief innate in the flesh and bones of Wilhelm II.

Overnight, so to speak, Harden became the best known dramatic and literary critic in Germany. Soon after, he began the publication of satires (later collected), which he signed with the pseudonym "Apostata," to intimate that he had cut loose from all traditional orthodox partisan ideas, and, without regard for what would best please his readers, would say what to him seemed right. Under this banner he uttered terribly harsh truths, mingling passionate feeling with biting wit, against the ruling class in Germany, and especially the Kaiser and his court.

These satires were eagerly devoured, and their remarkable success suggested the idea of creating a special periodical for Maximilian Harden. He brought out the weekly *Future* (*Die Zukunft*). What that periodical became for the choicest spirits, not of Germany alone, is most clearly seen from the judgments of the philosopher-poet, August Strindberg, which, without knowing Harden personally, he passed upon him and his work (*Letters to his translator, Scherling*).

"MY DEAR MR. SCHERLING:

"It was my intention to congratulate Harden at the turn of the year, but I am afraid of saying something awry in my poor German. Please thank him for the hospitality that he has shown me in his magazine, and assure him of my limitless admiration. It is needless to tell him how important he is in the life of Germany. That he himself knows. He speaks once a week to the German nation, and is heard.

"If ever he were condemned to drink hemlock, it would be for Socrates' crime: 'I am not an Athenian (German) but a cosmopolitan.'

"Every number of the *Zukunft* brings such a wealth of ideas that I do not venture to read it through, for fear my own creative thought would be cut off or misled.

"Tell him, I should count it a high honor to be busied in one corner of his workshop.

"That is my sincere feeling, which I cannot suppress.

"Your

"AUGUST STRINDBERG.

"Stockholm, January, 1904."

"Die Zukunft is a Parliament, a free Reichstag for Europe, a permanent Congress, and he who wishes to know the future, can study it in *Die Zukunft.*

"AUGUST STRINDBERG.

"Furnsund, July 4, 1904."

"MY DEAR MR. SCHERLING:

"To see the first section of my *Swedish Nature* taken up into the *Zukunft* delights and honors me; and yet that work has cost me long years. I have been astonished at Harden's omniscience. Is he a mediumistic writer, or has he a Dæmon who dictates to him? His article actually bristles with wisdom. How can that solitary man have seen and heard it all?

"AUGUST STRINDBERG.

"Stockholm, August 24, 1904."

Nothing like the effect of the little brown numbers had ever been seen in Germany before; perhaps never attained in all Europe since the Junius letters. Without exaggeration it can be said that every European diplomatist read them in the hands of court-flunkeys, and that in the "Special train" of the "Old War Lord" the time was whiled away with this reading. The weekly brought with it one of the weightiest and most stimulating supplements. Here Behring first made his diphtheria serum known. The best writers in all departments of science, on international politics and sociology, were contributors. Masterpieces of Tolstoy, Maupassant, Bjornson, Fontane, Heyse, Spielhagen, Brentano, Zola, Anatole France, Schaeffle, Lemaître, and a whole Pleiad of more recent authors, appeared here. Naumann who was Bismarck's special physician, Rathenau, and others were first introduced by Harden. The congratulatory address presented to Harden on the tenth anniversary of *Zukunft's* foundation bore such names as Bjornson, Meunier, Forel, Kraft-Ebing, Lamprecht, Witwe, Mauthner, Rilke, Lagerloef, Kienzl —to cull merely a few out of the host. The "glorious misfortune," if it may be so expressed, was that in spite of all it was properly only Harden who in these pages was sought out and craved, and that every number in which he did not appear as chief contributor (which happened very rarely) brought disappointment with it.

In the contest which Wilhelm's immeasurable vanity carried on against Bismarck, the creator of the Empire, Harden took sides for the man of genius and against legitimacy (here disgraced by a crowned head); not, as might be imagined, because Bismarck's policy in all its details had his approval, but because he was enraged at the mendacity with which an empty-headed play-actor drove out, as he would a tiresome servant, the man to whom his house owed everything. And the pitiful thing that posed as "public opinion" in Germany was even then deceived. It huzzaed for the Kaiser, and reviled the Chancellor. Harden was the first to point out in Bismarck the "visionary," the "musician," the "statesman by instinct" of the Shakespearean type.

When the ex-Chancellor, who sat in loneliness, under a ban, in his home at Friedrichsruhe, had twice invited Harden to visit him, he did so, and often thereafter lingered as Bismarck's guest on his estates.

In a famous suit it was legally established by testimony that during one of these visits Bismarck had brought to him from the wine cellar the bottle of "Steinberger Cabinet" which the Kaiser (after a reconciliation with the ex-Chancellor, who had meantime attained a fabulous popularity) had sent as a tonic to the invalid, and had said to Harden: "I made up my mind to drink it with you, because you feel just as kindly toward the Kaiser as I do." The grimly serious meaning of the ironic-sounding sentence made a sensation at the time.

Even toward the great man whom, as man to man, he heartily loved, Harden always maintained his independence. On account of the social problems, which Bismarck viewed as a son of the Junkers in 1815 naturally would, they came into actual conflict, which was finally ended by a renewed invitation to Bismarck's home.

The court circle was filled with frantic rage against Harden. The first attempts to have him condemned for *lèse-majesté* were shipwrecked, and finally resulted in an acquittal which had for Harden the significance of a "civic blessing," for Wilhelm II that of a veiled warning.

The judge who had so spoken was dealt with. A lawyer was hired to distil an indictment out of thirty-two (!) volumes of the *Zukunft*. The highest rewards were assured to the state prosecutor then in office in case of success. And with all this expenditure, to which was added intimidation of the judges, the difficult task was accomplished, and Harden found guilty of *lèse-majesté*. Twice he was imprisoned for a series of months in the damp desolate fortress "Weichsel-münde" (Vistula-mouth).

But not for a moment did he give up the struggle, nor weaken in it. At the time of the jubilee for the 25th anniversary of the founding of the Empire (January 18, 1896) he wrote that if the government were carried on a while longer as Wilhelm was conducting it, then a real "Völkerbund" (Union of the peoples) would take form, and tear down the present seemingly unconquerable one.

Quite alone, against Kaiser, courtiers, government, military, courts of justice, officialdom, and, alas, the larger portion of the press (which never forgave him that when it was necessary he had also censured it unsparingly as an institution and in its representatives) he carried on the fight, against the "ring," His Majesty's favorites, "Eulenburg Moltke & Co.," and was victorious at last—after hardships too long to be described here—over all the Powers.

Albert Ballin, of the Hamburg-American Line, wrote him at that time: "If the Kaiser had not been so badly advised, instead of causing a criminal suit to be brought against you, he would have published in the Reichs-anzeiger, officially, the thanks of the crown." It was Ballin, also, who brought it about that the imperial government (secretly, to be sure) repaid to Harden the entire costs of the suits. Harden did not accept this payment until it was stated by letter in the name of the Imperial Chancellor, that thereby the justification and beneficial nature of his fight had been recognized.

Harden foretold the war, wrote in the *Zukunft* in

April, 1914, at a time when no one in the world had a thought of it,—*"In this summer!"* He could not prevent it, nor could he ever believe in German victory. In the third year he wrote that "only by political— not by military—action could an end be put to the war, unless Europe was to sink into midnight darkness!" With the most violent energy he opposed the submarine warfare. On April 12, 1916, he wrote a letter to Bethmann-Hollweg, then Imperial Chancellor, which he printed in the *Zukunft* on October 26, 1918. "The wound which Tirpitzism has inflicted on the Empire's body must be made complete. In this hour of fate I implore your Excellency not to be pettier than your destiny!"

Harden's note appended in the *Zukunft* to this letter ran: "Von Bethmann believed Helfferich and Zimmermann (who cannot escape the imperial courts); and the submarine warfare, to England's salvation, brought America into the war!"

Harden labored unwearyingly for an understanding with the United States; he sounded the warning, that that country, and it alone, could determine the result of the war, could bring about peace by mediation. He arranged, as a last means, for the reception of the American ambassador at Headquarters (Letter to Bethmann dated April 22, 1916; see *Zukunft* of October 26, 1916. "This letter obtained for Hon. James W. Gerard the invitation to Headquarters").

In the articles *If I Were Wilson* and *The True Wilson* Harden divined beforehand, from his whole character and career, the chief lines of the program which Wilson later announced. Both of these articles were recorded verbatim in the American Congressional Record "for eternal remembrance."

But no less unweariedly did the possessors of power labor in their zeal of persecution against Harden. Many times an edition of the *Zukunft* was confiscated; twice its publication was forbidden for five months; every imaginable device and threat, which included even the bookkeeper as an accomplice, and intimidation of the public, contributed to the economic ruin of the once prosperous periodical. The publisher did not yield an inch, made not the slightest concession to the militarists.

In October, 1918, when he saw chaos approaching, he, after a severe struggle with himself, resolved to break the reserve which had grown to be second nature with him, and telegraphed to the Kaiser, without the least courtly ceremony, asking if he could speak to him in the interest of Germany. Wilhelm put forward "engagements" as an excuse, and asked him to talk with the head of his civil cabinet. ("I may most respectfully impress on you, to give us notice by telephone of the date and hour of your visit.—Delbrück, Secretary of State." Oct. 7, 1918.) To this old gentleman Harden uttered the final words: *"Only a prompt and great action, which makes the nation master of its own fate, and at the same time brings peace, can still preserve the monarchy, within the limits of that of England. For a Kaiser who is in hiding is protected only by the greater unpopularity of his eldest son, and by the fear of the Bourgeoisie at the prospect of a Red revolution of the Russian type."*

The head of the Cabinet promised to repeat all this to His Majesty. Did it come to pass?

At Harden's urgent request, on the evening of November 8, the ministerial director, Simons (the same who is now President of the Imperial Court and President's representative, and who had asked for Harden's opinion on the situation), induced Prince Max of Baden, the Imperial Chancellor, to order Gen. von Linsingen, who desired to stifle the uprising in blood, "to take command in the marches" (i.e., to lay down his command immediately); and his deposition was reported in the course of the night to Harden by telephone. A bloody civil war was thus avoided.

Harden also originated, during the years of the war, the phrase, which since then has been spread abroad so widely, *sans paternité*, "Never again war!"

On the day when Wilhelm II abdicated, he said to the Count, who laid the document before him in Amerongen: "Now you must send Harden to Versailles. He is my greatest enemy, and has been from the beginning; but you have no better peace-maker."

The Socialist gentlemen who were in power were not of that opinion. When the proposal was actually made, even in immense public meetings, they said: "Harden? *No!* Why, he says that Germany is the one chiefly to blame for the breaking out of the war. Surely we can't send him there!" The first word of those whom they did send there was that the assertion of Germany's guilt was a lie.

"Whom the gods will destroy they first make blind."

Not until long afterward did the Nationalists sate their rage against Harden. Three hired assassins had to lie in wait for him. With eight wounds on his head, after terrible loss of blood, he was carried to the clinic of Prof. Moritz Borchardt, whose surgical genius saved his life. . . . But Harden had to give up the publication of his weekly, which was wholly dependent upon him, and he has not yet been able to resume it as his health has not been sufficiently restored to undertake, with safety, this immense task.

Harden's eminence as an orator is well known. For hours at a time, speaking entirely without notes, so that the hearer sees the very dawning of the thought, he holds the attention of crowded audiences of the highest intelligence in the chief cities.

The twenty-fifth anniversary of the *Zukunft* occurred at a time when the Supreme Command forbade publication of the magazine; so many good Europeans made Harden's sixtieth birthday the occasion to tell him in a little book what they think of him, how they feel toward him. All the noblest names are there.

I will close this account of Harden's life with what one of his devoted friends said of him in that book:

"On his birthday, which, quite incredibly, is his sixtieth—this world never saw so youthful a man of three-score—we in spirit clasp his hand: and may he long be actively at work in the fulness of his strength!

"Behold ye him. No man's subject hath he been."

II

WOODROW WILSON

THE first lances were being broken in the three-sided contest between Taft, Roosevelt and Wilson, when I expressed doubts as to the election of Roosevelt, who at that time enjoyed extraordinary popularity in Germany. It seemed to me that a people with so strong a youthful urge toward rationalism, and yet so happily idealistic as the folk under the starry banner, would not for a second time select for their chief ruler one whose very face seemed drawn in the lines of a caricature such as one sees upon the fences, and who, despite his clear intellect and unquestionable executive ability, suggested rather one who shouts "Fire" than one who calmly ponders his daily duty. Thereupon one of the shrewdest and foremost captains of finance in the United States answered me, privately, that he, too, could not grow enthusiastic over the "great Teddy," but nevertheless might prefer the man of practical experience to the theorist, ignorant of worldly affairs, who would enter upon the highest office filled with every sort of dogma and prejudice and might need years to find himself at home among realities and to subject his habits of thought to their stern demands. No man, he said, who had the true interests of the United States at heart could demand that their whole economic, political and social structure should be con-

14

tracted, expanded, moulded into ever new forms at the caprice of such a man.

Much the same, too, was the first utterance of prejudiced opinion in Germany concerning Dr. Woodrow Wilson. Bismarck, once the target of their fiercest hate, and later, in the full splendor of success, their idol, had often uttered a warning against the politics of professors. And now this land, which lacked the background of long tradition and knightly legends, this folk of busy farmers, manufacturers and tradesmen, was to entrust its most important affairs of State, its supreme political destiny, to a professor who had absorbed theories but who remained uninstructed by experience. With the supercilious self-satisfaction of him who believes in hereditary omniscience, in the divine right of royalty, and who with eyes still tearful shouts for joy when Amurath follows Amurath, when Frederick, the son, follows Frederick, the father, we awaited the drama that must presently develop beyond the Atlantic. Psychology is not the Germans' strong point. Anything different from what he knows at home is unpleasant to him and appears, at first glance, hateful. He is often loud in his criticism instead of striving to understand alien habits and mode of thought.

I believe also that sufficient attention has not been given to the perilous fact that the common people of various nations, illiterates in the realm of higher culture, often know each other only through the comic papers. Now wit, even though it bears the same relation to genuine humor that saccharine does to sugar, or canned beans to fresh, is most assuredly a precious possession; and yet, with those who make a daily business of grinding out wit, it produces a mental illness which dulls the senses of sight and taste.

For their ever open market they need simple forms and sharp contrasts of color; out of the manifold variations of feature which enable the thoughtful observer to form some conception of a people's spiritual character, they make a single coarse type which is recognizable from a distance, but of the nature whose essence it attempts to set forth it really offers only a few blotches, warts and pimples. For many years, in the atlas of this comic-weekly world, the Frenchman was a garrulous little fop, half phrase maker, half hairdresser; the German was a heavily-cloaked, bearded, bespectacled, cave man; the Englishman a stiff figure in loud checked cheviot, and the North American, who is still stupidly and ignorantly dubbed the Yankee, was presented as the weazened dollar-chaser and worshipper of the golden calf. Are there really droves of such a type beyond the Atlantic? Does not every country which is ruled by capitalism have a caste which devotes all its strength to acquisition, to the heaping up of wealth? Can any one who is not actually, or wilfully, blind fail to see what incomparably generous gifts are bestowed by American idealism upon the poor in spirit or in body?

All these criticisms and warnings of good sense proved unfruitful. It was in vain that Paul Bourget, decades ago, and, more recently, German scholars enlightened by personal observation, had refuted the silly fiction that the United States was ruled by King Dollar in the East and King Cotton in the South and that these had killed the spirit of the Lincolns and Washingtons and had left of their ideals barely an empty phrase. People whom America had enriched, in their endeavors as manufacturers, tradesmen or traveling artists, in far briefer time than would have been possible in Europe, but who felt under no obligation of gratitude, kept this fiction in circulation from year to year. Have we a right to complain so bitterly when we are branded as militarists, boches, huns, pirates, and are judged by the actions of a handful of snobs, if we ourselves, even in days of peace, employ only the four words, "Dollar," "Trust," "Corruption," and "Monroe Doctrine" to designate a nationality of such youthful power and future possibilities as the United States? The last of these four words in particular, if not traced to its limited, historic origin, to its meaning and scope, is falsely interpreted as the expression of a selfish presumption. We shall never come to a friendly understanding by a road paved with such gross misconceptions. They are but slogans for careless daily use, false conclusions that can only lead astray.

This was the mood in which the war found us. The flood tide of savage wrath against our foes at first prevented the thought of far-away America from coming to mind. She, it was said, when the question was raised at all, will not be against us, will never be found in the camp of our foes. Beneath the threshold of consciousness one could detect the hope of a profound hostile feeling among Americans against the British, a survival from the days of the struggle for independence, a feeling which one day might, perhaps, unite the star-spangled banner with our war flag. This hope was

cherished principally by men outside of politics. *Vani-
tatum vanitas!* But to one beleaguered by foes there
is an allurement in any tonic proffered by quack or
apothecary.

Many rejoiced when the German Kaiser resolved to
give Mr. Wilson an account of what had happened at
Louvain and found the President's reply, which fore-
shadowed something like an international investigation,
all too cold. The belief lasted that the great republic
in which so many descendants of Germans and Irish-
men live, and which had won its freedom by breaking
away from England's control, would never take action
with England against the German Empire. This belief
persisted until the tidings came that America was fur-
nishing arms and munitions of war to those who were
allied against us.

Then the storm broke and drowned the voice of
sober reason. In all wars of recent times, even though
Germany declared her neutrality, German industrials
have furnished guns and ammunitions to one party or
the other and have claimed the right to do so as an
essential condition of permanent efficiency. The
Americans would gladly have furnished such supplies
to Germany also if the blockade had not hindered the
delivery. The Americans did not desire a legal status
which, in case war were forced upon them, must
hinder them from purchasing needed arms from neutral
countries; they did not desire that every state, in order
not to be overpowered by those who were armed to
the teeth, should be compelled, even in time of peace,
to heap up a supply of arms. Such an accumulation
is a temptation to decide every quarrel by war instead

of bringing it before an arbitration court of disinterested nations. These and still more far-reaching explanations of America's actions were stated with especial clearness in the note which Secretary of State Lansing addressed to Austria-Hungary. In vain.

Who, in such terrific confusion, can keep his soul, his brain, wholly free from the cobwebs of delusion? The common people saw only that out of American howitzers and mortars, American ammunition was crashing down into the ranks of German men; that in this industrial war America's mighty productivity was helping our foes; and they vowed that such aid could not be reconciled with the duty of genuine neutrality, but was inspired by ignoble greed for gain, which we must, at least for the time being, repay with hatred.

The flames of hatred were fanned by rumors, the verification of which in time of war, with our foreign mail and telegraph delivered over to the caprice of the censors, was hardly possible. In Germany it was whispered, and presently cried aloud: "This is not a case of limited delivery of arms such as Krupp made in former wars. The United States has become a single great forge of weapons and a munitions factory for our enemies. They have transformed the greater portion of their entire industrial equipment, even that which used to produce pianos and sewing machines, for this profitable activity. The war would have been over long ago if such sales had been forbidden."

I never believed the report. Manufacturers whose business was crippled, in the New World as well as elsewhere, hoped for salvation through the opportunity afforded by war. But the transformation of an industrial plant, its adaptation to the needs of a new product, is so costly and laborious that it is carried out only where the former business and the market for its output have ceased to exist. Why should the industrial regions of the United States, to which, besides their own hemisphere, the entire territory of Germany and Belgium stands open, and which can offer their products to the greater portion of the English and French markets, determine upon a costly transformation which would deprive them of the opportunity to extend their circle of customers, and which, after the war, would again have to be transformed to their original industrial purpose at renewed expense? Perhaps the imagination of our merchants charged to the account of the United States all the shipments which came from Canada, Australia and South America.

To me the estimate of the *World* seemed credible, according to which the coalition against us had drawn only six per cent. of their munitions from the United States. The issue of the war, it was argued, could never have depended upon this percentage. I have always regretted that the government of the Republic did not itself issue a statement covering this point and that its silence seemed to confirm the rumor that only America's aid made possible the continuance of the war. Is it not quite conceivable that the parents, children, brothers and sisters, wives and sweethearts of our warriors flamed out in rage against a class of men who, themselves out of danger, in comfortable security, abundantly increased their capital and income by providing mountains of murderous instruments for use against the sons of a land from which they had re-

ceived only kindness? The criticism which crept into
the White House from the camp of the Western powers
was unheard by us; it was forgotten that North America provided millions every month to feed Belgium and
thereby indirectly lightened for us the burden of the
war. Day after day nothing was discussed but the
profitable traffic in arms which, it was declared, was
unmistakable evidence of American hostility toward
Germany. Conscious that they had never done, or
even wished, evil to the country of Washington or
Lincoln, the common people felt themselves grievously
wronged; and they shouted their loud approval of those
who declared that Germany, beleaguered on every side,
must leave no weapon untried which might cut off the
transportation of arms from over-seas to her enemies.

The bitterest wrath was directed against the President who, honest Germans argued, could demand, even
compel, Congress to place an embargo on the exporta-
tion of arms. As he made no move in this direction he
was considered Great Britain's handy man who sought
to harm us. In the heat of emotion, robbed of reasoning power, the thought did not occur that such action
would have been interpreted by our opponents as an
attempt at favoritism, or that Congress could refuse its
sanction. And so, while the press of the Western
Powers scornfully reproached Mr. Wilson with being
misled by German evasions and with replying to criminal actions with polite notes, we ourselves, engaged in
violent submarine warfare at the time, accused him of
breach of neutrality and looked upon him as a pawn of
the English.

Accusation and condemnation became so loud and

were turned with such avidity into the ugly distortions of the comic sheets that serious thinkers became ashamed of the brawling and the abuse.

No one, however, can brew a potion which will change folly into wisdom.

Burn up ninety-nine per cent. of this so-called literature, bound in war covers and feeding upon the war! Throw all these poems, speeches, novels, essays, boastings and pamphlets where alone they may still be of some use—into the paper mills; and devote yourselves once again to those books from which you may derive spiritual sustenance. Then perhaps clear reason and human dignity will return. The art of Rodin and Hodler, Maeterlinck and Verhaeren, Kipling and Wells, Forain and Raemaekers, Spittler and d'Annunzio is not judged by their wrath against Germany. By the same token Mr. Wilson, the scholar and politician, should not be considered a monster because he prefers English customs and institutions to those of Germany. And it has never been proved that he did show such preference.

In the State of Virginia a mother of Irish ancestry bore him; his father was the native grandson of a Scotsman. He had therefore not inherited any blind worship of England. We find him as a student at Princeton denouncing "Cabinet Government"; he censured the secrecy and lack of accountability with which the business of government is conducted and because of which, from year to year, the people's desire for active participation in governmental affairs becomes increasingly sluggish. Following this he published a book dealing with "Government by Congress," which earned him a call to teach at a young ladies' seminary. For eight years, as its president, he ably guided the destinies of Princeton University which, being an institution favored by young men of wealth and family, might be designated as America's "Bonn." Then he resigned because he believed that the terms of acceptance by the university of a twelve million dollar endowment were opposed to the educational interests of his high school. Rather than besmirch his ideal he left.

As the undaunted leader in the fight against ugly misuse of power, he was elected governor of the State of New Jersey, which he freed from the yoke of the Trusts. He has written with a high degree of ability on the life of Washington, the history of the American people, the affairs of State, and in his collection of essays, "Only Literature," expressed greater wisdom in his estimate of politician, poet and author than has been uttered in many a year in either hemisphere. Then, as neophyte in the highest office in the Republic, he made obvious mistakes. But, among the various heads of government, is he the only one who can be so accused?

Twice the people of the United States gave the highest office to this earnest, cultured and morally upright man. And he who was dubbed "the Theorist" dared to grasp powers which many a "practical man," anxious to cater to the masses and currying the favor of Wall Street, would have hesitated to approach. Gradually even the Germans came to look upon him as one who held his convictions inviolable and acted only according to their dictates. He who has such a reputation is immune against the psychology of caricaturists and jokesmiths.

Germany had no particular reason to look to Mr. Wilson for any great degree of fondness or friendship; she was not in a position to demand or beg anything of the country or of its President.

But is it not reasonable to believe that all humans, during a period of inconceivable stress, accepted as a dispensation of Providence the fact that the leader of the greatest of neutral powers was nurtured in the pure atmosphere of science rather than in the fog that envelops those who are engaged in the battle for wealth?

In every path he trod, be it ever so steep and narrow, this man felt a duty toward humanity, and consequently, with all the power of his soul and his will, he would strive to achieve that happy juncture where the performance of this duty was compatible with the interests of his fatherland. Only one attainment could still lure the professor who had become President— the ascent to the ever unclouded pinnacle from which the light of those who have brought happiness to humanity shall shine throughout human history.

As early as 1916 I expressed the hope (in the *Zukunft*) that his heart would respond to the desire which held all mankind. And the Wilson my inner mind perceived spoke according to his works, his will and his conscience.

.   .   .   .

The son of Nun, whom you may call Joshua, Jeshua or Jesus, inherited the leadership of the tribe of Ephraim after the passing of the great Moses, lord of Israel and the brains and brawn of his people.

Joshua was enabled, through the power of breath blown
into the trumpets of his priests, to bring down into
dust the walls of Jericho and conquer and lay in ashes
the city of Ai. He defeated five kings—those of Eglon,
Hebron, Jarmuth, Lachis and Jerusalem. He commanded his soldiery to tread upon the throats of the
defeated ones with their heels. "Thus," spoke he, "will
we deal with all our enemies." Then he commanded
them to be killed and hanged upon trees. There they
hung until the sinking of the sun. Only then did
Joshua order them to be taken down and thrown into
the cave in which they had hid from him; and the entrance he then ordered to be blocked with boulders.

The sun that had witnessed this great victory, had
stood in the heavens longer than upon any other day.
For while the Lord, giving aid to his chosen people, had
sent down a storm of hail upon the Amorites, Joshua
lifted his voice in pious wrath and cried, "Sun, stand
still in Gideon, and, moon, stand still in the vale of
Ajalon." And the heavenly bodies stood still until
Israel wreaked its wrath upon its enemies. The sun
cast its rays upon the earth for almost a full day.
And none equaled him whose voice had forced obedience from the light of day.

What in remote times was a day's work is now the
accomplishment of an hour. We received tidings that
beyond our borders our enemies proposed to add an
hour of sunlight to their day in order further to insure their revenge. Joshua's name today is Honnorat.
He was a member of the French Chamber of Deputies
and his proposal won the approval not only of his
people but was also accepted with favor by the menac-

ing German Empire. In both countries, and consequently in all others affected by the war in western Europe, clocks were turned back one hour, and every worker's day was prolonged for sixty minutes. We need not be concerned here with the fact that the purpose was economy, that lighting costs were reduced by many millions, and production vastly increased. We see humanity wiping an hour out of its life in order to sacrifice it upon the altar of hate. Joshua needed for his victory a double day. For he had not the means to illuminate the night. Today the embattled peoples can accomplish this.

The power of money, wrapped in the magic cloak of invisibility, urged them on because it feared a relaxing of effort, and so they plucked an hour from the night. Thus they would not become indolent, and the cloak would not become threadbare. Rage could no longer content itself with the ancient measures of time.

The steel-clad multitude of descendants of the Jesus of Gideon had forgotten the warning that went forth when Jesus of Nazareth hung on the cross, heeded not the darkness that covered the earth when Jerusalem and Rome, mighty in strength of spirit and of arms, combined to destroy the noblest of humans. Has Europe been stricken dumb so that it failed to see what became of the empires conquered by Joshua and those who later became Israel's leaders?

Then let the voice of reason recall us from this raging madness!

(Wilson) "That continent which, after the birth of Deda and the Holy Scriptures (Old and New Testa-

ment), and after the death of Buddha and Christ bore
the richest fruit, is weary, and the attempt may succeed. And if the call comes to us now, as, during Holy
Week, we ponder upon Crucifixion and Resurrection,
it will find eager response. Give ear, oh humanity, to
the message of a human being.

"This message is directed to the United States of
America and, at the same time, to all countries, to all
the peoples of Europe, combatant as well as neutral.
It seeks to give expression to conditions as they exist,
to extract from these twenty-one months the sum of
possibilities and to point the way to what is necessary.
In other words, the purpose of this message is to bring
peace. No assumption to seek paths upon which I
have no right to tread has led to this desire. If another
spokesman appeared I should gladly remain silent.
Who will relieve me of this duty, which burdens me?
Thirteen nations are in the turmoil of war. Even the
concerted action of nearby neutral states would be too
weak to weigh in the balance. The Pope, whose pro-
scription is underestimated only by the fool, is without
material force; besides which, as head of the Roman
Catholic Church, which has a multitude of followers
in both camps, he is hampered in his desire to act. No
fading light, but only one aflame with youthful strength,
can lead the wanderer lost in the forest.

"Europe's spirit and industry have implanted in our
soil untold seeds, and for this she deserves our gratitude. And this we would give in unstinted measure if
Europe could be saved by heeding our counsel. But
this can be of use only if given in passionate desire for
justice and with unrestrained candor. Painful truth

must be told, but none will be wilfully offended. Europe stumbled into this war as a child walks upon thin ice, believing it will bear its weight and suddenly finding itself struggling in a torrent. Is not a strong arm needed for the rescue?

"The duty toward extending this helping hand becomes stronger as the danger of our being drawn into the whirlpool draws nearer. We are still neutral and free from the prejudice that fastens itself upon those who are held together by a consciousness of race unity. Those who have looked upon our people can discern traces of the form and face of all the races of the world.

"Perish the thought that we should ever desire to mould Europe into our own likeness. Let us not attempt to dictate the destiny of that continent which for centuries has given laws to peoples and given form and substance to the history of mankind. But we are the spokesmen for the United States, not of North or South America, but of white peoples, which desire a speedy peace. And now the hour for action has arrived. You of Europe may take your clocks and turn them as you will; you may prolong the day or shorten it; continue, if you wish, to heed the fools among you who tell you of our weakness and of our braggadocio; no steel can ever chisel this hour from the body of your fate.

"We are still neutral. This is denied in Europe, in both camps. Both resort to abusive articles and caricatures which bring a feeling of revulsion even to friends of strong satire. They attempt to hold up to ridicule and contumely the President of the United States.

Many greater men have silently borne such insults for years. Out of the morass of these paltry jokes to catch the applause of the rabble I look to the words of the one German the bravery of whose soul, whose determination and manly charm remains unequaled and whose works have become the New Testament of the art of statesmanship: 'The honor I carry in my heart is sufficient for me and no one shall sit in judgment upon it. My honor before God or man is my property. I give myself credit for as much of it as I believe I have earned, and I decline any addition thereto.'

"Millions of my fellow citizens have entrusted to me the guidance of the affairs of State. Had they desired to bestow this office upon a man with the unrestrained temerity of a cavalry colonel or a submarine commander, they would not have chosen a scholar. I can perform my duty only as my conscience dictates and I cannot, without being certain of the ground I stand upon, overthrow a fixed resolve in order to shine by a display of hasty action. At least nine-tenths of our citizens desire to live in peace and friendship with all peoples, especially with those of Europe. This desire must be the arrow which points our way, so long as it does not conflict with the honor and interests of our country. Has the wrath of the people broken this arrow?

"The Western Powers accuse us of enduring German crimes against international law with pitiable weakness and jeer at us because we ask for information and accept excuses when American citizens are killed. In their opinion it was our duty to defend Belgium's neu-

trality, of which we are one of the guarantors, in order
to safeguard the dearly acquired benefits of civilization
and either to have lifted our voice in admonition or, if
need be, take up our arms. Germany and Austria-
Hungary scold us because their enemies are supplied
with American-made arms and munitions and because
they believe us to be hampering their conduct of the
war without justification, and because, as the formula
goes, we 'are mixing in affairs which are none of our
business.' Such two-sided accusation falls to the lot of
all those who strive for righteousness.

"During the long period of the war the United States
has not made even the slightest move which sound
reasoning could construe as a misstep against neutrality. Great Britain is conducting a commercial war
against Germany, enforces a blockade against food and
raw materials and says: 'This method of procedure
against beleaguered cities and nations has had the sanction of usage in ancient as well as modern times and
conforms entirely to the conceptions of the present
day. We live upon our island, are not a nation of land
warriors, and desire that dispute between nations be
settled by arbitration. We cannot use a sword to
tame a wild beast that attacks us, but we can subdue
it by weakening it. When it has been deprived of the
means to live, blind rage will be replaced by a weigh-
ing of realities. Whosoever draws comparisons between our methods and a knightly passage at arms is
either blind or is a liar. The war of today which
employs siege guns of the heaviest calibre to rain
shells into human ranks, mines, chemical flame pro-
jectors, explosives and poison gas, and makes use of

lying and deception has nothing whatever in common
with knightly combat nor even with wars of the nineteenth century, limited as they were to the use of foot,
horse and cannon.   Is there greater chivalry in burning out one's enemies' eyes or lungs, in bombarding
unfortified cities and villages from the air, in attacking
defenseless ships bearing human beings or cargoes of
goods, in knifing or dropping bombs or torpedoes, which
kill and maim, upon women and children, the old and
the ill, is this more chivalrous than our attempt to stop
commerce of our foe and force him to cease his shell-
ing?   It would not be more humane, and at the same
time would serve no purpose, to bombard his ports, because naval armament is not effective against strong
coast fortifications.   Our blockade, however, is effective; for it has had the effect of driving the German
flag from the seas and without our permission no ship
can go through the Channel or into the North Sea.
This fact remains, despite the ability of a few clever
fellows to run the blockade.   Their counterparts lived
in the time of the corsairs whose deeds are preserved
in literature.   The effectiveness of a land blockade
would not be lessened because a small but intrepid
patrol had found a small breach in the lines and even
managed to return to its base.   Germany's sole aim
in building up her fleet was to break just such a
blockade, despite the fact that she denies any intention to attack us.   The task of her fleet was, as it is the
task of every one blockaded, to hurl itself with all its
weight against the blockader and overpower him.   This
was the destiny prescribed for it by its creators.   Submarine attack upon unarmed ships of commerce is

not permitted by international law and is contrary to the first principles of humanity.'

"Submarine warfare does not violate the sovereign rights of any government, but day after day it does violate the rights of humanity and international law. It must violate such rights unless it is confined to a tax upon war vessels.

"Unfortunately the use of a false flag is still permitted and consequently every ship flying neutral colors may be a vessel belonging to the enemy. It is not possible to tell from a submarine whether a merchantman has two or three guns concealed somewhere; and the mines strewn upon the seas by the under sea craft do not make inquiries as to whether or not the ship they blow to bits is a neutral one. For this reason the promise to treat neutral and unarmed ships with consideration, to warn them and to protect crew and passengers from the deadly fire, is almost impossible of fulfillment.

"Since the horrible end of the *Lusitania* this is the point around which revolves the controversy, now almost a year old, between Germany and the United States. A twofold poison has been injected into this dispute. Manufacturers all over the union have delivered artillery, shells, munitions of all kinds to the British, French and Russians. To do this was entirely legal. It was not their fault that Germany, whose trade they would gladly have had, was blockaded and could not place orders with them. In all modern wars German industry, despite the neutrality of the empire, supplied arms and munitions to one or both combatants. American industry cannot be deprived of the same opportunities that were permitted to the Germans without limit.

"American business men and officials have proceeded according to well-established legal rights, the use of which, however, has drawn down upon them the bitter hatred of the Germans. On the other hand, the further poisoning of the issue was brought about by the error of those who have found friendly acceptancé in the family of our estates, but many of whom believe an injustice had been done the land of their forefathers. They believe themselves justified in sowing the seeds of dissension in order to avenge what they considered an injustice. We have official records to prove this and also to prove our leniency in the matter. We had done no injustice to the German Empire, and we demand obedience to the laws from him who comes to dwell among us. Why did he come? Undoubtedly because at some period in his life he became aware of the greater freedom and opportunities for gain offered by our country. Had he desired to remain heart and soul German or Irish and in all circumstances to uphold the land of his birth, then it was his duty to remain at home, to bear the disadvantages under which he lived and to assist in improving political conditions. It would be an intolerable presumption were he to accept the benefits offered by our country and then, at the first sign of storm, to disclose himself as a raging German or a furious Irishman. Past examples would only add fuel to the flame which I would see extinguished. Therefore I will only ask this: Would Germany have permitted Japan's agents to foster dissension among

Prussian Poles during the Manchurian war, in order to intimidate Germany through fear of revolt to forbid the sale of munitions to Russia?

"I can well understand the difficulty for a nation fighting for its life calmly to weigh realities; in its distress it forgets how often it supplied the enemy of its friend with arms and munitions. But I must demand of Germany that it publicly disassociate itself from partnership with ill advised patriots who, no matter how strong their feelings may be, are either guests among us or have been admitted to citizenship, and who are either taking advantage of our hospitality or undermining the public peace. They are not only useless to the German Empire but actually do it great harm. No serious minded person will blame these people for hoping for a German victory or for assisting it in the form of charity. But no one who is true to his country can permit them to raise their banner above the Stars and Stripes, to use the machinery of our politics as a tool to further their pro-German objects and to make their vote, a gift presented by us, dependent upon a pledge of pro-German activities on the part of candidates for office.

"I must further demand of Germany an unequivocal expression as to the steps it intends to take to safeguard the rights of our citizens and to protect American lives and property.

"The question of friendship or enmity between two great nations can no longer be left to the whim or the nerves of some young submarine commander. Concessions on either side will not be looked upon as weakness; what the moment demands is an expression of sincere desire to maintain friendly relations between two peoples who have no ineradicable grounds for enmity. It were folly to attempt to utter threats against a people of the acknowledged bravery and strength of the Germans. Besides which the leaders of the Empire are fully aware of the consequences to follow a severing of relations. Our entire hemisphere, north and south, would become enemies of Germany,— and not alone for the period of the war. All German ships in our harbors would be taken, and so a substantial acquisition in tonnage would accrue to Germany's enemies. Throwing our weight into the balance would furthermore prolong the war indefinitely and our 'inner front,' represented by those of German, Austrian or Irish descent, would disappear at once in the true American patriotic ardor of these very people.

"We did not rage in behalf of Belgium, because our money could insure the provisioning of Belgium, and this was possible only through the coöperation of Germany. We did not take offense during the long-drawn-out controversy between Germany and ourselves because in almost every case the facts were not clear and because we wished to spare the world the horrors of unrestricted submarine warfare which would have followed a declaration of war. The Berlin government furthermore gave us acceptable assurances of its earnest desire to come to an understanding. We are also fully aware of the tremendous difficulties confronting Germany and could not expect that the second winter of war had already given birth to the decision which sought to bring about the spring of peace—to place diplomacy above strategy, to defend the su-

premacy of the political council against any encroach-
ment by the military commanders.

"If such supremacy had been assured there would
have been no war which, despite the heroism it daily
calls forth, is nevertheless a horror and disgrace to
white humanity. Is it meet once more to dig the roots
of the matter out of the blood-drenched earth? All
are to blame, the only difference being the weight and
the time of their offense. The offender, of course, is
not conscious of this fact. At the same time he who
has only seen the latest offense and who has not studied
carefully the long chain of causes may be too hasty in
his judgment. Germany abruptly declined to consider
arbitration of the Austro-Serbian dispute, even after
Austria had finally accepted this proposal of the
powers; it started the war which, according to the in-
controvertible testimony of San Giuliono and Giolitti, it
had already sought to begin in 1913; wilfully violated
the Belgian neutrality it had once demanded and guaranteed, and by a rapid and devastating penetration had
grasped a pawn in the shape of France's industrial
region. Consequently Germany is guilty; proof of
this is found in a comparison of all documents published on the subject. But a reading of the book of
history prior to July, 1914, should not have been neg-
lected. France could not forget Sedan, Metz and
Strassburg. She did not charge the loss to the account
of the 'damned empire'; she did not determine upon
a new war; but she did provoke the victor of 1870 by
loud and continued threats of revenge, though it had
no further desire to take from her so much as a blade
of grass and did not begrudge her the second largest

colonial empire; also she offered her alliance to any
and all through whose sword she could hope to recon-
quer Alsace and Lorraine. The tie between herself
and the Russian Empire would have become strong
much sooner had not Bismarck with untiring effort
broken it again and again. During a period of grace
stretching over thirty years Germany has not been
served with unselfish genius, but during that time she
has succeeded, by dint of unparalleled ability, in at-
taining an undreamed-of prosperity and a huge portion of the world's commerce. Germans have settled
in every part of the world and are busily at work.
They are more diligent than their rivals, working for
wealth as well as for the honor of their country's flag.
But they forget that in order not to arouse envy of
their remarkable accomplishments in every field of
endeavor they must maintain a quiet dignity. They
are also unmindful of the fact that their enemies, at
whose expense Germany has achieved greatness, are
still alive and active. Her sword rattled. Above the
clash of shining armor one heard announcements of
intentions for still further aggrandizement. Instead of
limiting herself to coast defenses, fast cruisers and tor-
pedo boats, she built a war fleet with a cruising radius
far beyond the North Sea which would pay adequate
dividends only if it could break one of the more prominent jewels from the British crown. England felt she
was being outstripped in industry and technique, fears
for her commerce and colonies and sees her supremacy
threatened in Egypt and India; everywhere Germany is
at her heels. She cannot sit idly by and wait for the
black day to come when she will be compelled to

accept Germany's yoke, and, because suspicion and selfishness have prevented an understanding in naval matters, it suits her convenience to emerge from her splendid isolation and join the alliance of Germany's foes.

"And he who would dig at the roots of the war must not overlook the fact that it was Germany's violent interference in French rights in Morocco (rights which had been acknowledged by Bismarck in 1880) which roused the French nation from an indolent leaning toward socialism and a tendency toward flabby acquiescence for the sake of peace. Furthermore he must remember the unbounded commercial upheaval caused by the incidents of Tangier, Casablanca, Algeciras and Agadir.

"Germany proclaims, all too eagerly, her desire for the preservation of peace; at the same time she increases the strength of her army and navy. For what purpose—when no one seeks to rob her of territory and none can be found to draw his sword for Alsace-Lorraine? Ostensibly to widen her frontiers. The only protection against this is encirclement. Russia, driven from eastern Asia by Japan at the behest of Great Britain, fears German militarization of Turkey, from whom it seeks to take Armenia and the Dardanelles. Hope of alliance with the strongest powers and eradication of the accomplishments of Prussian generals in the Ottoman empire is the bait she swallows. Her further aim is to dominate the Balkan states, liberated by the shedding of Russian blood, through religious unity and by her own spiritual influence, to intimidate or break up the Austro-Hungarian empire, and so wipe out the ignominy of her defeat in Manchuria. The wars in Tripoli, Albania, Macedonia and Thrace are results of alliances formed as a consequence of the Moroccan quarrel and were fought to prevent the penetration of German power, culture and business into southeastern Europe and to place it under Slavo-Italian guardianship. If this program succeeds and Italy obtains a foothold in the Adriatic, then Austria-Hungary is hemmed in between Slavs (Russians and Serbs) and Latins (Italians and Roumanians), and its national body is crippled because of the desire of its alien members to return to their blood-brothers. Then it will be impossible for Germany to plunge into a mighty war. All this only because they fear attack, the purpose to dominate by the youngest of European powers, and the loss of what they have acquired. Germany, having grown tremendously in population and wealth, and considering its vast accomplishments in every field, cannot rest content on the present basis of allotment; and because she will not trust her fate to the ill will of enemies, and realizing that her mighty weapon may rust for lack of timely use, and sensing that the fateful and favorable hour has struck, casts aside diplomatic intervention and draws the sword against France and Russia.

"The decision which she believed was dictated by necessity for self-defense exposes her to the dangerous misunderstanding which the creator of German imperial power warned against when he said: 'If we become aggressors, the full weight of the Imponderables, which is far heavier than material weight, will be on the side of the opponents whom we have attacked.'

"So it is preventive war?   The classical example.
Two groups of powers mistrusting each other.   France
fears invasion and treatment as a hostage, while at the
same time Russia sees herself prevented from reaching
ice-free water for the period of another hundred years.
England has pledged herself to remain aloof from any
aggressive war upon Germany, but has not met Berlin's
demand for a declaration of neutrality in any war
which might be 'forced' upon the German Empire;
because the fear existed that any war brought about
by aggressive dealing might appear to have been
'forced' upon any one of the participants.   Germany
did not want to be hemmed in, did not want to leave
matters of arbitration in the hands of a hostile majority, and did not want to be weakened by the three-
sided attempt to throw Austria-Hungary into confusion.

"The statement that throughout she desired to bring
about war, not as a matter of self-defense but for conquest, is a slanderous one.   Only insanity could breed
desire for a conflict of such incalculable consequences,
and from which, in the end, nothing could be gained.
Likewise it is false to accuse England, France and
Russia, who at most were only half-prepared (and, in
fact, needed a year to complete their preparations) of
any designs at invasion.   They desired a diplomatic
battle, not a conflict of arms, and resisted a hasty war
with all the power at their command.   But its outbreak
could not be halted; because at the decisive hour the
will of the strategist was stronger than the will of the
politician.   Bismarck's words: 'In the preparation for
war always remain a step behind your opponent' are

regarded by the responsible military as the idle chatter
with which a shrewd writer of notes desired to partici-
pate in the rough work of the warrior. If Mars was
to reign, they believe, only their own expert word must
carry weight; and the beginning of this scarlet sway
was to be left to their judgment alone. From time im-
memorial, since the dispute engendered in the days
of Agamemnon and Kalchas, between the sword and
the mind, doubts as to the truth of everything that
has come from the pen have retained their hold on the
minds of war leaders. Despite the assurances of the
Tsar they will not believe that Russia, even with her
mobile army, will restrain every step, even every gesture of war until the last possibility of an understanding has disappeared. Nor will they believe that England will avoid the turmoil even for the sake of con-
venient, and at the moment even profitable, neutrality.
They see nothing but fraud in Grey's solemn promise
to throw the weight of England's whole power and
his own personal influence into the balance toward an
honorable relationship between the Triple Entente and
Germany, if peace can be maintained.

"They need not concern themselves that the estab-
lishment (in 1815) and the neutralizing (1839) of the
Flemish-Walloon Belgian state arose from the British
desire to protect the Island Empire against invasion
from this, to them, dangerous part of northwest
Europe's coast, and that Germany's attempt to use
Belgium as a base from which to make war upon
France is looked upon in England as a forerunner to
an attack upon itself which it must ward off. To them
the only important matter is not to delay mobilization,

to give their country every advantage to be had from a leap forward and to choose the ways by which they can quickly pluck the fruit of victory.

"No strings can tie the warrior; negotiations waste precious time; the country calls.

"The condition of any major state which yields to such a spirit is called in modern parlance 'militarism.' It not alone constantly urges ever increased armaments but implants the idea in the minds of the citizen, the scholar, the merchant, the artist, that the only fit manner in which a dispute among nations can be settled is armed conflict, and that other methods are unnecessary and dishonorable. It enters the very vitals of the nation.

"England, France, Serbia, Hungary, Austria, Australia and Canada bear ample proof that heroism and a war-like spirit can be maintained without the rule of militarism. And Germany's deeds illustrate, as has never been equalled in human history, that constant and thorough preparedness is a pledge to speedy transition into a state of war. Many will look upon the voluntary arming of three million Britons, including colonials, and the perseverance and self-sacrifice of Serbians and Frenchmen, as greater heroism. Between Antwerp and Trebizond twenty million heroes are embattled, and most of them are the product of non-militaristic nations; and because militarism is an incentive to war and will spread beyond control if it is not eradicated, the war is to be carried on until it is destroyed. This is the determination of Germany's enemies, and the wish of all neutral powers.

"Theirs alone?

"After the undreamed-of slaughter, to which already today five million corpses and at least ten million cripples bear witness, the cry for peace between Hamburg and Bagdad is louder than any other.

"Is it possible to destroy militarism?

"To me it is a certainty, the consummation of which is only delayed by the imbecile endeavor of a power to delay the severing from its body of a member which it considers indispensable to the function of life. This power would be forced from the first day after the conclusion of peace to lay upon the altar every sacrifice of wealth and blood for the reëstablishment of its body politic and its honor.

"Consider, Grey, Briand, Sasonov, the depths of misery in which you would languish if this mutilated power were immortal Germany seeking with all the passionate power of its mind and muscle to free itself of shackles and planning revenge for injustice! Remember, Bethmann and Burian, that the weak are more sensitive than giants and that Serbia arose from the grave! Peace, as war, leaving in its wake crippled nations, would merely bring an armistice and we do not want a peace that is an armistice, but an armistice that will bring lasting, honorable peace and that will become Europe's resurrection. We want it today; because today peace is possible and therefore necessary.

"If, in the end, reason controls, those who have placed themselves on a level with God, and their enemies on a level with the devil, will be ashamed of themselves. Who will wager that an armistice would not again lead to war? And who would benefit? For the French, Alsace-Lorraine and the Cameroons; for

Germany, Courland, Polish or Lithuanian territory; for the Austrians and Hungarians, Serbia, Czernagora, North Albania? That were sowing the seeds of new wars, instead of planting a strong peace, and would bring with it the certainty of friction and strife at home.

"What European state within the past one hundred years has benefited by the incorporation of foreign peoples into its own body? Russia, Austria, Prussia, the Netherlands, the German Empire?—No! Enlightened minds look upon annexation as a means for expansion which has become incompatible with European custom and thought. The morsel, having been swallowed, may become indigestible; and while the swallower might be glad to spit it forth, honor compels its retention and even the risking of life in its defense.

"German banks and industrial concerns rule (control, they say in New York) many foreign undertakings, either openly or secretly. They acquired the majority of shares, but not the buildings and grounds. And they were careful not to appoint German officials nor did they display the imperial flag. Why do nations proceed less wisely? Might gives right; the appearance of might gives offense.

"I visualize the time when nations will be joined in a community of interests, will amalgamate in order to reduce the costs of government. Instead of two authorities there will be one. This step is for the present conceivable only where related peoples are concerned, after the shackles of war have been removed and nothing can hold back the spirit of democracy; and I see the day when even the great powers will make common cause and there will be but one fleet, one submarine squadron, one standing army. Why not?— seeing that even today it is impossible for them to take from one another territory of any permanent worth and that the liberated will of peoples will not even permit them to think of it? Greater wonders than these have come to pass.

"The first and most timid demands now call for the appropriation by governments of all industries that can possibly serve war. If they are unable to replace the private owner or acquire the services of men of the calibre of Ballin, Lloyd George, Stinnes and Thomas, the state can lease these plants as concessions, in return for high but secure dividends. The flood that has overwhelmed us has also swept away the superstition that only he who is lashed by greed for profits is capable of unusual accomplishments. And never again must there arise a class of men to whom profit will flow from the veins of bleeding warriors.

"No parliament will then grant appropriations for armaments the expenditure of which will not enrich the state treasury. A government not so pledged would beg in vain for admission into the league of large and small nations banded together for the protection of life. This international assurance society would require a strong police force or militia. Otherwise it could not command obedience to its decisions. And a judgment which cannot be carried out is worthless. Being itself without income, it further needs funds— the moneys to be invested at interest. How pile these up from a devastated and impoverished continent? How, I demand, are war loans to be obliterated, how pay for reconditioning of land, the rebuilding of cities and villages, the replacement of implements, and provide the cripples and helpless dependents with comforts, not alone bare necessities, to the end of their days? Twenty-one months of war have cost between one hundred thousand and two hundred thousand millions of marks; add to this the cost of rebuilding and the burden to be charged for maintaining invalids and dependents. Cash indemnities, even such as might be compared to an acorn lying at the foot of a huge oak, cannot be hoped for by the triumphant victor. And the payment of tribute, extorted by the occupation of territory for decades, was possible during the periods of Rome's glory and decay, but today is as impossible as the forcible removal of whole tribes of people, which many have dreamed of. No nation engulfed in the flood can expect to obtain compensation other than through its own thrift. The power which reduces its annual expenditures for land and naval equipment by one billion will begin to see the dawn of financial order after the passing of a generation. What, therefore, is to be done?

"What has never been done before anywhere. Only new ideas, not regilded old ones, will light the way. After the first flood Noah eked out his existence by the cultivation of vines and as his son Ham witnessed the naked shame of the drunken vintner and was cursed to become the slave of all slaves, in like manner the Old World would become vassal to the New if it did not succeed in covering its nakedness with the mantle of brotherly love. Europe's war guilt shall be made a shrine of atonement.

"The loan certificates of all European participants in the war who will agree to abide by the decisions of a court of arbitration must be transformed into legal tender guaranteed by the debtors. But there shall be no possibility of debasement through debauchery and fraud as was done by the assignees of the Jacobin convention and the French Directorate. And how long must this condition endure? Until those who have been weakened by war are enabled to redeem the international legal tender with their own metal or paper. Forty years at the earliest, sixty years at the latest, after the conclusion of peace.

"A common European citizenship can be built on this foundation; this is the tie that will bind them together without leaving the scars of bondage; nor will it throttle them. Europe would be liberated from the unbearable condition into which its finances have sunk; it need not starve the arts and sciences, it need not permit the decay of industry, technique, commerce and household economy; it need not drive its citizens overseas with the threat of additional tax burdens.

"Even those who consider us nothing but sly traders, without ideals and a sense of honor, cannot doubt that we, both North and South America, will accept the new paper money in payment, though it be only for the sake of gaining customers and making sales. France, the ever gracious, ever joyous, leader in the art of social culture, will be freed of the desire for revenge and made neutral territory by its own demand, in the same manner as Belgium, for the rehabilitation of whom Germany will pay one-half, while France and England will pay one-quarter each. Great Britain, land power and sea power, having thrown off the irritating desire to be Europe's masterful and sulky guardian, roughly awakened from its indolent slumber, its sluggish comfort, and having opened coaling stations and opportunities to Germany for emigration, will be honestly reconciled and remain in the front rank of those guarding the freedom of the seas, the code of which has been purged of the right to take prizes and other abuses reminiscent of the piratical age. Finally Russia, cleansed, after the hurricane, of the Tartar wrath and dissensions, will have easy access to the ever-open sea; cured of the mania for expansion beyond inner seas and mountains on the ground of common religious belief; pledged to the court of nations not to deprive the Baltic, Finnish, Polish, Ukrainian or Lettish peoples of their rights of citizenship. Austria-Hungary will be a union of nations functioning on a plan somewhere between the German and Swiss, in which Serbia and all Serbian peoples, provided with good ports, will be accepted as an independent federated state and which every Balkan state may join if it desires. Germany: You will see it bloom. When peace has returned, and we no longer snarlingly quarrel as to which submarine shot is permitted and which is forbidden; when there is universal freedom and good will, and human rights are not treated as a beggar in rags; when Europe can stand at the graves of those who have fallen and justly say: 'For this you died; not for bits of land which we coveted yesterday and would be rid of tomorrow; nor for the futile task of attempting to absorb alien tribes. You died for freedom's light, for the honorable and lasting peace of the

fatherland, for mother Europe. And a more nobly
consecrated death was never implored by German
maiden of her betrothed.' Then those who remain behind will no longer have need for setting back the clock
in order to lengthen the light of day."

.   .   .   .

On Sept. 7, 1916, the United States Senate resolved
to incorporate in the official record of its session "for
everlasting remembrance" some articles I had written
in April. (These articles contained a respectfully sincere criticism of our enemies as well as a defense of
the German aims and actions such as had not yet been
heard abroad and which, according to the judgment of
the German Ambassador, were of value to the German
cause.) They cover pages 16380-88 in the Congressional Record, volume 53, No. 223. The conclusion
was that the Senate had permitted him, whose conscience led him to point out what he considered were
the rights and duties in the premises, to speak to the
President. And thus Wilson spoke. The mental picture I had drawn of the President through his writings
was true to its original.

He who has read Bancroft's History of the United
States will realize how difficult it was for American
psychology to understand the spirit that swayed the
German people. The adaptable German, echoing
Steuben's joy in the newly found freedom, quickly ac-
customed himself to his new surroundings and soon
became ambitious to be an upright, independent
master of his own fate and not merely a busy servitor.
But those Germans who settled beyond the seas did
little to enlighten their brothers in the old home con-

cerning conditions in the new; and in the old there were still strong powers which saw advantage in discrediting America. Here was a huge country which fought for independence, against slavery, for freedom; in which all nationalities, all beliefs and all individuals were given ample breathing space; and which at the same time had attained the greatest degree of wealth and happiness. It did not suit blind princes to point out to those at home so dangerous an example, nor did it fit in with the plans of parasitic courtiers.

The republic of Washington and Lincoln became the oasis of peace in a world of armor, and appeared worlds removed from the thought of mixing into the affairs of the Basalt lands, through which there still stalks the specter of knights and robber romance. A professor, a democrat and pacifist, became President; after the expiration of his term of office he was reelected, because the people saw in him the preserver of peace who under all circumstances would "keep them out of war." His Secretary of State, Bryan, and his most intimate friend, Colonel House, were pillars of peace. Despite the deep sentiment for Belgium and France (which was less than we really believe it to be, and still less for England) nine-tenths of the states were opposed to war. The funds appropriated for the conference of neutrals, and those collected to further the work of the Women's Peace Party, the National Association for the Preservation of Peace, the Anti-Militarist League and federations of workers, as well as the peace organizations supported by Carnegie, Henry Ford and other rich men,—all were stirring the fires of pure human sentiment. Despite all

this, on the first day the new Congress assembled, the
President announced the resolve to throw the entire
weight of American war and industrial power into the
balance against the German Empire.

To this he was driven by a fervently cherished
ideal. All efforts to refute the enemy through words
or to heap scorn upon them proved without result.
How could he overthrow a state of mind, the innermost
workings of which were not even understood? Mr.
Wilson himself emphasized the fact that he possessed
a "single track mind," and did not seek the fame that
comes to them who are considered shrewd, but sought
only simple human understanding. From the first
hour of war it was his aim to be the mediator of peace.
Was it because such office might make his name immortal? Perhaps. Was it because he had always
seen in the preservation of peace the greatest charity
that a human being can bestow upon humanity? Certainly. During August of 1914, says President Wilson, he gave daily assurances of his readiness to bring
about peace. Despite the fact that at home he was
looked upon as a confirmed pacifist, he did not
abruptly reject demands to strengthen the army and
navy for any emergency that might arise. He believed, as did every other courageous statesman, that
the most certain result of the war would be general
disarmament, and knew that his efforts would be given
greater force if he did not speak as the representative
of an unarmed power. "It is cheap for you to dis-
arm," the answer might have been, "for you are
already disarmed, and the proposal is made solely in
your own interest." Consequently he asked for large

appropriations. These served two purposes: In the first place they enabled him to refute the charge of the militarists at home that he was a "flabby professor" who would permit the country to remain defenseless against attack (of Japan, Mexico and perhaps even Germany). In the second place they served to warn Germany of his determination to resort to arms if she carried out her twice announced intention of instituting vigorous submarine warfare without sparing neutrals. He considered that he had not the proper means to combat England's blockade; he reasoned that, while her actions were contrary to international law, yet it was the mildest of war expedients, while at the same time he knew that an attempt to place an embargo on exports would be fought by Congress because it would destroy the trade of farmers, manufacturers and merchants. Besides this, his chances for reëlection as well as the hopes of the Democratic party for continued power would vanish.

He therefore confined himself to the writing of admonitory notes (the sharpest of which, unfortunately, brought forth a masterly reply from Grey). For the moment he did not hope for results from a conference of neutrals; but he leaned toward the idea, since the desire for peace became stronger from month to month. But neither Colonel House nor any of the doves he sent overseas returned with as much as a leaflet of the olive branch. And only a trifling intruder could offer mediation which was not asked by both sides. As the man who "kept us out of war" and whose campaign slogan was "Peace, Prosperity, Preparedness," he was reëlected.

And what did he hear from Germany? Only abuse and challenge from those among us who were running amok: "America is the arch enemy, has been so from the very beginning and war against this despicable, profit gluttonous enemy cannot be avoided even by the weakest of procrastinators." Responsible people said: "We cherish the friendship of the United States and will not permit submarine warfare to be undertaken except within the limits of our mutual agreement." December brought with it the "peace offer" of the Central European powers, an expression of readiness which, however, was silent upon all essential points. The empires would have liked to enter into negotiations. Did they insist upon the retention of Briey, Courland, Wolhynia, parts of Serbia and Roumania and did they still seek predominating influence in Poland and Belgium? It was just as difficult to obtain a clear answer to these questions as it is to grasp a piece of slippery soap in a tub of water. The track along which Mr. Wilson wanted to proceed was now blocked. He set the switch so that he could move along another. He brought forth the peace proposal, the call for which he had looked for from both sides, and defined his idea as to future world order. The mild, not the burning, sun of peace without victory should ripen a sincere desire toward friendly understanding.

Wilson's message of Jan. 23, 1917, expressed the thought contained in my address of April, 1916, to the President of my imagination. The Allies looked upon the scheming peace offer as a verbal bridge upon which Germany intended to cross into unsparing submarine warfare. And quietly accepting the possibility of war and certain of the support of his country, he answered with a list of conditions the sound of which was more serious than their meaning. This quiet offer of mediation was politely declined by the Imperial German government.

The rejection of the offer of mediation was speedily followed by an announcement of more intense submarine warfare, which came as a great surprise to the President. He had clearly indicated that American neutrality could no longer be reconciled with such a form of warfare, and his almost rude rejection of the attempt to compare the English blockade, to compare seizure with destruction of ships and crews and to make this a basis for compromise, was silently swallowed by Berlin. Was Germany seeking to call forth a new enemy? The President, who had even entrusted the Secretaryship of War to an unbending pacifist, Mr. Baker, formerly mayor of Cleveland, did not believe, despite the evil succession of events, that they had any such hostile intent. Only yesterday his ambassador (Gerard, of French descent, whose ancestor was Steuben's friend) was so elaborately fêted by Berlin dignitaries that he had definitely vouched for their good will. No sign of deception anywhere. Today the word was passed that limitation of the submarine campaign was to hasten the conclusion of peace. To this end, thinks Mr. Wilson, I have still one more trump card, but only one. And on Feb. 3, he severed official relations with the German Empire. What followed? Armed neutrality.

Suddenly a message was intercepted, a message from

Secretary of State Zimmermann to the German ambassador in Mexico. The ambassador was instructed that, should the United States be driven from her neutral position by the unrestricted warfare which was to begin on Feb. 1, he was to inform General Carranza, President of Mexico, that, with England weakened to helplessness within a few months, he could offer him an alliance with Germany, which would assist him financially and would permit the conquest of the states of Arizona, New Mexico and Texas. At the same time the ambassador was requested to urge Carranza to use his efforts to bring Japan out of the enemy group and into alliance with Germany.

In modern history there is no example of a lack of knowledge of existing conditions to be compared to this.

Had Mr. Carranza desired to add to the United States of Mexico, with its sixteen million inhabitants, the very rich and beautiful territory comprising Arizona, New Mexico and Texas, with five million inhabitants, he had no need to ask permission of Germany, which could offer him no assistance in carrying out such a plan. His first task was to defeat General Villa, who was in control of the Americo-Mexican buffer territory. (Did the Wilhelmstrasse know this?) After that he could launch out upon the Leatherstocking-like adventure of making war against the richest nation on earth, against one hundred million people in whose service is the best artillery, the highest technical and industrial development, and who would rather bleed to death than permit Mexico to take three states from them.

President Carranza rejected the proposal. He declined to transmit the offer to Japan. Wilson felt he had been offered a personal affront. While he had been busy polishing his peace proposal the Berlin government had decided upon unrestricted submarine warfare; while the Chancellor was glorifying himself as the guardian of the friendship for America which had been inherited from the time of Fritz, the President was aware of the letter which in the event of an open break offered foreign property to the Mexicans,—three flourishing states under the Starry Banner,—and begged Señor Carranza to bait Japan into an attack on the west flank of the United States. The upright enemy must comprehend what light was shed upon Germany's behavior by such glaring deception.

Both branches of Congress were aroused to wrath because of the letter, which even the most lenient judge will interpret as merely a senseless attempt at bluff. The last doubt disappeared. The pacifist President forced himself to the announcement of war. South America and the islands of two oceans—five continents—acclaimed him. High finance, which he had wounded by the introduction of the eight-hour day for railway employees, flocked about him to do him honor. His bitterest opponents of yesterday, Hughes, Roosevelt, Elihu Root, Taft, paid homage to him who held the confidence of the nation and was the brains and heart of the country.

After the announcement of the election of Harding the secretary to President Wilson reminded the newspaper representatives of the latter's motto: "It is

better to be defeated in a cause the resurrection and
victory of which is certain in the end, than to be victorious in a cause which the future will condemn to
destruction." *Condemn to destruction*—such is the
mocking echo.

And the echo says further: "Condemned is, and will
be tomorrow and in all eternity, the disaster you have
wrought,—pedant, weakling, hypocrite!" As a defeated man, of whom no song is ever sung, as one
who is shunned, mocked, hated by millions, Mr. Woodrow Wilson departed from the White House and the
city of Washington,—the same Wilson who only two
short years before had left for Europe on the *George
Washington* followed by a burning adoration such as
had never before been offered to mortal man. He had
succeeded in changing the mood of mankind where
Northcliffe and his shrewdest advisers had failed; the
peoples of the world were more eager for his words
than they were for those of their own military or
governmental leaders; morally and militarily he had
ended the war, insured victory, by sketching a world
condition which was attainable only on the ruins of
German imperial power and by the calm force of the
preparations for American participation which made
possible the landing of at least two hundred thousand
men every month by the spring of 1918. With a
towering preponderance of men, artillery, ammunition, airships and tanks, Generalissimo Foch in the
summer and autumn could almost entirely annihilate
the German reserves and could husband his own,—
these reserves of his which, according to the false
declarations of the German intelligence service, had

already been destroyed. And since in July General Ludendorff, blinded to actualities by desire for success, had failed to grasp the opportunity which still offered a slim chance—that of withdrawing to shortened lines of defense,—the German army, still fighting bravely, but led by desperado strategy, was threatened with the most stupendous defeat in the history of warfare. In order to escape a defeat which between the Meuse and Limburg would have delivered into the hands of the enemy 160 decayed divisions with all their equipment, our army command constantly repeated its plea for the speediest possible armistice and pledged Mr. Erzberger to the acceptance of all conditions.

Out of the New World came the Professor-President as though with warming spring breezes to thaw out the winter numbness of the Old. A godlike atmosphere surrounded the man in scholar's garb who had lifted himself above the crowned and the chosen of Europe. His arrival inspired wonder and awe equal to that with which the seventh German emperor, Henry, was greeted upon his arrival in Milan. Recall how of Henry it was said that he would purge the earth of iniquity, restore its holiness to the Roman Empire and insure to all mortals the eternal blessing of just and righteous rulership. As an angel of the Lord and the redeemer of the world Dante worshiped him on bended knee and cried: "Rejoice, ye slaves and sufferers, and welcome the heaven-sent shepherd who will lead us to safety." He implored the emperor to hasten to Florence and at the Arno to recall to his duty the black sheep that was leading all Italy astray.

At Milan Henry set upon his own head the Iron Crown. He conquered Lombardy, but he entered into a compact with the French to deal gently with the Guelphs, whom he had come to punish, and only after being crowned in the Roman Lateran and after the revolt of the Romans did he ally himself with the Ghibellines. Too late! On his march to Naples, derided, jeered; and then, almost friendless, he died in the village of Buonconvento. Three years it was since his solemn and triumphant departure from Kolmar. Three years—just the flowering period of Wilsonian fame. Was Wilson also too noble a character to combat the host of deceivers, as history judges Henry to have been? The Hotel Crillon at Paris became his Buonconvento. There was life in him when he departed from it, but he had become a lonely figure.

A smile had often crossed his lips when, during the sessions of the Council of Four, he had observed Clemenceau, sitting by the fire-side in his peasant boots and gray suede gloves, lift his bald head and open eyes almost hidden by bushy brows, and utter some harsh word of scorn. He smiled because he considered himself the stronger and so permitted the Tiger to play the rôle of Brennius, who, deeply suspicious and scornful of humanity, vowed that force alone would bring it to its senses. Maybe. The program which was being prepared in this chamber by the good will of man would teach him his error. For the victory of the New World over the Old was as assured as the rising of the sun.

In the godlike sense of happiness which his acceptance as a redeemer brought him, the President sometimes undoubtedly forgot that his powers were limited to executing the will of the American people. The United States, which we still looked upon as a land of raw materials and foodstuffs, are in reality world suppliers of manufactured materials. They are in competition with Europe, which owes them approximately thirteen billion dollars, that is, twice as much as the gold reserve of the entire world. Because the greater part of the materials delivered to Europe remained unpaid America was compelled to send overseas almost half a billion in gold and silver, so that payment could be made for raw materials.

To the idealist the continent of Europe was a great disappointment; to the business man it was a poor devil who could not pay his debts and daily begged for assistance.

This sentiment was first expressed in the Senate, the center for the expression of the opinion of large business interests. Here the President, bent upon the erection of a structure founded only upon his pure aims, found very little coöperation. This was the revenge for his failure to ask that powerful body to share the responsibility of making peace and for treating it as a mere adjunct of government.

The Republicans in the Senate begrudged Wilson his victory; the Democrats who supported him cautioned him to delay his decisions no longer. Belgians, Poles, the people of Lorraine, Russians, Czechs, Roumanians, South Slavs, Armenians, all called to him for assistance. The scholars Lavisse and Aulard, Bergson and Boutroux appealed to him. He listened to them all,—but to no German. And none made even the effort to gain his ear. The flame that cast its light upon the Starry Banner faded out. Chaotic sounds issued from Germany. Did the President harbor the thought that Germany trusted him? He was reminded that only yesterday it had scorned and berated him in word and picture; that the eternal deceivers had attempted to use him as a tool for their cowardly machinations. It was "proved" to him that the treaty exactly covered the Fourteen Points and gave to the French, whose misery was a reality to him because he had personally seen and felt it, only what they deserved. If he was still doubtful a hundred, if necessary a thousand, reasons for action could be presented. If he should spare the empires masked as republics, then the newly created and resurrected states could not live. He was deceived into overestimating Germany's capacity for production. Sinners, he thought, deserve severe punishment; they must go through purgatory before the gates of mercy leading to paradise are opened to them.

The first German whom he received in Europe was wilfully impolite; he denied the guilt of the imperial government, and accused the President of having broken his word. The President was on the defensive; the game of Paris is won. But the League of Nations was saved. Beside it the treaty of peace became passing matter. The League was "the great achievement the world expected from the Conference." A campaign of oratory was contemplated to reveal this to the people at home. Illness, the result of his tremendous exertions, struck him down before the gospel he preached could once more awaken the glow of belief. And his bitter opponents at once had a clear road.

They asked: "Is it not true that the Democratic party has been guilty of stupidity every time it has been at the helm?" The people of the United States nodded affirmatively and turned abruptly away from the President. Britain, France, Italy—all nations opposed him; and to the Germans he became once more the hypocrite with horse teeth that he had been to them until the collapse of their army.

But it must be remembered that he felt and thought, —not only spoke,—as no other government head had done before. The poorest and the mightiest hearkened to his word, which gave aim and object to the war and which, for a brief moment, seemed to break down the barriers of class. And he would have been unconquerable if also in Paris he had addressed all the world and had not left it to the Bolsheviki to send forth their call over mountain and sea.

A change in the tide of opinion concerning Wilson has already set in. Be assured of this: On a not far distant day the young giant America will enwreath the portrait of the man who placed upon it the burden of honor to fight for an ideal without the hope of material return. Never before in human history has this occurred. It remained for America to do it. The parchment upon which treaties are written will decay. And immortality is the lot of only one conqueror— the spirit.

As a wanderer in the Elysian fields, which are very far away from his Paris Hotel Crillon, he could confirm to Axel Oxenstjerna, a fellow wanderer, who was

Sweden's chancellor in the seventeenth century, the truth of the latter's statement that the world is governed with an incredible lack of far-sighted wisdom. And were Wilson to arise from the dead he, who was so often nailed to the cross with brutal words, would be driven to a second death at the sight of what has been wrought in Europe. Before his last convulsion of pain he might readily speak as did Nietzsche's Zarathustra: "Only when all of you have denied me will I return to you."

And is there not even today a halo about the head of the man who, though he was unable to bring about the moral ennoblement of peoples, nevertheless strove for this achievement with holy earnestness and pointed the way toward its attainment to generations yet unborn? America, conscious of her debt to him, will some day bow her head in reverence before his image.

III

LLOYD GEORGE

In March 1921 there appeared a statement in the newspapers that at the end of the announcement that Mr. Bonar Law no longer felt that he was strong enough to remain leader of the Lower House, your voice, Right Honorable David Lloyd George, was stifled in gushing tears. That seemed to ring in our ear from the world of melodrama. Doubtless it was, too, elaborated a bit for effect. Still, your ability to say, to do, with unfailing accuracy at each hour what is most effective needed no heightening from the clever reporter.

A keen-edged word of yours on the Suffragettes once won you, from the mouth of those wild dames, the cry: "If I were your wife, I would give you poison!" Quick as lightning your retort shot back: "If I were your husband, I would take it!" And a convulsion of laughter shook the assemblage. So it is always. Whatever the ladle can get out of the bowl is dipt out. And when a good friend goes, a little tear, at least, must drip into your voice.

Your sorrow over the parting with this friend was surely sincere. Where could you find offhand another so bound to you in personal loyalty, yet belonging, hair and hide, to the Tories? As late as the spring of the year 1914, no Tory would stay in the same room with David Lloyd George, foe of the Upper House, social reformer, tax-extorter. He had brought the Asquith ministry into such ill repute that the old nobility and upper gentry associated with none who belonged to that cabinet, with no one who was even on casually friendly terms with it socially.

The Canadian, Bonar Law, was the genuine Conservative; lower-born, but almost more dependable than his predecessor, the skeptic Balfour, who was a Cecil, and so secure in the saddle that he dared reveal in the daylight his friendly devotion to you. With Balfour you lost the certainty that you could at all times control the party machinery of the Conservatives. You had no other ally. In the House of Commons, in both islands, throughout the empire, a great following, but no party.

Whigs? They hardly exist any longer. "Whig," says Bucher, "is supposed to have meant originally a Conventicler in Scotland, inclined to rebellion, and Tory, a horse thief in Ireland leaning to Papistry." The religious contrast, the merging of several states into an empire, the victory of the aristocracy over the crown, the succession of a new royal house, the peculiar character of an aristocracy which recruits itself, without objection from the common people, and gives over its junior members to that people,—all these circumstances, with the existence of the Parliament, worked together, to develop under these names two parties, who agreed only in this: that power was to be shared by them in alternation.

That is the sole abiding element in the contrast, which has assumed the most variable forms: Popery and Protestantism, Stuart and Orange, common and parliamentary law, court favor and popularity, war and peace, permanence and change, centralized power and self-government, corn-laws and free trade. In the war with America the names were passed on to the Indians, who scalped one another under the battle cries of "Whig" and "Tory." Always it was difficult to define the difference between the two parties, but they always did "connote something."

The Whigs, who for nearly a hundred years have been called Liberals, made as a party the same mistake as its German namesake. Instead of coming to a prompt understanding with the self-assertive and strong individual, that he should leave the party free and yet not dam the current of his own influence, they put forth all their strength in the struggle against the man who towered annoyingly above the common run. To be sure, Joseph Chamberlain was, Lloyd George is, no Bismarck. But the feud against them both, rising to sheer stupidity, has enfeebled English Liberalism.

The Coalition, in 1916 a necessary war measure, is now an empty shell. The man in the street is asking: "What is Lloyd George going to do now?" Will he create a new Centre party, return to the Liberals and try to rebuild their power, or commit himself absolutely to the Conservatives, with whom he is at bottom closer akin than Disraeli was?

The speech to the "New Members," the shrill battle-cry against the Socialists and their "heavy artillery," Asquith's independent Liberals, pointed to the Right. Three days before, you had made the commercial treaty with Lenin's Russia—with the Bolsheviks,

whose "bloody hands" you had sworn you would
never clasp.

"What does this man in whom the empire's fate is
embodied really believe? Can we let him, whose will
and energy were in war-time indispensable and unlimited, continue in control?" Such questions were
on millions of lips. The retirement of Mr. Bonar Law
closed a chapter in your life, and surely a foreboding
embittered your farewell to your most faithful supporter.

You are one of those enviable men who see, always,
only what the desire of their brain wishes to see, that
is, always one side only of any proposition: viz., that
which makes it acceptable or to be rejected, for the
end you are seeking at the moment. If sleepless, behind such an eye, there bides a clear keen intellect,
then not much is lacking to make a good partisan adviser. If such a man's desire leads him out of the
law-courts into the open, and he learns the twin arts
of eloquence and demagoguery, no crown hangs too
high for him.

You can do more. You can work (which, in your
home-land, before we aroused it, not every man could,
even on the battlements). You can endure chill wind
of the people's ill-will (as opponent of the Boer war
you were exposed in many a gathering to their yelling
frenzy); what is needful but distasteful to your folk,
you can knead so industriously, and sweeten so deftly,
that it tastes to them all like plum pudding.

Have you perchance a drop of blood not Celtic in
your veins? "Conventional Cant" has not ossified
you. I do not see you in London social gatherings

where "All wear masks, say what they do not believe, eat what harms them, and speak ill of each other on the way home." (So Gordon sighs, and would rather squat like a dervish in the Soudan with the Mahdi, than do service every night in London to the false god Society.)

Your strong point is that you (like Robespierre, according to Mirabeau's judgment) believe everything that you utter. Almost everything, at least at the instant when it rushes from your lips. When you make a new patent-law, bring order into the confusion of the Thames harbor, obtain higher pay and old age pensions for workingmen, fight the land monopoly and the brandy-makers, you feel yourself to be the Redeemer of the island-empire, you consider every opponent a villain, and are convinced that no other genius ever produced such ideas as yours.

"Between luxurious wealth and humiliating destitution the cleft has grown so wide that the social conditions of the present day cannot endure. Where many souls are ruined in order that a small group of human beings may prosper superabundantly, the ideal of righteous kindliness is lost, and the world-order destroyed." Such thoughts, you (sometimes) fancy, arise out of no brain save yours. To us, after Stein and Bismarck, Marx and Lassalle, the utterance seems "small talk"; mere chatter after Carlyle, the Webbs, and the other Fabians. You think in official decrees; he who is not guided by them may go dwell with the cattle.

Wartime is the very element in which men of your type flourish. To them the world's political history is a harsh melodrama in which kindliness and purity, in their angelic perfection, strive against hellish malice. To put all the Peers of England under ban as oppressors and rascals would certainly be difficult. That all Germans are barbarians, criminals, Huns, cannibals, others than children enjoy hearing. And so you were the man, Right Honorable, to hit upon the watch-word that hammered into all heads the unique character of the war:

"Mazzini once said that every war not waged in defense of a great truth, or to unmask a great lie, was the most terrible of offenses. We Allies will not grow weary of exertion until the lie that 'Might is Right' shall be buried so deep in the earth that it can have no resurrection. There's your fat for you, German Michael. (No other can pass the Channel.) Why do three emperors, four kings, many republics challenge you? Because your stubborn wits roar at civilized humanity, 'Might goes before Right!' "

Bismarck said it? Never. In his speech against the address of the Prussian House of Representatives, which accused the Prime Minister of having violated the Constitution (on the 20th of January, 1863) he did say: "The life of a Constitution, in the judgment of an experienced statesman, consists of a succession of compromises. If a compromise is thwarted because one of the parties concerned insists on carrying out its own views with doctrinaire absolutism, then the succession is broken, and, instead of the compromises, conflicts arise, which then become mere questions of Might. He who has the power in his hands goes on in his own fashion, because the life of the state cannot for an instant stand still." Representative Count von Schwerin answered: "The speech of the Prime Minister culminated in the words: *'Might goes before Right*. Say what you will, we have the power—therefore we shall carry out our own theory.' This statement I consider to be one which the dynasty in Prussia cannot permanently uphold. The greatness of our country, and the reverence in which the Prussian ruling house is held, rest rather on the statement: *Right goes before Might. Justitia fundamentum regnorum* (Justice is the foundation of kingdoms): that is the motto of the Prussian kings, and so should it remain."

Bismarck (who was in the hall during Schwerin's speech) said: "As I am told, the gentleman understood me to have declared that 'Might goes before Right.' I do not remember such an utterance. (Vigorous contradiction.) Despite the expression of disbelief with which you receive my correction, I appeal to your memory. If it is as accurate as my own, it will tell you that I advised a compromise, because otherwise conflicts arise, which become questions of power, and the possessor of power, because the life of the state cannot stand still, is compelled to make use of it. (Great disorder.) I did not characterize that as an advantage, I make no claim for impartial judgment from your side; I only wish to correct, for the record, what was misunderstood."

This he did again, five years later, when Twesten had misinterpreted a sentence in his speech: "I am not willing that, by the previous speaker's midwifery, out of my word another wingèd one be born, as, out of another, what also I have never uttered sprang: 'Might goes before Right.' "

It was actually written by a much earlier Boche, Luther, when he translated the minor prophet Habakkuk,—not so accurately, in my opinion, as the Catholic Allioni, who reads: (Habakkuk I, 2-3) "Why, O Lord, dost thou show me iniquity, and set robbery and injustice before mine eye? Judgment is rendered, but *the opponent has the upper hand.*" (Luther's version is: "Violence goeth above right.")

. . . But can the true voice of conscience announce that: "The lie 'Right is born of might' is dead"?

"Conscience" (so your smile replies) "permits or forbids nothing." "We only imagine that we have such an organ in our nature," says Jeremy Bentham. Bain declares that it should create in man's heart a copy of the government's command. And Butler, "Conscience would rule the world, if, to its Right, Might were added." There is a pair of words you may enjoy juggling with. From the Heaven of Ideas the truth shines into the bishop's brain,—that forceless right is little worth. Out of the womb of Might, Right is born. Can grown-up men question that it is she that moulds and shapes it, gives it swift currency, and compels its recognition?

I refrain from the righteous jest of discussing thoroughly what morally purified Right, cleansed of all the dross of Might, gave your people authority in Ireland, India, the Soudan, the lands of the Boer, Canada, Australia, Gibraltar and elsewhere. Might did it all. So long, and only so long, as Might flutters the pennon of your empire has she the ruler's Right!

"When Man deliberates what he should, what he should not do, behind it hides the question what will benefit, what harm him. The beneficial he calls good, and what he fears will harm him, evil. Duty is the necessity of acting, or refraining from action, so that one's own happiness may be perfected, or at least undiminished. Reverence is the consciousness that a man has indeed the power to do us either good or evil, yet spares us the evil. Benevolence: the pleasure felt in the consciousness that, while fully gratifying our own desires, we can also fulfill the wishes of other men. . . . He who gives, hopes the gift will return with interest. . . . What we desire we call good, what terrifies us, evil. God's rights are never questioned where he is considered almighty."

Only Nietzsche (whom you, Sir, know from the newspapers, who in truth was the most defiant critic of the young empire, but is booked in your memory as a blind Germanist) can have written those sentences? No! It was Thomas Hobbes, your beloved fellow-countryman; he who, before the Jesuit Busenbaum (though after Machiavelli), perceived that, for a permitted end, all means are permissible.

"For what profits us a Right, if the necessary means to assert it be denied? Everyone has the right of self-preservation, and therefore also the right to utilize all means, not to disdain any one without which self-preservation would be endangered." Your virtue should ply her spade to bury the "Leviathan"!

And still you are digging the vault all too narrow, else room will be lacking for later creations. Six clods for every Utilitarian! A special tomb deep in the

earth even for the pure Baruch Spinoza, not because
it was his pleasure to urge spiders to fight each other,
or to push live flies into their webs, but because he
dared to say: "Every man has just so much Right as
Might; the limits of Might are those of Right as well."

"But where," asks the man from Wales, impa-
tiently, "are the Germans in this parade?" They,
Sir, speak otherwise than Hobbes, Locke, Bentham, or
that elder David,—Hume.

"The concept 'Right' is a negative one. That of
'Wrong' is the positive, and equivalent to Injury, in
its widest sense, done either to a person, to his property, or to his honor. Human rights are to be defined
accordingly: Each has the right to do whatever in-
jures no one else. The state is in its essence a means
of protection either against external attacks upon the
whole body of members or, from within, by individuals,
on one another.

"From this it follows that the necessity for the state
rests essentially upon the acknowledged injustice of
the human race. If justice ruled in the world, it would
suffice to have built one's house, and no other protection would be needed beyond this evident right of
ownership. But since injustice is the rule, he who has
built a house must also be in a position to protect it;
otherwise his right *de facto* is incomplete, because his
assailant has the *'fist-right.'*

"Now this conception of right is, in the political
world to be sure, theoretically abolished, but in practice it continues in full force. The beasts of prey
among human beings are the conquering nations—and
their successes and failures are the material of his-

tory. Voltaire is right in saying, 'Robbery is the purpose of all war.' Yet every government declares that it will only take up arms in self-defense. It should frankly and shamelessly appeal to Machiavelli's teaching, that between nations the rule is: 'What you would not have another do to you, that do to him.'

"Right in itself is powerless: in the natural course of things Force prevails. To supply Right with Power, so that it may rule, is the problem of statesmanship."

So writes Schopenhauer. After the philosopher let us hear the teacher of law.

"Right is not a logical conception, but an expression of power. Every right of a people or of an individual is maintained solely because the requisite power stands ready to support its assertion. Every right on earth has been fought for. That is why Justice holds in one hand the scales, in the other the sword."

These words are Jhering's, a great jurist. In the guilt of the lie which your war would bury deep, these two righteous men do not share. But you charge that we, each for himself, took part in the crippling of all morality? Burke says: "War of itself looses all the bonds of moral duty." Our arming was itself a violation of peace? Fox declares: "The unarmed man is a bad guardian of peace. True statecraft bids even the peacefully-minded to arm himself against sudden outbreak of a will that strives in the opposite direction."

It was a crime that we accumulated means of defense without constant noise and bustle? Hear Canning: "Like to a magnificent mechanism that after long disuse suddenly reveals the power of its machinery, is our England; while it seemed at rest, without the will to act, it was accumulating the force without which it could not take advantage of future opportunity." It is Canning, again, who warns against mercy and half-way measures in warfare: "For, where only violence can bring the decision, weak hesitation is cruelty."

Harsh methods of conducting war are shameful? "The spirit of peace has no place in war, which, as the final appeal to force, must not be moderated. Slack conduct of war wastes, not saves, blood and wealth; it would be worse than parley or submission."

The last was Macaulay's utterance. I have cited Britons only as witnesses. Will a hard-headed business man of your type seriously blame us that we fought with every available weapon?

Fulton's submarine boat was frowned upon by Pitt, as a dangerous weapon against British sea power. The Coessin brothers devised one that provided space and air for nine men. It was tested and approved by Lazare Carnot in 1811. Swiftly and cheaply, the "Organizer of victory" wrote, France could construct under-sea craft. Nothing came of it; but no one then thought of outlawing this means of warfare. Great ships, capable of carrying heavy cargoes, became possible after the dynamo accomplished the extraction of light aluminum in unlimited amounts from argillaceous earth.

As hot suffocating gases poured out of an exploding shell, "The idea naturally suggested itself," as Professor Anschütz said, "of pouring heavy gases, irritating to the mucous membranes, without explosion, by mechanical means, over a wide area of the enemy's position so as to drive out the combatants."

Explosives, your people thought, would soon be scant with us when no more saltpetre came from Chile. A vain hope! Ammonia is produced from nitrogen and hydrogen, and ammonia mixed with air becomes saltpetre. Despite the blockade, which shut out the familiar materials, the hardest, toughest steel was assured. Chemistry discovered the color for German uniforms best suited to the battlefield, the means of illumination for clock-dials, metal for the threads of pocket-lamps, found substitutes for benzine and rubber, solidified liquid fats, produced serums and disinfecting materials (so that none of the pestilences that raged elsewhere crossed our borders), obtained curatives from thousands of synthetic carbon-compounds.

Why, O David of Manchester, reared in Wales, did your chemical industry, that fifty years ago seemed invincible, let itself be beaten by ours? Why did only six men of complete scientific training serve your state, while we had two hundred and fifty? Why were your submarines, aeros, cannon, explosives, fuses, telescopes, metal plates, films, not better than ours?

Once, long ago, you were united in a mighty empire, and could not but be so far in advance that seven-league boots were unable to overtake you. Then the globe would have heard no complaint about unethical German behavior. After the declaration of war, to cut off our supply of saltpetre from the Chilean province Tarapaca was your sacred right. When we plucked deliverance out of the air, and on every front

proved superior to our enemy's cannon, then we were
outlawed with the cry: "These Huns think Might
makes Right!"

In the second year of the war I asked the question:
"When civic life returns to earth, what will be the
relation of the Prussianized German with the nations,
with all mankind?"

M. Bergerat, once the cheerful genial Caliban of
Figaro, made answer then:

"If, twenty years after the conclusion of peace, a
son of these Germans of today offers his hand to us, to
Englishmen, Italians or Russians, our gesture must say
to him, 'Away with you. Depart forevermore from
us! What your fathers did can never be effaced.
Oceans divide you from us since then!' For almost a
half century the German has devoted himself, body
and soul, to the invention of a war undreamed of elsewhere, which should combine all harms and leave nothing to chance. Robbery, incendiarism, butchery, violation—without shame he taught himself every barbaric
art and went back, consciously and deliberately, across
twenty thousand years, to the fighting methods of pre-
Adamite man-apes. That, he asserted, was to be the
real warfare of the future.

"Now the German wishes peace. What would it be
like? If no one survives to proclaim his victory, then
there is no distinction of vanquished from victors.
What we are living through is no human war, the sport
of ancient heroes or of the great commanders, in which
the poet's imagination bids the gods take part. For
this war no Homer will arise! Who would sing of

factories? In this Darwinian strife for the life of the species, this war of numbers against violence or trickery, no issue is thinkable save one: Extermination! Neither reconciliation on the battle field (as after an honorable duel) nor softening of hatred by time. Ill were it for mankind, if the peace that follows this war should not bring with it annihilation!"

One day after the publication of these sentences M. Aulard, France's most famous historian, cried from the tribune:

"Let there be no illusion. Only blood brings us victory. How often have we been assured that our mastery of the sea would force the empires of Central Europe into famine? But it only compels Germans and Austrians no longer to over-eat! Those gluttons are but forced into a better manner of living, and so, without gorging or guzzling of beer, into nimbler thought and action, through the new hygiene. Will Germany, for lack of food, arms, men, collapse and confess defeat? A perilous delusion!

"And if 'twere to come true: if Germany, starved out, disarmed, were compelled to beg for peace, I should see in that the most grievous peril, the certainty of near, of horrible evil. What terms of peace could we impose upon a people whose army has been victorious, has occupied French and Russian territory, the whole of Belgium, Serbia and Montenegro? Surely, only a peace that might, perhaps, give us back Alsace-Lorraine, set free Belgium and Serbia, but would leave Prussian militarism, in all its might and glory, intact. The Prussianized German Empire would remain a constant menace, a constant peril for mankind. Sooner than we it would recover from its loss in men. By the fruitless and negative victory our alliances would be weakened, and after brief respite united Germany would pounce upon the contentious Allies to crush them decisively. "From this it follows that genuine victory, which will assure durable peace, and so the destruction of Prussian militarism, and secure the maintenance of the balance of power among European nations, can only be won when the German army is smashed, broken to pieces, its prestige and splendor taken from it. The number and the valor of our soldiers assures us this real victory on the day when we have cannons, machine guns, flying machines, poison-gas, in sufficient amounts, when closer unity and better method are secured, and when an elementally mighty effort of power and will utilizes our admirable warriors and complete munitions of war."

So wrote a thinker, on the threshold of the nineteenth war month.

And you, O Vulcan of the island Romans, you didn't worry? When your colleague Asquith grew feeble, and like Saul of old, "dried his eyes on the hangings of his room," you, more vigorous than that yellow weakling, the David of Rembrandt, plucked at your harp until from its strings the spark of your own eager faith fired the old man's blood. Again in January, 1916, you roused yourself to undertake a David's task.

"Beside our unconquerable fleet is growing up a mighty army, armed and equipped as few continental armies have ever been. And behind the fronts a new England, a flawless industrial organism, with marvelous machinery, an ideal organization, and a people proud of their hereditary freedom, rejoicing in their unity won by self-sacrifice. Our national wealth increases, replacing ten-fold what the war devours. So we need not fear that that war will long go on. I count it possible that it may last two years more. It ends when victory shines upon us."

—And—"when the foe is flayed, yea, destroyed"? So could, so really should the psalm have closed! Overthrow of the German army, extermination of the sixty millions that toil with brain or hand behind it.

A hundred years before, a minister of a British King George had heard that melody,—from Frenchmen then.

"The Prussian monarchy is by its very structure forced into ambition. That ambition must be bridled. If the Allies grant her the ten million inhabitants that she had before her fall, she will soon have twenty, and dominate all German lands. The German Confederation offers us the means to stifle her greed for power. Her possessions can not be extended if the little states are preserved, the central countries enlarged."

This was Talleyrand's plan to hem Prussia in, the germ of an alliance by England, France (the France of Louis XVIII) and Austria against Russia and Prussia. Lord Castlereagh allowed himself to be won over. For the Berliners he had honeyed words, but no will to aid them. England might have pushed aside at that time the memory of all the Great Fritz had

done and made herself fast friends with the chief
power in Germany.

But you, Sir, with all the munitions of war heaped
up about you, were you never yourself disturbed when
the cry of terror against Force was raised? Oh, no.
"Germany is the arch-enemy of the human race. After
victory the German warrior-caste would only seek for
new conquests. Europe would sink into helplessness.
Our sea-power would be wrenched away from us, the
French and Russians would no longer be allowed to
maintain the armies needed to defend their frontiers."
It was the voice of Europe's counsellor that pleaded:
"A halter for the transgressor!"

But at home, after dinner, swollen with your knowledge of human nature, you shook with laughter at the
threat to put that speech to the test of your own conscience: "Oh, just stuff for jurymen and popular belief; doesn't affect the price of gold."

Agreed. But what is it that will happen?

My answer, in the spring of 1916, was:

"Europe is bleeding to death. We refuse to stop,
today, to count how many men have fallen and been
crippled; everywhere the most vigorous in the van.
Yet a year more, two years, fresh devastation; im-
poverishment to crush our grandchildren, burden our
latest descendants; stunting of industry; degeneration
of our whole manner of living, back to the conditions
from which the creation of the empire uplifted us.
Loans are future taxes for the citizens of the hostile
lands. The state will become a business partner who
pockets half your profits. Government monopolies,

restrictions on manufacture and trade, official surveillance, lessening of demand, high barriers against
offerings of large supplies! Does private industry pay
today? Is not, rather, the time drawing nigh, that
is promised in the Socialists' manifesto?

"The longer the fighting and the destruction of
values lasts, the heavier grows the cloud over any hope
to recoup, as victor, the costs of the war. What people
could adjust itself to ten years' serfdom under con-
querors garrisoning their land? Their very souls
would be at last outworn! Aversion from wedlock,
home, daily civic duties. Somewhere the whole framework of a state would collapse (one only?), and once
again there would be losses and miseries for those near
or far. Do you dream that your social reform, your
relief plan, could be saved from the hurricane? Will
not the gulf between hastily-clutched Mammon and
naked misery be yet deeper after the war than in
those days when you thought the world-order destroyed?

"In your Lower House it has been said that the
war is an event comparable to the fall of the Roman
Empire, the invasion of Islam, the Reformation, the
Proclamation of the Rights of Man, with all that
came after, under Robespierre, the Directorate, Bonaparte. If it goes according to your notion, if the fighting continues, does it begin to dawn upon you that
your colleague at Westminster did not exaggerate?"

Yet again, I repeat, it was in the spring of 1916
that I wrote that.

And has not the gulf between riotous wealth and
degrading poverty grown yet wider than in the year

of your "Poor man's budget"? Has what the war devoured of your people's wealth been tenfold replaced? Out of a deeper root of realization than yours came my prognosis, without official station though I was, who, midway in the second year of the war, wrote that from month to month the hope was more heavily overclouded for any adequate recovery of the victor's costs.

You were forced into a war against Ireland, waged it with such merciless cruelty as only the blackest mythical legend ascribed to the German army,—and had to deal with the Sinn Fein as you would with a hostile power and grant to defiant Ireland the rights of the greatest Dominions. Egypt, where for forty years England's will was absolute law, won her freedom, and chose a banished rebel for her ruler. To Major General Younghusband India seemed more grievously imperiled than ever before. America, that threatened your sea power more grimly than ever Germany could have done, and China, wandering in impenetrable darkness, alike rejected your commercial treaty. The demand for your manufactures was dead; the world-rule of the pound sterling destroyed; what were the Isles of the Blest now hear the cry of want from two millions of unemployed. To the shrill battlecry against Socialism and Communism you add, without pause for breath, the rash announcement that the new Moscow gospel takes the force out of the principles of the gentle Labor Party and that Lenin's speeches are hardly to be distinguished from those of the war minister and Bolshevik-hater, Winston Churchill!

Never did the sigh steal through so many British hearts: "Nobody knows what he believes in! Does he himself see a goal and struggle with strategic skill to reach it, or is all his activity merely part of the needful daily exercise of a tactician? Is the solicitor-general of the Allies in wartime growing to the eminence of a creative statesman, or is his strength fading out, like Clémenceau's, before the completion of his task comes into view?"

You have no party and no longer any psychology. In wartime you did have one which, whether genuine or not, was invariably effective. What has happened to it undazzled eyes can see at a glance. Only on the platform to a popular audience, never before the woolsack at Westminster, will you venture the assertion that the lie of the origin of Right from Might is so deep buried that it can have no resurrection. In every task you have been successful. Can it be, then, that in the highest of all you have disappointed the confident hopes of men?

You seemed a creature of exhaustless natural energy. Will you content yourself with the short-lived fame of one who, in an unwelcome war, fanned the fire of a host of peoples even to the high noon of victory? Much longer lasts the laurel of the Bringer of Peace. Does not your ear, else so fine, so wakeful and keen at the dawning of uproar, hear the storm of longing that calls for the Redeemer, the Messiah? He will ascend, in the splendor of the flame of God, not in the robes of the Counsellor, to the highest seat. That seat, Celtic David, is empty as yet.

In London, in the morning of the year 1921, you

intended to create a peace; and the attempt failed.
You were determined that this time, even over the
highest obstacles and hurdles, you would attain the
goal; but even the magic wand of your persuasive
skill struck no spark from empty heads. It vexed you,
too, that the broad picture you painted of horrible
deeds done in war by Germans made not even the
shallowest impression on Germany's soul. As it is
with a grown-up who leads stupid children, all in vain,
over and over, close to the spot where the sweet
Easter eggs are hidden,—so was it with you. Hence
that discourteously shrill complaint over the non-ap-
pearance there of any German statesman competent
to act upon so important a subject.

Yet to us, debtors in all else that we are, you owe
as yet the proof that you yourself possess the breath,
the brain, the breadth of soul, for such an undertaking—the flame of God, not the most pugnacious counsellor's unwearied keenness of scent.

To a large portion of your great speech every just
man could not but give his assent. What you said
as to the responsibility of the Imperial government
was here in Germany not heard aright (in some quar-
ters, heard with intent to misinterpret).

"That Germany distrusts us is more easily explained than our distrust of her. The Germans need
an army, as we need a fleet: for defense against hostile
onslaughts. Although their land lies between two
strong military states, they have never striven to create
an army superior to the defensive power of both neighbors; but we absolutely refuse to give up our 'Two-

power standard,' and we have built dreadnoughts that were quite needless, to assure our superiority on the sea. Our claim has no just foundation."

That was publicly uttered on the next to the last day of July, 1908, by Lloyd George, Chancellor of the Exchequer. You cannot have believed, then, in our wearisomely crafty preparations for war.

The mere comparison with the Peace of Frankfort proved that your intention in London was to repeat the principle—"He who declares war takes on himself the responsibility, and if defeated, the whole burden of reparation." Our standard-bearer took the sentence in a more ethical sense than it was intended and swears that "The revival of the 'guilt-question' will furnish the shroud for the Versailles agreement."

These disguised Monarchists (the unmasked ones deserve all the respect due to pious believers) shudder at any mention of the fact that the imperial government, by unrighteous and hasty action, in thirst for glory and blindness, in the summer of 1914, burdened itself with the chief guilt for the outbreak of the war. They seriously believe, in spite of Wilhelm's letters and marginal notes, despite two declarations of war, invasion of neutralized Belgium, and the lies as to conspiracy, attack, bomb-throwing, etc., that day after tomorrow, out of two worlds, the confession will resound: "We were mistaken, or were deceived by villains; and it is our stupidity that has dug the graves of many millions."

Such a childish fancy does not help us forward. No more does it to drag out and throw the light on all the mistakes that have been made before, at, and after, the London conference. (Jurists without juristic instincts, and with a craving for applause: most terrible of terrors!)

We are threatened, all of us, with a danger, from the results of which this quarter of the world could not recover within any time that can be descried. Did you foresee that danger, or did you only wish to "get rid" at last of the wearisome business, to chain the French to the anchor of mere hope, and throw a towrope to the Germans on which, drenched like a poodledog, but with unbroken bones, they might come safe to some scant beach?

Great Britain's demand on Europe, at present, is only for money: but Europe demands more from Britain. France fears that, cheated out of the reparation payments, plunged into insolvency, she will be overwhelmed by her stronger neighbor's thirst for revenge. Germany fancies herself dragged down into the dust, clutches again at the straw "Necessity knows no law," and lets herself be beguiled into thinking she shows heroism by refusing to pay her plain duty-debt.

"Thirty annual payments? No! Twelve milliards in the spring, the first one in March? No! You're peddling out the coal that we deliver to you? Shameless misuse! No plan, to point the way toward an understanding. The Entente may split its lungs; we won't budge!"

Is this state of things to continue? Imposing fresh penalties will only fan the glow of hatred. The negotiations must begin again tomorrow. Not in public; that is always with a glance, or a squint,—at the gal-

lery. We need to discuss it quietly, like sober business
men. Frank talk, with no virtuous posing, and nothing held back. Serious consideration of the necessary
and the possible, not of what once was. Germany's
people cannot and will not be a swarm of beggars, a
festering sore on Europe's body. Once on free soil
they will again listen to the voice of Conscience. Let
everything they accumulate above bare necessities go
to Reparation (which France sees as quite too simple
a matter). Two peoples that control the ore and coal
of Western Europe, and for whose wares immense
regions are ravenous, can, even without hearty friendship, help each other quickly to prosperity, if England only restrains her selfishness, and learns to look
with friendly eye on a Franco-German economic trust,
or even confederation.

The statesman who accomplished such a lofty task
would need no party. He hallows by justice his possession of power. For the Bringer of Peace the laurel
blooms imperishable; does that laurel hang too high
aloft for your reach?

Lloyd George craved the laurel. It was his desire
that summoned the nations to Genoa. There was a
double purpose: to grind out a world film useful for
the Parliamentary elections, and to found a League
on which Harding's America would look more favor-
ably than on Wilson's. Despite uncommon success in
war and peace, the Prime Minister (to whom the
people had never given a familiar nickname, as they
had to Palmerston, Disraeli, Gladstone, Chamberlain)
was no longer beloved of all men at home. Wilhelm

wasn't hanged, Germany couldn't pay, and the election bacon, which should have gone to the smoke-house before Easter, was getting rancid.

Ireland, Egypt, the Caliphate, India—like the white leaves from an artichoke—were being stripped off from the stalk of the British Empire, and in the fat earth the moisture was drying out. Constant protests from the Dominions, quiet industrial crises, stagnation of trade, unemployment, overburdened budgets in the state and the communities, sullen murmuring on every side:

"All the fault of the hasty untrustworthy demagogue. Yesterday a Radical, three-quarters Socialist, today a most pious Calvinist and original Free Trader, on familiar footing with the dear Lord himself, chews the cud of Cobden's and Bright's principles, and would root out all Socialism, trunk and stump. If he, in spite of his oath 'never to clasp the bloody hand of the Moscow murderers,' hadn't begun to chaffer with Krassin, we would not now, on all sides, from Canada to Asia Minor and the South African mining regions, be tormented with Bolsheviks. His hope that America would cross off the four billion dollars we owe her was builded on the sand. The soup he served, against the advice of the Cambridge professor, Keynes, and other learned specialists, at Versailles, has turned the stomach of our trade!"

This is not all true. The notion that the aches and pains of industry, of the export trade, were brought on by the shortcomings of the Peace Treaty, sprang from a hasty and superficial survey of the situation.

Throughout four years, fifty million people, those most useful for manual labor and the arts, had worked only upon means of destruction. On this side and beyond the ocean entire industries were built up which no one had needed, so long as their products were to be obtained from Germany. Meantime the old German industries were not, as might be imagined, given up, but were developed in the heat of the ever-renewed pressure to produce what was needed for the army and for the folk at home. In wide fields heretofore satisfied with imports, various peoples became in the course of the war providers for their own needs. So there was a multiplication of the chief industries, increase in productive capacity, and (especially, but not only, in Eastern Europe) a terrible decrease in the demand and in means to purchase.

From all this, was not the heretofore unheard-of business crisis, whose beginning worries the world, clearly inevitable? Heretofore men have groaned over the "severe crises" whenever the scales of production and consumption were not to be held in perfect equilibrium. Now the latter swings high, and far below the other sways softly; and a miracle, one not to be expected from Conference or Consortium, must come to pass in order that the generation now alive may see the end of this worst of crises, and the return to healthy industrialism.

The development was not forced upon mankind at Paris, it was not sealed at Versailles. Yet to the man on the street, because the newspaper spreads the lie before him daily, the Peace Treaty is the devil's spawn that sowed misery in his world. And Mr. Lloyd

George, last survivor in office of the "Big Four" who made the peace, is a suspected contemporary.

Despite the lack of any one far-beckoning leader's name, victory at the polls was altogether too uncertain against all these hostile forces: the Tories, weary of the yoke under which they had bent so long, when even they had been forced to take a hand in the unfettering of Ireland and the stripping of leaf after leaf from the Empire; the Labor Party in the tumult of its desire for the New Day; the free lances of the Churchills, Grey-Asquiths, and Robert Cecils, electoral battle against all these was altogether uncertain.

So the Genoa film was planned to assure electoral success. Three dozen nations made up "the noble supernumerary mob"; there were eminent managers; the press of the world provided the orchestra. He would be the stupidest of rogues who could not win profit from such a pageant.

The David who slew Goliath transformed himself into the David of the psalter, of the harp. The champion of the "knock-out" became the Saviour from whose benignant hand mankind, languishing in agony, was to receive peace. If only the First Lord of the Treasury could lead the tamed Bolsheviks to make an oath to his Gracious Majesty, to renounce henceforth all plotting, stirring up of sedition among the masses, all mole's work; if he could but demonstrate that Christ died on the cross and rose again, the martyrs perished in torture, the papacy was spiked to Peter's rock, and its all too earthy material disintegrated by the lye of the reformer-spirit,—all this in order that trade might bloom unblasted, that no limit be set to

the sale of oil, iron, wool and other earthly goods; and
if this First Lord of the Treasury should be applauded
by the unanimous voice of public opinion, and if he
were able, for the three vernal months at least, to plant
firmly the faith that all sorrow should soon be turned
into joy and the deadness of the market transformed
into abundance like Pactolus' stream,—why, then, the
nation that shared in the sunshine of his fame would
make up its mind to grant to the world's darling a
continuance of its confidence!

That was the goal. "Whatso Reinecke doeth and
writeth, that abideth evermore rightly done and duly
recorded. Hereof shall each and everyone take due
notice!"

First disappointment: M. Briand sauntered out of
the presidency of the Cabinet, in which the First Official and the Senate would not gladly see him longer.
This amiably clever Bohemian of politics was a good
comrade, not always easy, and sometimes ruder than
was to be expected from one so comfortably bedded in
the favor of princesses, but nimble, pliable and—especially since his loss of prestige at Washington and
Cannes—hardly replaceable as a medium of communication and as general manager.

President Millerand showed the Welshman, who
scolded him as if he were a schoolboy, that even in
Elysium there may be porcupine quills. President
Poincaré is a heavy cautious student of documents,
who listens to the mood of Chamber, and allows himself neither to be fascirated nor betrayed into fire-
works.

These were two experienced watchful attorneys of

the Bourgeoisie, who understood alike the peasant and the laborer, and were opponents to the English advocate of the middle class, who wounded the pride of France by the all too gracious proffer of a treaty of (very long-distance) protection against invasion.

The disappointed Prime Minister snarled out his rage at the check upon applause for himself that had come from the Parisians. But already he had a plan prepared to pillory France as the disturber of the peace. The shrewd man made his approaches craftily. He published, after three years, a memorandum in which he had sounded a warning against the all too sharp corners of the Versailles treaty, against excessive robbery of Germany and enrichment of Poland. That the warner had cheerily let all the evil come to pass, and angrily dismissed his financial adviser, Keynes (who saw in his chief always the mischief-maker, never the counselor of moderation), did not hinder the master of magic from turning the spotlight on his own kindliness, and denouncing the Lorrainer (whom old Clémenceau had actually excluded from every deliberation upon the treaty) as the arch-villain.

Second disappointment: the Rapallo pact; a gross violation of the basic principles announced at Cannes, to the observation of which all those invited to Genoa had bound themselves. Water to the Frenchmen's mill! Better, indeed, could not have been devised, even by them, to whom it was essential to maintain that a "fair trade" and honorable frankness were no more obtainable from Germans today than yesterday.

"You only needed to sit tight, coöperate with us in quiet good faith, and you could have been sure of important gains." In a tempest of abuse and condemnation David's fury was discharged.

After that, from the fair Italian city only Lloyd George's voice resounded over the land, over the sea; from consultation-rooms, from dining halls, from the parks (where the fragrance of Ceylon's tea is wafted about the palms). He praised and blamed, caressed and pinched men's ears, blessed and damned. The Pope (who had written a curious parish-priestly letter to a government secretary) was "a most excellent man," so his Don Sturzo was invited to the breakfast-table of the Welsh heretic. "Don't spoil the Riviera for those splendid Moscow fellows! It's true one of the Czar's gold rubles, just one, buys 2½ million Soviet rubles; but 'tis but a bat-blind Frenchman who draws the conclusion that they're doing us! They accepted the principles of Cannes and now flout them, yes; but who should worry about little matters of property rights in a land where many a Belgian, German, Frenchman, but only two or three Englishmen, have claims for restitution and reparation?"

Yesterday, "my dear Tschitscherin," wars were impossible, and conferences therefore needless: today David's eye, rolling in uncanny frenzy, sees the despair-driven Germans arming the starving Russians for the most appalling of all wars (which would surely have to come as quickly as lightning, and in impenetrable darkness).

Nonsense became sense. If such a spring-flood were thinkable, if the advance of the Russo-German armies were not early checked, say, by the bluecross gas produced in the west, then the Right Honourable would have no right to scoff at the distrustful fears of his war Allies.

He roared,—Only, no halting! The masterpiece, the European compact, must be brought safely under shelter. That which it is to bring with itself has long stood already in the Covenant, the statute-book of the League, and also at the end of the Cannes program. No matter about that; not until tomorrow will it become history.

M. Poincaré must come hither. How can he have the audacity to be making speeches at home, while the fate of mankind is taking shape? Here must he, the father of all evil, acknowledge what villainy he is plotting for the time after the last of May.

Great Karl, who stretched his hand over all the earth, sun—Louis, who in himself mirrored the state—they were but timid dwarfs beside this All-embracer, whom the Tories (that he might gloriously reveal himself?) left to roar alone, without Balfour the file-leader and Curzon the guide. The shriller his outcry, the more venomous his insinuations against the Parisians (read Reinecke's moral sermon on Isegrim's wickedness), so much the more sincere was the regret to see a man of such high achievement degraded to the rank of a circus barker,—and so much the larger, it is true, grew his audience.

Only, all this was but the cranking of a film, not a discussion on the world's business by equals, striving to lighten the destitution of mankind. A Conference you call it? In a Levantine cabaret a debater yells and stamps to win applause. The film was of a sort that pleases only in Germany. The "common sense"

of Great Britain turned gruffly away from the noisy
shouter, who in the war had won approval everywhere, but since then had sowed trouble, and (as M.
Poincaré quietly and shrewdly pointed out) well nigh
roused all Islam against England. Twice he himself
failed of election. He had to fall in behind Asquith,
at whom he had so often scoffed.

Since then he has written articles which, despite the
fullness of his life-experience, rose not an inch above
the level of tolerable editorial leaders. Through them
all rang the wish to secure the scalp of Raymond of
Lorraine, in whom he sees (not without reason) the
author of his own downfall. (Is it this Indian impulse that beguiles the Sioux to elect to honorary chief-
ship the white man who roars through America as a
peripatetic orator with a megaphone?)

Too quickly, at home, he assumed again the Saviour-
rôle. He who yesterday ate Socialists raw, or fried,
now finds Mr. Jason Ramsay MacDonald the elect of
heavenly wisdom, who shall bring home the golden
fleece of world-peace (and by harsh bullying of
France weaken himself and his party in popular
favor). Is the German, "the Hun," the detestable
butt of the notorious "knock-out" speech, today the
noble sufferer upon whose prostrate body the sinful
pride of the Gaul "tramps to and fro"? Does he believe what he says? Yes, while the breath lasts with
which he utters it. But the proposal to give the martyr
just one of the ships taken from him, one bit of what
were German possessions, the tiniest scrap of colonial
land, he would reject with gusty laughter. To other
men he preaches magnanimous renunciation (he who

would raise the tariff for German goods to prevent their importation).

Out of the many husks of his talents stands revealed at last his own original nature. That this man may climb once more to the bleak peak of political power is thinkable; but not that he who confuses Silesia with Cilicia, who sees in the Poles of Upper Silesia interlopers or miners invited in by Prussia, who stands with no key of understanding, without even an instinct, helpless before the riddles of the Russian continent, will ever again, with a swarm of obedient secretaries, far away from the traditions, the doctrines, the whole atmosphere of the Foreign Office, prescribe the paths of the British Empire. For England knows him; knows him for one who even beneath the snows of age retains his personal charm, but in the inmost heart of his effort always holds, always wished to hold, only himself.

IV

CLEMENCEAU

In the Hall of Mirrors of the palace at Versailles, which once was the abode of the Most Christian Kings, the Peace Congress, from which mankind hopes for the creation of enduring world-peace, is presided over by an old man, yet unbowed by the burden of age. An Asiatic? At first glance he seems one. With his yellow skin, his saddle-nose between prominent cheek-bones, and his Tartar moustache, he recalls Mongolia rather than La Vendée. But even so did many a Celtic chieftain, many a Gaulish Brennius look. Does M. Georges Clémenceau feel today that he is like that Brennius who, after his victory on the Allia, forced the beaten Romans to weigh out their tribute, a thousand pounds of gold, with false weights and, when they complained, thundered in their faces the words of scorn, "Vae victis"? Does he now also wish to teach a deadly foe that the vanquished have no rights, are delivered helpless to the victor's every caprice? I cannot believe it. Between the fight at the Allia and the battle of the Marne lie three and twenty centuries. Between them shines the teaching of Christianity and all the efforts of the spirit of humanity,—of Sully, Bernardin de Saint-Pierre, Rousseau, Kant, Washington and now Wilson, who have striven to secure honorable peace for the world, to make the insolence of physical force bow beneath the banner of justice, and, upon an earth fragrant with the imperishable flower of sincere brotherly love, to assure due reverence for the individuality of each nation as of each human being.

Was this Vendéan of eight and seventy, whose whole life was a battle for justice, for freedom, for the advancement of humanity, to stand aloof from all those efforts, untaught by the purest wisdom of all the ages of culture? He had never been at ease under the imperial rule of Louis Napoleon, and though he had brought back a wealthy wife from America he lived a retired and simple life as physician of the poor at Montmartre, and in the Paris city council was a champion of the weary and heavy-laden. At the age of thirty, during the rule of the Commune, he was the mediator between Versailles and Paris, between the rebels and the hostages. In the Chamber he was Gambetta's successor as deputy from Belleville. Always a fighter. Zola, when he was editing *La Justice* in 1880, ranked him (in *Figaro*) already above Gambetta:

"M. Clémenceau is a man of the scientific spirit, and of serious importance. He marches with the century and his place is in the foremost rank of the new men. He speaks clearly, simply, logically, the language of an orator. To my mind his speeches, because they are plain, without a dash of extravagant rhetoric, are superior to Gambetta's. And yet this delegate is almost isolated, quite without influence in the circle of his colleagues. I am sure that even the commonplace Floquet will attain to the tiller before he does."

And so it came to pass. The radical, the poor man's physician, had his first day of greatness when Brisson presided over the Assembly and Fallières, destined later to be President of the Republic, was Minister of Education. It was then that against the Prime Minister, Jules Ferry, who was being furiously attacked on all sides by yelling assailants, he raised the cry "Away with you!" (*Allez-vous-en*). From that time he was known as the "destroyer of ministers." A divorce scandal lessened his repute. The Panama debacle swept the friend of Cornelius Herz, the promoter, out of the Palais Bourbon. He was accounted a taker of bribes from England and from the looters of the canal. If he opened his mouth he was put to silence with the silly gibe: "Aoh, yes!"—Destroyed?

He smiled, feeling himself unconquerable. Again he started *La Justice*, then the *Bloc*, and finally took charge of the *Aurora*. He that would not listen should read! Clémenceau became generalissimo of the Dreyfus crowd; he sounded the call for resistance to governmental violence, condemned militarism and the courts martial (to which as Prime Minister in war time he later assigned all trials for treason). He became senator and like all Dreyfus's champions, world-renowned. But only late in life, at sixty-six, was he a minister. For a half century he fought, without wavering, for the liberation of men's minds from priestly domination and militaristic arrogance, from the cowl and the sabre, often, especially against hated ministers, like one who loves the fray for its own sake. Gambetta, Ferry, Millerand, Jaurès, Delcassé, Poincaré, Ribot; whoever has won a name, has felt his blade. *Batailleur* (lover of strife) like Cyrano de Bergerac, with whom he also has in common the keen rapier of wit, and also

oftentimes *bretteur sans vergogne* (a shameless bully).
But he, the antique Jacobin, the last of the race of
Danton, is none the less always a true Intellectual.
(He has even written a drama, which the wicked
Boches put on the stage in the Berlin Theatre chris-
tened with the name of the arch-hater of the French,
Lessing.)

It is true that in 1907, as Prime Minister, he did let
Marianne feel the weight of his bony fist. The vintners' uprising in the South was beaten down by force
and craft combined. A regiment which refused to
obey others was sent to Tunis as a punishment. In
Marseilles baker apprentices, in Paris the electrical
workers, were dispersed. Wherever a spark glimmered
soldiers were ordered to march against bourgeois and
workingmen. On May Day the capital was like a camp
awaiting the call to battle. Jaurès, the orator, foamed
with rage but was overwhelmed with invective. He
never won a victory in his strife with this foeman. The
end sanctions all means.

Clémenceau in 1871 had voted against the pre-
liminary peace, and his hope of vengeance for Sedan
was never buried. All German ambassadors from
Hohenlohe to Radolin dreaded him as the instigator
of *Revanche*. "He will have a thumb for the eye of
the German who gazes longingly toward Morocco."
By treaties with Japan and Spain, he secured quiet
about Atlas, in Indo-China, on Madagascar; then he
went fearlessly to Udjida, where the Algerian soldier,
after the long hesitation of the Parisians, had hardly
hoped to set foot again. He praised every general
who "in the garrulous warmth of the banquet" made

a stab at the neighbor to eastward. And yet, in this radical Democrat and enthusiast for the tricolor, there still lived the man of lofty mind. *Labor, Justice, Dawn, The Freeman.* With such names were christened the journals which he edited. Is he minded now, as one of those who brought final victory, to set a crown on his life-work?

His first ministry ended ingloriously. Six days after the triumph accorded him by the national festival at Longchamp in 1909, he was overthrown by a word of Delcassé, overthrown by the fury of his own retort, which revealed that France, in the first year of the Morocco crisis, was unprepared and so was forced to submit herself to the "most shameful humiliation." The recess of the legislature was at hand. A hundred members were on a journey through Norway. Conservatives, Liberals, and Social-Democrats united against the cabinet and defeated the vote of confidence proposed. As the blue ballots piled up in the baskets and the fall of the government became a certainty, Clémenceau grasped his papers and said with a smile: "I'm off (*Je m'en vais*)." Brisson was again presiding over the Chamber, as he was on Ferry's day of doom, and Fallières, seated beside the victim on the ministerial bench, this time received, as head of the state, from Clémenceau's hand, the request for the dismissal of the cabinet. "Wasn't it sensible that I didn't move out of my private home? With my umbrella I came into the minister's house, with my walking stick I go out. So,—no moving expenses. My successors would do well to show like prudence." One final jest, and the dictator was again a newspaper writer. A jester and a brawler he remained. "My majority was under the midnight sun. And how could I budge, between two colleagues, one of whom (Caillaux) was posing as Napoleon, the other (Briand) as Jesus Christ?"

Eight years later this man, who had never duly recognized Joffre, the Marne victor, who had scolded Viviani and Briand, Ribot and Painlevé, railed daily at President Poincaré, mocked at Wilson, pulverized the Caillaux and the Malvys in the mortar of his scorn,—wrote above a leading article in *L'Homme Enchaîné* the heading, "A Government is demanded!" That was November 15, 1917. That afternoon M. Poincaré requested him to form this government. On the 16th, at noon (not at five P.M., as the stirring old man had promised the reporters), it was formed.

His first speech to the House was a shrill, defiant trumpet call. He had no faith in conciliation, the brotherhood of nations, the conversion of the world, the gentle reign of justice. The union of nations, which M. Bourgeois had for ten years been recommending, was child's talk to him, and his raillery maliciously punctured almost every sentence in Wilson's peace program. It was at that time that I said:

"Only victory that smashes the foe into helplessness can sate him; swift victory over the arch-enemy, the Prussia-led German Empire on the Franco-British front (all else is rubbish to him). He, he alone, is the government; as prime minister and minister of war he plays the final, the highest rôle; and he will strain every nerve, every heart-beat, every effort of his will, to rise, at last, in the eyes of the whole world to the greatness of which he has always felt himself capable. He may win much for his fatherland; he may on the other hand lose terribly. Until the dice shall have fallen from that yellow bony hand, the miraculous coming of the spiritual union of mankind is not nigh. Solness the Masterbuilder ventures upon the rooftree of the house that his dream has builded. If he falls headlong, Youth will raise a joyous shout; Youth, that does not wish to see its abode constructed by feverish old men nor to have the home it longs for furnished with mouldering desires; Youth, that listens not for the voice of weary officials and cold-blooded phrase-makers, but for the beat of a great heart. Like the tiger's tooth, even so shall decay also (what our poet in the Song of the Bell calls more terrible) mankind's delusion. Then out of the glimmering ashes of a patriotism made ignoble by craving for power and greed of conquest—as the phœnix of the international socialism that has perished in the fire,—shall soar Heavenward the consciousness of human kinship."

M. Clémenceau, old as the hills to behold, played the game and won! Now shall the miracle be wrought?

He looks about him in the Hall of Mirrors, and over his deep-furrowed yellow cheeks there creeps a sunset glow of sparkling triumph. This room, where Vanity can behold itself so gloriously reflected on every side, was dedicated, by an inglorious Louis, "*à toutes les gloires de la France.*" The phrase still displays itself upon the walls that echoed back, on the

18th of January, 1871, the proclamation of the German Empire. This day, however, they hearken to, and behold, the loftiest glory that the political history of France has ever recorded upon its pages. And he who has bestowed this glory upon his native land, after long deprivation, is the man whom his countrymen once disdained as a receiver of English bribes, smirched by the Panama scandal, whom they drove out of the Chamber of Deputies into the Senate, of whom even his followers said that he was indeed a mighty opponent, unsurpassed since Paul Louis Courier as a pamphleteer, but no statesman, one who could overthrow, cripple, destroy, but not build up, heal, create. Had he not now healed his country of the ills from which she suffered for almost half a century? Had he not begun the rebuilding of France in the splendor and greatness of the Bourbons' or Bonaparte's time? An old man, and even with a bullet now lodged between the lobes of his lung, he can yet enjoy a triumph such as a mortal has hardly experienced since Napoleon; a civilian, perhaps, never. He crosses his sinewy arms over his meagre breast, lifts his shoulders high like one who draws a deep breath, and even now resembles in every essential the portrait of him painted forty years before by Edouard Manet. There is none of the kindliness of age in the eye, the countenance of the Celt. Sternly he gazes from the President's chair at the glimmering lights of the Hall. *Vae victis!* The words flame from his eyes. A sign from him opens the door to the *délégués boches.*

Across many a mile my voice sought his ear:

"Into your path of action, your range of feeling, I

have tried to grope my way. The defeat of 1871 embittered and distorted your life. To hear the souls of the vanquished breathe in anguish about you was a horror and a torture to you. You sat in the parliament of Bordeaux and signed that protest against the wrenching away of Alsace and Lorraine from the beloved body of your homeland, a protest that rang out like a bell consecrated to the god of vengeance. All the other signers of that protest sank into the grave. You, alone, lived to see the war of vengeance. You had wished it, yearned for it; and it was as if that yearning desire had stiffened your body, hardened it to steel, so that the scythe of the Black Reaper could only graze you, not mow you down; as though it fell with a clash from its metal sheath. It seemed as if even the boy Cottin's bullet could not seriously harm the aged man it sought. If all the other men who sit about this table could swear before God and mankind that they had not willed the war, Georges Clémenceau may not take the burden of that oath upon his conscience, and will not. Need I recall to your mind all the bitter, hostile words that you have hurled at Germany, all your warning summonses to a war of retribution? You attached yourself for a little while even to the sorry knight Boulanger, because it seemed that he might prove the sword of your hope. In March, 1907, as Prime Minister you embraced General Bailloud, who at Nancy had in public given vehement utterance to his assured confidence in the early reconquest of the lost provinces. Their loss always seemed to you unendurable, their annexation a deadly sin which must be avenged, punished, even at the cost of a "zoölogical war" as Ernest Rénan called it, prophetically in his famous letter to Strauss.

"You lived to see the war, you carried it on,—you, as Minister of War and Premier, gave it such vigor as no war has ever before roused in France. You became, in a higher sense than Carnot, the organizer of victory. That we Germans know. I could show you letters of German generals and princes who sigh: 'If only we had a German Clémenceau!'

"Now you are the most eminent head and mouthpiece of those who should organize world peace. The power of your patriotic longing for victory, which enabled your aged body to endure the hardships of a daily journey to the front, has also turned to steel your spirit, which never had enjoyed indolent repose.

"Long-lasting remembrance is assured to the President of this Congress. Uncertain only is whether you wish to live in the memory of humanity as 'The Tiger' or as one who shared in the creation of a new union of mankind, as the representative of an old world impelled by greed of power and lust for vengeance, or as a master builder of a new and glorious temple of international harmony, founded upon the consciousness of kind. *That is the question.*

The sole survivor of Bordeaux restores Alsace and Lorraine to his fatherland. Do you have the least idea how bitter, for the Germans, this parting is, this encoffining of forty-seven long years of governmental labor? Although their lack of genial manners and of insight into racial psychology has been most terribly revealed precisely there, yet the Germans have accomplished much for the organization and the prosperity of those provinces. If anything could give us consolation, it would be the certainty that your France means to treat Teutonic Alsace tenderly, not to Gallicize her by violence. Strassburg, city of Erwin von Steinbach and of Goethe, the old imperial cities within whose walls, in the time of your Revolution, resounded the fame of French generals from German stock— Kleber, Kellermann, Rapp—these never were and never will be French. Instead of repeating Prussian mistakes and suppressing language and ancient usage, which is the very essence of individuality in this beautiful land, secure for it uncontrolled self-government— perhaps on the Galveston system—and yourself, in your own lifetime, prepare it thereby for the lofty mission of becoming the mediator between our two peoples, who, because they need each other and can supplement each other marvelously, like flame and fuel, must, therefore, learn to understand one another.

"There is a bitter smile on your lips and I know what words they would utter. You indulge in no illusions and cannot, as the executive of a people smitten to the marrow, offer mere phrases to their stomachs or brains,—and mere phrasing is, to you, anything that does not assure a renewal of the former development. How savagely did you, as the *Homme Enchaîné*, ridicule the Gospel of President Wilson! Yet gradually its magic mastered even you, and it is as its expositor that you sit where you do. That you may not forget.

"Time presses. Let me speak in utter frankness, not alone for this Germany, though in it dwell, in truth (you will hear no lie from me), not Boches alone.

But it is the cradle of a most honorable culture, not merely the Kultur of the discredited professors, and it gave to the Occident, to the whole Western World, its most fragrant flower, Music. No, not for Germany, but for all the world—and, finally, for yourself.

"You are not content that Alsace and Lorraine have returned to their own, though it is what only your boldest dream returned to hope. You desire the Saar basin and, if not political, at least economic mastery over the left bank of the Rhine and mountains of millions.

"It is not incomprehensible. France, in victory, is far, far more vitally wounded than in 1871, when overthrown. Thirty-six million inhabitants,—and of these, three millions of the most vigorous and productive, fallen or perished as a result of the war. Her chief industrial region, the treasure-house of the Republic, laid waste, her Paradise of planted fields and vineyards trampled under foot, her coal mines flooded or crippled for years. How could France, that has spent for munitions of war alone, twenty-eight thousand millions of francs, recover herself without Germany's money, labor, raw materials, to help set her on her feet? Even the Socialist disciples Longuet, Cachin, Mistral and their school, ay, many a peasant family that would remind one of Zola's *La Terre*, would cry aloud if the German gold-milliards should fail them: 'A fig for glory, for Alsace, for Lorraine! We will not endure that we and our children and our children's children shall be bowed down under the burden of taxation. We have not with resignation taken upon ourselves the agony, the horror, of this the most tremendous of all wars, only to groan in even profounder misery afterwards than ever before.'

"Your government, sir, would have to fear something grimmer than Jacobin revolution, ay, a very earthquake of upheaval, if the hope of your people for gain at our expense were suddenly dashed. Not in arrogance does it demand such a measureless amount. Your government must be able to credit to its yearly budget billions of German money: for, whenever that government called upon the French nation for fresh sacrifices it added as a consolation 'L'Allemagne payera.'

"But Germany cannot pay all. To be sure, she still has about sixty million people; her machinery is not smashed nor looted, as is that of northern France; her industrial areas and her technical apparatus are unharmed, quite intact, save where the blind fury of her own children has destroyed them. That is why victorious France fears this beaten people and expects that it will rebuild its military machine and, after the Americans and Britons, who hurried hither over channel and ocean, are at home again, will begin a most cruel war of revenge, and with the larger tale of men will overwhelm *la douce France* before aid from overseas again arrives.

"That is impossible. Anyone who saw Germany yesterday, even though it were with the eyes of hatred, will tell you today that, within any time now to be foreseen, she could become dangerous for the French only in case she were forced into toilsome slavery and so driven to slaves' resistance and to unnatural alliance with her traditional foes.

"Our clothing, even of those of us still seemingly well-to-do, is shabby; our shoes are patched; our suits we have had turned because new material is not to be had; what is issued to us of rationed food, by card, at fabulous prices, does not suffice to still the appetite of a child, and thus we have lived for years. Not a drop of pure milk is any longer to be seen; we know not how the flesh of strong well-fed cattle tastes. The clover, that used to go to the pigs, we ourselves now get in our 'bread.' Now for the first time in years, since the shipments from America, a half-pound per week to each of us, we have realized what genuine wheat flour looks like. By May we shall have no potatoes left.

"Our men are sallow, anæmic, enfeebled; our weary women's skin is loose and wrinkled like the leather of unlubricated machinery-belting. The children, brought up without milk, wither away like trees to which sunshine and water are denied. In Germany's cemeteries the rows of graves are ever lengthening.

"We crave no sympathy,—but only a pallid smile can respond to the suspicion that this same Germany, in which a Spartan policy of the painless slaying of all the elders, invalids, cripples and drones has been in all seriousness proposed, can set up a war machine, can at any visible date create the apparatus without which even Russia's human ocean would be as useless as a brook too weak to drive a mill-wheel. And even that smile dies, when an enormous tribute is demanded from Germany, where twenty millions of people are all but condemned already to imminent death, and where a few milliards have been laboriously raked up for the most necessary food. Such is the face of reality with us.

"Could the destruction of Germany benefit you, Frenchmen, or benefit mankind? Never has the solidarity of all human interests shone forth with such tragic force, through all false veils and vain imaginings, as since the maniacal transgression of this war, which with unheard-of persistence and cleverness has overthrown the whole framework of human prosperity. The old Europe can never be restored. A new one can upbuild itself only on the foundations of humanity's consciousness of its own unity, on the harmony of the nations' souls.

"Do you, sir, the organizer of victory, wish to live in memory as he who dug the grave of the old world, or as he who helped on the birth of the new? As the inheritor of a patriotism beside itself with thirst for revenge and greed for power, or as the progenitor of a youthful heaven-scaling patriotism to whose eyes kindness is not weakness, forgiveness is not childishness, nor profession of love for mankind an empty phrase? Shall it be a saying among men once again, and this time repeated forevermore, what was said after your first ministry, after your merciless attacks with soldiery upon poor vintners, upon factory workers who, at worst, were but misguided and starving to death for their faith,—that your withered age, your chilled heart, could no longer feel for the world, with all its misery and its longing?

"Millions of woeful, millions of dead eyes look to you, hoping that he who sits in judgment may not be too small for his tremendous task, that can either crush him utterly or uplift him to the height of the Spirit of God's Grace. For justice, freedom, progress, you have battled half a century long. If now your life is crowned by victory over self, then shall the fame of your name throughout all the life of mankind overtop that of all the rest with which these walls have re-echoed; then will it, too, be indeed consecrated 'to all the glories of France.' "

At such utterance the old man smiles, braces his knuckles, always grey-gloved against the table-top, and whispers only: "Proceed!" The last of the Jacobins. The Prussianest of Frenchmen. A Samurai from La Vendée. He that drew his breath for freedom and human rights now utters only Bonaparte's watchword: "Be strong, win power; all else is delusion!" Delusion to him is whatever exceeds the surety of making the most of the next hour. . . . A Cyrano grown old, old, old, who stamps, with a grimace, upon the *panache,* the cockade he has torn from his hat. To slash not merely bombast, empty pathos, but all lofty feeling, is his delight. He desired his war, won it, and upon a hundred tablets read the echo of the Roman formula: "Citizen Georges Clémenceau has deserved well of the fatherland." He desired his own peace, secured with all its bristling severity;—and lost the helmet-plume of his fame.

What the old man's energy accomplished, inspiring with his warm vitality those at the front and those at home, is deserving of all praise. But gradually he seemed, the whole Clémenceau chorus seemed, to forget that the tremendous victory could not have been attained, if General Pétain had not restored the fighting capacity of the army and America had not with deliberate speed thrown the whole of her mighty power into the bloody game.

Not at all times, and not at every Parting of the Ways, did the stubborn one see aright the necessities and the possibilities of the war. The creation and maintenance of the Saloniki front seemed to him a vagary, a senseless venture, into which Joffre had drawn the fools Poincaré and Briand, 'because this over-estimated general wanted to keep the far more capable Sarrail at a distance.' At the finish of the great struggle it stood revealed how essential the army of Eastern Europe was, for its pressure tore Bulgaria and Turkey out of the fourfold alliance. So *notre tigre national* was not infallible. Indispensable? The splendor of the stars may have dazzled him into that belief.

Until December, 1919, it was accepted as certain that Paul Deschanel would become President of the Republic in January. Then suddenly the rumor fluttered up that Clémenceau wished to be a candidate. Wished? Wished? Oh, no. He assumed the heroic, paternal rôle of self-sacrifice, which the burning desire of the people, of the land, did not permit him to refuse. He hoped, without taking the trouble to go to Versailles, without lifting a finger, to be chosen by a gigantic majority, and after that would perhaps at once, or after a couple of weeks, have renounced the Elysian delights. Possible, that he craved the office only as Zola did the frock-coat and palm of the Academician,—as the crown of a storm-beaten life.

Hated, outlawed, insulted, accused of treason, the fall from the Tarpeian Rock, and then, at eventide, enthroned upon the Capitoline! It has allured many,— though not quite the greatest.

Before passing harsh judgment on such a belated push for position, it must be duly considered, how reluctantly, everywhere, the very oldest are to decide on departure from a field of action. The farewell to statecraft, theatre, concert-hall, the idle lingering amid the memorials of hard-won fame,—the herald of death. "When in the morning I have trimmed my nails, my day's work is done," sighed Bismarck. Clémenceau grown old could write his Memoirs. (Long ago a little book of his was announced, "Three Jewish Tales," of which the first, "Moses," is praised.) But to him who for fourteen months had been World-arbiter, literature could offer but a pitiful substitute.

So it was that he said, with a groan, that he had, to be sure, longed for a restful old age in his beloved La Vendée, but a faithful steed must, if need be, even die in the traces. But this attitude did not win favor.

"Must it be so? Is France, while the world resounds with her praises, absolutely limited to the one man? What has she yet to expect from a man of nigh four-score? An all too agèd Cyrano. And from the north, at that,—a bully out of Brittany, still sparkling with the wit and audacity of his Gallo-Celtic prime.

"('What have I against Mr. Wilson? I admire him heartily. My veneration is dimmed a little only, because he issues fourteen Commandments, though God Almighty himself got on with only ten!')

"He was a marvel of good fortune as the war glimmered out: but bewildered and blind before the problems of the day and the morrow. Of industrialism and finance he has no conception. 'Empiricist' he calls himself, in pride, because he has learned nothing and will not be stigmatized as dilettante.

"Je fais la guerre! There was a time for that. Ever cantankerous, and again easily moved to tears by clever ticklers of the lachrymal glands.

"What would such a man in the Elysée accomplish for us? Six months ago, when Pichon complained of illness, he gibed: 'Don't whimper: you'll be well enough for a good while yet to become President of the Republic.' Everyone who had risen to the Presidency he scoffed at without mercy. Now he will have it himself? Wants to turn the spit and rule the roast, to entertain every minister with epigrams, thunder and lighten in every state council, crash his messages into Parliament and thro' all the land, defend every chance word of his peace-treaty as if it were a reconquered province, and—as the calm sensible Waddington long ago said of him—'start up a dangerous surprise every fortnight'? Too much he can do, but one thing never: keep quiet, content himself with the calm dignity of an arbiter.

"But that is precisely what the President of the Republic must be able to do. His power is not so slight as you fancy; and Clémenceau could, simply by trying to make the dignified fiction of his powers a reality, imperil the state."

Did M. Briand talk like that? He did, in a whisper, coax M. Deschanel out of his decision to retire in M. Clémenceau's favor. Through Parliament floated

Nietzsche's longing at Bayreuth: "Deliverance from our deliverers!" A majority decided for M. Paulus Deschanel:—and the day before the decision Clémenceau withdrew his name. To bring about an open downfall for the favorite of the Bourgeoisie, the middle class, would have been for many a member of the Versailles Congress grievously distressing. But the old man seemed to demand the choice as a duty to be performed, as requital for the sum total of his deeds; he seemed loyal to his vow, not to strike with the lightest tap the office-seeker's drum. A Coriolanus, disgusted at the very idea of disclosing his wounds to the glance and touch of the common people? Parliament was like France in '71, according to the historian Hanotaux's happy phrase, "dégoûté de ses sauveurs." It wished to become at last once more itself the shaper of destiny and to have a pliant will with which to deal. It knew that the presidential powers (often misunderstood, never yet fully exerted) offered to any strong man opportunity for grave extension. And to be merely the representative of the nation, which demanded a vigorous body and serenity even in days of storm—a cheerful sunny disposition—M. Clémenceau, with his stormy brain and ever-flashing wit, was certainly not the right man.

To avoid the defeat, he withdrew: went, to show that he was no invalided man, to India (for a tiger-hunt); roared as an orator through the United States; and since his return finds his place in the people's favor filled by the man most hateful to him, the Lorrainer Raymond Poincaré, to whom he had denied all share in the task of peace-construction.

As to that work, the Treaty, for which *le grand patriote* is and wishes to be responsible, all men are now disillusioned, the greediest no less than they who with the eyes of pious desire gaze toward new shores. And the soul of mankind declares:

"This man, also, was too small for his greatest hour." It was for M. Clémenceau to say to himself, and then to the Tardieux, the Mandels, the Ignaces:

"The war can have for its issue only the rule of France on our continent, or a Franco-German alliance. England, that waged the war in Lloyd George's—that is, in a political—spirit, will oppose either. The hegemony of France would in the long run be even harder to maintain than that striven for by Wilhelm. Therefore our endeavor must be to interlock Germany's interests so firmly with our own that the new political boundaries of France shall never again be threatened, the possibilities of her economic development shall be widened, and the United States of Europe (united at first economically) be brought into being."

M. Clémenceau had no such feeling. He thirsted for atonement, revenge, punishment of those whom he hated; and with tremulous hand he discrowned his life. Here was, indeed, a Force—but it could not shape Beauty that should deserve to live. Here was Fire—but in the glow of its rage it could only heat men's spirits, not cleanse them, in its own elemental purity, for noble aims.

V

THE HINDENBURG MYTH

In the East, holy men and holy books tell how a man became a Buddha. In occidental countries, in Germany, for instance—the home of Luther, the Reformation and Kant's *Critique of Pure Reason*—one can learn how a carpenter's son became God. But who of us has ever seen a God on earth or even dared to dream of seeing one!

Yet this is just what we have experienced.

In this modern and scientific age, when the radio carries the most distant sounds to the ears of the whole world as clearly as if they were the close and intimate words of a lover, when the light motor engine allows wingless creatures to fly over ocean, desert and mountain, when the lightning exchange of news from continent to continent seems to give man a certain degree of control over present events and future developments, in this day of colossal business enterprises, man, eager as of old for miracles and personal wonders, has visibly created and beheld a God.

It was autumn, 1914. (Don't worry, ladies, for neither politics nor tales of war shall weary your ears.) The people of Germany were hearing of nothing but victories in the west and in the east—not a word of their armies' enforced retreat on the Marne. They were confident that, long before the leaves turned yellow, Paris would fall and that before Christmas their victorious army would return home.

119

An official circular letter signed by the Prussian general von Viebahn requested information as to the number of windows in Berlin on the *Pariser Platz* and *Unter den Linden* that could be reserved for special guests to witness the triumphal entry of the troops into the city.

Victory is really as near as that, think the recipients of von Viebahn's letter, and their contagious joy and confidence spread quickly to others. Only a very few in Germany knew that the advance in the West had come to a hopeless deadlock; that the army had been forced into a trench warfare that might last for years and years and that the Russians in the East, due to their overwhelming numbers, were becoming more menacing from day to day.

William the Hasty dismissed the Commander-in-Chief of his Eastern army, in spite of the fact, which was later proved, that this same General, von Prittwitz, and General Gaffron had acted wisely and taken the proper precautionary measures. Nothing would do but that he must send for Colonel Ludendorff, who had distinguished himself before the war on the Great General Staff and, later, in the daring attack on the fortress of Louvain. But a Colonel who was not even of the nobility could not be given the position of Commander-in-Chief. Such a French and Bonapartian move as that by which Colonel Petain was raised to that office in 1917 was not at all in keeping with the Prussian system and tradition.

Who then should be given the highest command?

To prevent friction and quarrels the distinction had to be conferred on a regular officer, some passive, easy-

going general who would permit caustic, hard-headed
Ludendorff, a neurasthenic, with a will as well as
muscles of steel, to have his own way; who, in short,
would never interfere. So many generals were already
in active service (with six million men at the front)
that the choice became very limited. The first man to
be considered, a former commander of the Imperial
Guards, was sick in bed at his home in Hanover but
there was, in the same city, old General Paul von
Hindenburg, now on the pension list. His request to
be taken back into active service at the beginning of
the war had been refused. It is quite certain that, at
a time when there was such great need of generals, the
conscientious Chief of the Great General Staff would
never have decided against accepting Hindenburg back
into service if experts had been of the opinion that
this sixty-six year old general had any special ability.
But Hindenburg is the type of the regulation Prussian
officer and now they could afford to remember his request and consider his case. This quiet old man would
not disturb or irritate the inordinately egotistical and
self-assured Ludendorff by any dictatorial interference.
This was the deciding factor and Hindenburg was appointed Commander-in-Chief.

Colonel Ludendorff went to Hanover to meet him,
explained the military situation to him, and, on the
way to the front, outlined his strategy. At Tannenberg, a Russian army was annihilated! The series of
victories in the East had begun!

And then this quiet old man was showered with
glory. His fame spread from one end of Germany
to the other. In every heart, on every tongue, there

was but one name, Hindenburg. He had freed East Prussia; he had shattered the Russian armies and warded off the Russian menace; he had given fresh courage to the wavering Austrians. The first Commander-in-Chief, von Moltke, had taken refuge on the barren rock of his Christian Science, after breaking down under the burden of work and anxiety that was too much for his already shattered physique. The army had no confidence in its second Commander, von Falkenhayn, appointed to succeed von Moltke; and the people saw in him only a favorite of the Kaiser's who had suddenly been pushed into the limelight. The idolized navy, which found its popular embodiment in the familiar figure of Admiral von Tirpitz, with his long, flowing, white beard, was forced to remain in hiding; and, though daily news of some victory or other came from France, no more advances were reported.

But, "just be patient," was the comforting advice given out from headquarters. Hindenburg would soon have done the job in the East and would then turn and crush the enemy in the West. He was reported to be the greatest commander of all time. Bonaparte and Frederick the Great, Cæsar and Alexander, compared to him, were like the antiquated Italian Montgolfier flying machine compared with the Zeppelin, or like an old Carthaginian chariot in comparison with the modern tank. Germany's hour of glory draws near. Hindenburg has promised it. Hurrah for Hindenburg! Hindenburg forever!

All sorts of stories were told about the popular idol. Rumor had it that he was in great disfavor with the

Kaiser at one time because he told that conceited Majesty some unpleasant truths to his face, and that only the need of the moment compelled the Emperor— much against his will—to put in power the only man who would not flatter him. But Hindenburg's genius had long been recognized by experts—so the stories ran—who knew that for years he had been occupied with the plans which he subsequently carried out at the Battle of Tannenberg, and which he had worked out in the smallest detail. But, if the truth be told, the Emperor, King, All-Highest, War-Lord, never had a more obedient, more pliant servant than this general, whose ability had never before been taken very seriously. The fact of the matter was that the people, in their hysterical mood of the moment, swinging suddenly from grief to ecstasy, gave blind credence to the most absurd stories about him.

At that time people were not hearing very much about Ludendorff. He was capable, energetic, and untiring; but he was completely overshadowed by the old Titan, to whom people were practically on their knees. In the furrowed surface of Hindenburg's broad skull— which, to be sure, is not insignificant in form, but which is. nevertheless not particularly different from other heads of the Slavo-Prussian military type, with the short neck set on a huge, thick-trunked body— painters and sculptors found traces of genius which for sixty-six years no eye had ever before discerned. Scholars and litterateurs made exhaustive studies of his family and his ancestral history and quoted his wise sayings in their notebooks.

These sayings often sound very strange.

"Since I was a cadet I have never read a book that didn't have something on militarism."

"War is better for me than a cure at a health resort."

"I hope it lasts until they have all bowed to our will."

Is this the death rattle of a declining world?

No, so spoke, over his beer, a scrupulous Commander-in-Chief who looks at life optimistically, a man who has at his service the most modern technical inventions and for whom the Sanscrit professor in the nearest university deciphers intercepted radio orders from the high command of the Russian army.

Restaurants, cafés, pharmacies, moving pictures, delicatessens, confectioners, dance palaces, all angled for clients by using the beloved Commander-in-Chief's name as bait. The manufacturers try to profit by him. There are Hindenburg boots, Hindenburg soap, Hindenburg writing paper, and in every large department store a special counter for "Hindenburg articles." Little by little a slight opposition arose wherever military men were closeted together. "After all," they said, "it was not such a tremendous feat to drive back Russians who were poorly armed, poorly commanded and frequently betrayed by their own generals. The first blows were the only very telling ones . . . since then there have been no decisive victories. Russia's internal resources have scarcely been tapped, and until something is done in the West, no one can tell whether the lucky old fellow really deserves this growing fame of his and the rank of Field Marshal which he won so quickly."

There was a great deal of jealousy at the Emperor's Headquarters. "Will there never be any end to this cry of 'Hindenburg'?" asked Wilhelm, who, even at the front, could not help having an eye to the effect he was personally producing. "When I march through the Brandenburg Gate at the head of my troops, am I to be greeted with shouts of 'Hindenburg'?"

In spite of the fact that more and more nations were declaring war against Germany, Wilhelm still saw himself returning home as the conquering hero. And his eldest son whispered maliciously, "Papa is jealous!"

Since they knew the real reasons for the Hindenburg renown at Headquarters, it was a simple matter to set about quietly undermining it. For the first time there seemed to be very little going on in the East. It would not do any harm, therefore, if they took the Field Marshal's Chief of Staff away from him and in this way put a stop to the blare of praise which was so disagreeable to His Majesty's ear. Ludendorff was suddenly transferred to Linsinger's army. "Now," muttered the jealous ones, "let us see whether these pæans will not die away as quickly as they rose!" But the Field Marshal declared that he would hand in his resignation (he knew that even a courageous monarch dare not let his most popular general go in the midst of a war) unless Ludendorff was recalled. Two weeks later Ludendorff was back at his old post.

When a Prussian Field Marshal who is held in the highest respect by the entire army, makes such gratuitous efforts to emphasize the indispensability of a subordinate, it is pretty certain that the ranking officer is only the instrument of the subordinate's will and that, without the latter, he is an empty husk.

Without a doubt this was known to the heads of the government and the army. When a cabinet minister, a Stinnes, Thyssen, Krupp or one of the lesser captains of industry wanted to arrange an economic deal, he would say, "I will go to Ludendorff," without even mentioning the Field Marshal. Little by little the rumor of the subordinate's importance leaked out, but in the eyes of the people who began to say "Hindenburg and Ludendorff" the latter was still outshone by the glory of the former as an incandescent bulb is vanquished by the midday sun.

The voice of the nation, officially throttled by the censor, spread the news by word of mouth that the management of the entire war—which was dragging along gloriously in spite of gigantic losses and the lack of any effectual victory—would be taken over by these two. The Emperor rebelled against sacrificing his favorite Falkenhayn, and had repeated quarrels, both petty and serious, with Hindenburg (that is, with Ludendorff). It was usually the Empress, anxious for the future prestige of her family, who effected a reconciliation. Once she even crossed the Rhine to meet her husband who was travelling from the West front to the East. During the night, she had her drawing room car secretly coupled to his special train, surprised Wilhelm at break of day, and persuaded him to visit Hindenburg at Posen and make friends with him. She herself took a snapshot of the Emperor and the Field Marshal, posed together, and gave it out to the public.

The German people, credulous, but tensely anxious and easily disturbed by the slightest unfavorable report, were now fully persuaded that the two men were the best of friends again. Soon after this, it was found necessary to dismiss Falkenhayn. He had to be sacrificed because Verdun had not fallen. Once more the word went out from the inner circle, "Ludendorff is the only man who can save the situation. That is the reason why he was promoted to Chief of Staff."

From that moment, General Ludendorff, under the title of First General Quartermaster, conducted all operations on a theatre of war extending over three continents, from Ostend to Trebezond, from Dar-es-Salaam to Helsingfors, from the Russian marshes to the Suez Canal. He was untiring in his activities. At seven o'clock in the morning he began telephoning the chiefs of the army staffs, checking up old commands, issuing new ones. He had every figure, name and date in his head and absolute power in his hands.

In his book, Ludendorff himself said that the Field Marshal never once refused to approve his orders. Hindenburg was not lazy, but he was protected from too great a burden of work by the affection of the men who surrounded him and, no matter what happened at the front, was never allowed to pass a day without taking his usual walk.

I once expressed astonishment that the old gentleman should accept the acclaim of the people year in and year out for services, the credit for four-fifths of which, at least, belonged to Ludendorff. One of the army heads replied, "When we were celebrating Hindenburg's seventieth birthday, just among ourselves, he made it fairly clear that all these honors were not due him."

Why only "once," and only "fairly clear," and in private? Because, if the people were to keep their faith in him as a savior who had been sent specially to them in their hour of need, the Hindenburg legend must not be weakened in any way.

But in spite of the unsurpassed courage of the Germans, their tenacious endurance, their ingeniousness and their devotion, the leaders of the army were finally forced to beg for an armistice at the most unfavorable hour of their complete impotence. For years they had purposely spread false reports and had repeated them so persistently that they had come to believe them themselves. But the submarine warfare, which had been, according to the newspapers, unfailingly successful, had not prevented America from landing her young men, powerfully equipped for war, on the coast of France. Foch's reserves, which the same newspapers had reported as decimated hundreds of times, burst forth from the woods at Villers-Cotterets and won a decisive battle. But so ineradicably had the faith of the people taken root in the Hindenburg idol that after the catastrophe the idol became a God walking upon the earth. This was the greatest miracle of all.

In the days just before the Armistice, the German people, terrified by the extent of the disaster and disappointment, experienced a sudden reversal in mood. Even the Junkers, privileged as they were, broke forth in hot denunciation of the existing régime. We have been deceived and betrayed, was the outcry of the moment. But the popular rage was never directed

against the old Field Marshal, shrouded in the mists of
his fame. Suddenly it seemed as if everyone had
always known that Ludendorff was conducting the war
and that therefore he was responsible for the outcome.
This feeling was aggravated by the fact that the Emperor, who had detested this irascible, arrogant man for
a long time, now dismissed him. The Emperor's un-
gracious manner drove Ludendorff to ask whether his
services were no longer desired, to which the Emperor
replied, "That is the case; your retirement would make
it very much easier for me to rebuild my Empire with
the help of the Social Democrats."

The Field Marshal, who time and again had re-
iterated his determination to stand by the creator of
his fame, stayed in the service.

"Aha!" the people said, "that shows that Ludendorff was the cause of all the trouble." The latter was
not spiritually strong enough to undergo the experience of this double ingratitude on the part of the nation
and the dynasty without showing the marks of it.
True, he did not "flee." Since he had been retired
from duty after fifty-four months of almost superhuman work, he had a right to get away from the
Berlin street riots and the mobs that were particularly
bitter against him and to seek rest and relaxation
in the peace and beauty of Sweden. But ever since
then, driven by unsatisfied ambition, misunderstood
and condemned, he has gone astray in the dark by-
paths of muddled demagogy.

Field Marshal von Hindenburg placed himself at the
disposal of the Republic for the duration of the army's
return march and held the post of Commander-in-Chief

until the army was disbanded. But no one could expect the old man to go on working without pay. Under his own name he published an absolutely worthless book which, however, earned large sums in English-speaking countries. At the most he could only have furnished the subject matter, for the book is written in the easy, impersonal diction of the average, clever reporter, a style that would have been over the head of this old soldier, too illiterate even to educate himself by reading.

It was on Hindenburg's advice that the Emperor left Berlin secretly, a departure followed by his desertion of Germany and the flight to Holland. But has this done Hindenburg any harm? Not in the least.

Since the demi-gods of Headquarters have changed their uniforms for office coats and are making earnest efforts to excuse and explain their actions to influential journalists, it has been much easier to investigate the Hindenburg myth. They were all devoted to the old Field Marshal. It was almost the love of children for their father. No one had an unkind word to say about him. But neither did any one deny that, from a strictly military standpoint, any other General who was not ambitious for personal power could have filled the position as well. When I asked whether Herr von Hindenburg did not occasionally intervene on his own authority and make changes in the orders and imperial decrees that had been issued, one of his cleverest aides, after considering for a moment, replied: "He always added the words—'mit unteränigem Handküss' (I kiss your hand obediently) in letters of acknowledgement to queens and princesses, because I never could bring myself to write the words. I do not remember any other changes."

When I tried to draw an impartial picture of Hindenburg and Ludendorff in my weekly paper and to convey a warning against blindly worshipping Hindenburg and as blindly damning Ludendorff (while the latter may not be a military leader, he is certainly a war technician of the first rank) angry readers flooded me with insulting letters, accusing me of having disparaged the "greatest general the world has ever known" and of blaspheming a God.

"The greatest general the world has ever known!" Even if I should reply with a list of this general's total achievements, what would it conjure up in the minds of the unbiased reader? A long row of glorious, but unproductive victories . . . nothing more! Even Russia was not conquered and disarmed by Hindenburg's army—which was forced to halt before Riga and had to abandon its plans for capturing Petrograd—but by its own Bolshevism. Prussia's greatest theorist of war, Carl von Clausewitz has said, "War is politics fought with other weapons."

Hindenburg's policies were as shortsighted, as fatally bad, as were those of his predecessor who decided upon the invasion of Belgium, a country which had previously been declared neutral at Prussia's own suggestion. He had not the faintest conception of the enemy's power of resistance nor of the resources they had to draw on. The arrogant craze for victory destroyed every opportunity for concluding a sensible peace. The deeply inculcated spirit of militarism which carried into other provinces of life the same harsh methods learned in the school of war hoped to force a decision by using poison gas, by the submarine warfare, etc., etc., and did not reckon with the fact that the enemy, stronger certainly by three-fourths of the whole earth, could employ the same means not only more quickly but more widely than the Germans. Through oceans of blood, through devastated lands, over mountains of cripples and corpses, the way led to the most terrible defeat history has ever known.

The systematic and absolutely useless destruction of farm lands, works of art and industries in Northern France, the transformation of blooming fields, splendid cities and healthy villages into an arid waste, binds the German people to years of reparation.   In everything they used bad judgment.

When the final breakdown became inevitable, the "civilians" who until yesterday had been oppressed were now pushed to the fore.   They were the ones now who must ask for the armistice, a task which has always devolved upon the defeated Commander-in-Chief.   As they were stupid enough to allow themselves to be made use of, the world naturally holds them responsible for the capitulation, although it was Hindenburg himself who sent a telegram commanding them to agree to any conditions and to make peace at any price.   To avoid confessing that catastrophe was due to the witless strategy, blindness, deafness and unreliability of the army command, they spread the lies that the spirit of defeat and betrayal at home had "by stabbing them in the back forced the army to lay down their arms just when they were on the point of winning the final victory."

Does the heart of the nation, defiled by such libels, cry out at last in angry protest?

The parasites of the "revolution," proud heirs of the Imperial rights under the guise of the Social Democrats, welcomed the vanquished troops on their return home as "our unconquered army." And if the army was not beaten, certainly the Commander-in-Chief was not. Even in the days of the wildest street rioting the "Wooden Hindenburg," a gigantic wooden monstrosity close by the Reichstag, in which people, for the sake of charity, bought the right to hammer nails of precious metal, was left unharmed and became the sacred shrine of many pilgrimages. The faculties of all, literally all, of the humanistic and technical high schools that had not already given the Field Marshal a doctor's degree, hastened to do so now. The Republic gave him the highest pay for peace times, placed a drawing room car at his disposal for journeys, and did not make the slightest complaint or express any astonishment when he held parades, proposed cheers for the dethroned Kaiser, presided in official garb at a meeting of an order of knights, acclaimed the fame and glory of the disbanded army, declared himself on all occasions for the monarchy and ignored the republican form of government. Every child in the smallest village, every maid in the most distant forester's lodge knew his face by sight, that head which the people call a "majestic brow of thunder" and His Majesty the Emperor and King, in his jealous rage, termed "a sergeant's mug." Wherever he appeared, he was greeted with acclamations and shouts of joy.

Foch, the victor, went about Paris in uniform almost

unnoticed; when Hindenburg, the vanquished, rode out, millions drunk with adoration were ready to strain their own muscles to draw his carriage through the streets. Ministers of the Republic beamed with joy when they were privileged to come into his presence while he was reviewing a club of old soldiers, a patriotic band of Boy Scouts, or some other monarchistic group. He might do anything he pleased. Only timidly, on tiptoes, as it were, did criticism approach this powerful figure. Whatever he did was right. Who dared assert that he ever made mistakes? They were all Ludendorff's fault! Do not evil spirits triumph at times in all the old myths?

And so it went for six years. The rosy dreams which the infant German Republic dreamed were shattered bit by bit. The victors of yesterday, who were not able to understand the complex nature of the German nation, a splendid nature but also dangerous in many ways, attempted to smooth out the mistakes which had buried the fame of Western European civilization. In Germany's new government there was more dilettantism than talent. The shopkeepers who, after years of insufficient pay and under-nourishment, were lifted overnight out of their little corners and placed at the head of affairs, naturally succumbed to the bribery of the profiteers, those *nouveaux riches* who had made their fortunes through the war, the madness of the days following the war, and the inflation of the currency. These wrought havoc.

And so in this land, officially disarmed and disgraced, the waves of nationalism rose higher and higher; their idol still the white-haired old Field Marshal. The first

President of the German Republic—a Social Democrat—called on his services for a tribunal. This man,
who for years had preached Revolution and the cause
of the Internationalists and had risen to power on that
platform, was content to bask in the sunshine of Hindenburg's popularity and in his unshakable optimism.
Even in his eyes, Hindenburg stood as the court of
last appeal. The Nationalists were not slow in grasp-
ing this fact. The day which they had foreseen was
drawing near. As a new President had to be elected,
and the people's candidate, an unknown man, received
almost eleven million votes merely by waving the
black-white-and-red flag of the old Empire, the Nationalists put up the Field Marshal as the second candidate.

He was seventy-eight years old and had never both-
ered himself with any but military affairs. By his false
judgment of both the German and the enemy's strength
in war, as well as by his fomenting of Bolshevism in
Russia, he had shown that he did not possess the slightest glimmer of political instinct. To be sure, he has
always declared himself a monarchist, a faithful and
devoted servant of the Hohenzollerns. To him all this
clamor for a Republic was a disease and Democracy
a plague sent down from heaven to punish man's arrogance and self-confidence, bringing disaster and suffering in its train. He believes that nations are never ripe
for self-government. They are always childish and,
therefore, like children, they must be guided, guarded,
protected and trained by the hand of a divinely appointed father. The man who thinks and talks like
this was put up for President in the country which

has often, with the boastfulness of youth, called itself the freest republic!

And he was elected . . . the defeated Commander-in-Chief of the war, who was largely responsible for imposing the tremendous burden of reparations on the German people, who even in the stupid and ghastly treaties of Brest-Litovsk and Bucharest was setting up a model for the Versailles Conference, the man who smuggled Lenin, Sinovief, and Kamenief into Russia in a German parlor car, the man who really stands first on the list of the war guilty.

From the democratic parties, which did not possess any really popular leader, came a protest necessarily short-lived. They lacked courage for a fight which they realized was lost in advance. The few denunciations they made, in the tone of rebellious slaves grumbling at their masters, were followed by hot admonitions from their opponents not "to drag in the mud of party strife the noblest figure of German history, the grizzly Warrior before whom every one should kneel in reverence."

The last touch in the apotheosis of the God!

Half a century ago a deputy in the French Chamber once ventured to speak in defense of the Second Empire, which had been responsible for the war of 1870 and the resulting disaster to the nation. But Count Audiffret Pasquier overwhelmed him with a speech which ended with a prayer. "May God spare our unhappy country this, the greatest of all humiliations: that the control of her destinies should once more pass into the hands that have so badly served her."

Every word in that courageous oration could now be applied to the régime of the Third German Empire, whose representative Hindenburg was and is, as he has always chosen to be and to remain. Yet today Hindenburg towers high above ordinary mortals.

In speeches and interviews, the texts of which have been thoughtfully handed him ready-made, the Field Marshal preaches the ideals of world peace, and of a brotherhood of peoples in the interests of mankind; and he makes obeisance before the sovereign freedom of the German Nation. The monarchist swears fealty to the Constitution (without, to be sure, one single mention of the word "republic"). The Nationalist who has so often said that what has once been German must again be German, seems ready to renounce Alsace-Lorraine. The General who denied reality to any power but arms and armaments now speaks of war as of the greatest of all evils. Any one else would be utterly discredited by such an unexpected change of front. But no one is bold enough to cast suspicions on the majesty of Paul von Hindenburg. Was there not one Paul who was converted in a second's flash? And Paul of Tarsus was only one of the apostles. He was not, like Paul von Hindenburg, of the divine lineage itself.

Who would dare go on strike, if Hindenburg has given orders to work? As a matter of fact, though Berlin working men are not easily moved, though they were suffering from the terrible lack of food, though they knew that Hindenburg could neither order them back to work, prevent them from striking, nor hinder them from doing anything they wanted, yet when their right to strike was challenged by the War Office they allowed their opposition to crumble and their strike to be nipped in the bud. The Castilians, who in the dark ages of mythology allowed themselves to be

led into battle by the body of the dead Cid Comprador
bound on his horse's back, had not greater faith than
these socialists of the Twentieth Century to whom Karl
Marx and his disciples had preached the doctrine of an
all-powerful economic determinism. Seven years after
the unsuccessful strike, almost fifteen million Germans
(more than the entire Workingmen's party together
with the Catholics, civilians, and anti-militarists were
able to get together) elected Herr von Hindenburg
President of the Republic, and his opponents of yesterday rallied around with assurances of devotion.

Out of the inextinguishable ardor of faith a God is
born. From the friction of long suffering rise the
flames, fed by the aspirations of the dynasty which has
lost its throne, of the classes which have lost their
privileges, of the longing to plant monarchistic in-
fluences in the heart of the Republic itself, if indeed
the Republic cannot be stamped out altogether. The
flames have gradually ignited the bark of a gigantic
tree; if this crashes to earth it will be terribly destructive.

A fine General, who has always served his King
and Kaiser, the chosen embodiment of his Fatherland,
in his straightforward way, rises in the glory of his god-
head, and is surrounded by a swarm of blissful slaves.
With a deep breath of relief German Nationalism has
attained the first of its desired goals. Not even a
slender wedge of upright Republicans bars their path.
Hindenburg Hurrah!

Soon we shall see who is the real power under the
cloak of peace of this disappointed and enfeebled War
God.

VI

STINNES

"HE wants to buy the Southern Railroad. In Rome he negotiated for his admission into the American Steel Trust. He's going to carry in with him the Minette of Longwy-Briey, the Ruhr coke, all the German and French iron foundries, steel works, the ore of Morocco and Sweden, along with the German imperial railroads that he has bought out and Sinclair's corrupting petroleum."

"Nonsense! He was in Rome to engage Mussolini as chief Propagandist (with a high rake-off) for the Latin countries, to recast the Papacy into an industrial corporation ('Successors to Peter, with limited liability'), to prepare, by providing a monstrous original capital and brilliant prospects of returns, for a fusion with the Greek Orthodox Church, Patriarchate and Exarchate, to offer a syndicate contract to Grand Master Senussi, the Mirdite Bishop and the Dalai Lama of Thibet, and eventually to build a paper-factory in the Vatican grounds, to drain out the Pontine marshes and create there a film city on a scale never before seen, a European Los Angeles equipped with every up-to-date comfort."

"He's financed the Friedericus Rex already. But all that's just odds and ends. He has the Alpine German-Luxemburg, Rhine-Elbe-Siemens, the Berlin Trading Company, dock yards and shipping equipment on the grandest scale. What not? Coal, ore, iron, steel, mines, smelting works, casting- and rolling-mills, electrical storage-plants, ocean, Rhine, Ruhr, and Elbe steamship lines, forests, dozens of estates, paper-mills, hundreds of newspapers with printing presses, hotels from the Moselle to the Moskwa, alkali, zinc, manganese, cotton, saw-mills. All over the world, houses, real estate, industrials, partnerships. He owns half of East Prussia, a large part of Southern Sweden, of the shore front in Emden, Bremen, Hamburg, Copenhagen, and a majority in the fattest stock-companies. He's going to modernize and complete France's canal system, in the coalless lands, Holland, Italy and Austria, he will electrify the railroads, and struggle with nails and bristle against the petrolizing of the world's industries until he has the chief part of the petroleum production under his sceptre, or has a profitable working agreement with Rockefeller, Rothschild, Sinclair, Urquhart, Kemal Pasha and the Soviets of Baku and Batoum. In Mexico, his daughter, just a young girl, has sought with a divining-rod for marketable oil-wells. In Argentina too he is said to have organized big business. His eldest son discovered America; during the war his younger one, then hardly twenty, instructed the ambassadors in Copenhagen, Stockholm and Hamburg, and saw to it that not a ton of Swedish ore, not a tub of Danish butter, nor a tin can of milk failed to be despatched through shipper Stinnes. Even in Austria, and farther East! In general, it is impossible to count up what he commands or controls. Of course it's well known that he has poured out a heap of billions to the Czechs, and secured mammoth concessions in return."

"That's what they say. D'ya believe Prague iron turns to gold overnight? Even your great Hugo can't work witchcraft."

"He must! Just look at the little black head with the smelling-porch, and think, when you hear his name, of Achilles, Socrates, Euripides, not of Reitzes, Karpeles, Teveles."

. . . "You're all on the wrong track again. That man, that you're chattering so much about, doesn't exist at all. The press has invented him, created a homunculus out of the ideal concepts of Stinnes-izing, Stinnes-ism. Only booby birds are afraid of a patched-up scarecrow watching the potatoes and peas. Boys just put in breeches don't know a snowman's just a thousand flakes stuck together, and melts under the first sunbeam. Rumor, the never-sated, always eager for the superhuman, ascribes what a hundred captains of industry and a thousand speculators did to this one fable-giant. Nothing of Stinnes ever has been alive but the Stinnes-myth."

Is it much exaggerated? Didn't it run on about in that fashion, on tongue, pen, typist's finger-tip, the talk of a year and a day?

Hugo Stinnes lived, in the body, at Mülheim on the Ruhr, where he was born, in Berlin, Hamburg, Prague, Vienna, Buda-Pesth, Carlsbad, Oberhof, Rome, Amsterdam, Zurich, on his South Swedish estate, by the North Sea dockyards, just wherever something was to be attended to. His father and grandfather were Ruhr shippers. The eldest invented (or found in use) the system of "vertical arrangement." Instead of building like businesses one upon another, that is,—in his case, instead of multiplying river-wharves, he built his own boats, brought in his own coal, to use for fuel and also to sell, and secured for himself in this way, by cutting out jobbers and middlemen, the whole profit from the enterprise.

The grandson developed the system on a grand scale. The fact that from his own woods, sawmills, pulpmills, comes his paper which his printing-presses use to produce his newspapers,—that is the most trivial illustration, hardly worth mentioning, the profit from his paper-making, compared with that from his coal, ore, iron, steel, tools and machines, electricity and ships, which he himself builds, complete. And the ruler of this empire, that waxed with each moon and shrank with none, called himself simply "Hugo Stinnes, merchant." Without the slightest vanity, but because he wished to seem, and to be, nothing else. (Which proves that a man who never quaffed from any spring of the Humanities, who looks at no pictures, reads no books, because "business absorbs all his imagination," is none the less in his own fashion, "cultivated").

A merchant he became when, with fifty thousand marks,—a meager capital to start on, even in the time of the gold mark, a time as remote as Solomon and Sheba,—he left his father's business and set himself up on his own feet. He remained a merchant, one who dealt, until 1914, as much in English coal as in German, without aid from anyone, without connection with larger houses, extending gradually from the smallest beginnings, and from a petty local start created his world-wide power:—not always, indeed, without wavering nor without mistakes.

His mother, an amiable matron, eager for the ideals of pious culture and the beauty enshrined in noble poetry, who worships the twin-star Herder-Schiller, is of Gallo-German origin. (She was Fräulein Coupienne when betrothed to the Mülheimer.) She may well have been anxious at times over this son, who was never content with the ordinary throng but sought ever wider spaces and remoter goals. "Does he not venture upon all too lofty ridges? Will not the wreath he weaves prove too large for his brow, and, falling on shoulders and breast, bind him in fast-withering though fragrant fetters?"

Doubtless from his mother he had his dark skin, the maroon brown of his hair and beard (which, always independent of fashion, he did not shave). Of the Jewish cast which the caricaturists give him, his face has not a single feature. He resembled the type of energetic men seen in the creations of Master Matthias Grünewald, or his head might well rise above the throat of one of the honorable guild-brethren whom the art of old Cologne has taught us to know and respect.

When I first saw him, many years ago, at a general meeting, which I had gone to Düsseldorf to attend because its subject had a political tendency, the visionary eye of an apostle shone above his lean cheeks. But the cheeks filled out, the lips came to protrude somewhat more roundly, and yet from the eye, which strove to pierce the depths of other men's mysteries, heavenly joy could smile, or the lightning of heathenish savagery gleam.

In those days he came only rarely over the frontier of the mining and smelting region; to Berlin, whose range of amusements has never had any attraction for him, to a ten-hour day packed with important negotiations, or in the school vacations into the mountains; to a children's health resort, by the round-about route over his own Luxemburg to Noordwijk, whose gentle "mighty melody" charmed this visionary also.

Mostly, however, he stayed close by his mother, in the old Mülheim cottage, that seems expressly made for the master of a little handicraftsmen's guild, in the warm cozy family life of a German bourgeois. In the early morning (his knit cap kept the coffee warm in the pot), at noon, and at nightfall all were united about the table. The father was at once the instructor (in the art of living), the friend and the comrade of the children, who, at the tenderest age, shared in difficult tasks, and afterwards had to sketch the outcome. The wife was her man's best—almost his only —assistant. Household furnishings, utensils, clothing, excellent, with the simplicity characteristic of the Lower Rhine folk of yesterday.

At an age when an industrial prince's and financier's heir-apparent would long ago have had provided for him a riding-horse, a motor-boat, a décolleté dancing-girl, a plump soubrette, a film actress with her boyish body and corn-yellow Titus-head, a private bachelor apartment with a discreet "servant to the master," and, of course, his own bank account,—here the brood

was glad to bide in the parents' nest. He who gave
instructions to German ambassadors carried his silver
watch on a steel chain. The father wore rough sailors'
shoes, an unpretentious sack coat, knitted neckties and
a never well-fitting but always fresh felt skull-cap.
He did not smoke, barely sipped a light wine, never
noticed what he ate.

Emil Kirdorf is housed on a big scale in Streithof.
The still older August Thyssen fits into Landsberg
Castle. Beside and below Krupp's hill-villa his directors build their own splendid villas—Hugo Stinnes,
merchant, bided where he was. His working-room was
no bigger than Michael Angelo's, whose handicrafts-
man's dæmon seemed to be astir at times behind the
Mülheimer's brow, and for a flash's space stamped
him with a likeness to Buonarotti.

The merchant's loftiest goal was to make himself
independent of the bankers, who as bestowers of
credit had taken to themselves the greater part of
the control over industry. Not before his fiftieth year
did he attain that goal. And then far surpassed it.
The mightiest men in high finance, even Have-quick
and Hold-fast themselves, hung upon his lightest word
or sign, as once did Gertrude's shabby majesty on
Hamlet's black-veiled glance. If the pressure to get
into any enterprise became notorious, straightway a
murmur of the "Stinnes-peril" fluttered through Berlin's Bahren Strasse. When chance threw his way the
cheap purchase of one-third of the shares in the
Berlin Trading Company, then, said Rumor, the sun
was soon to set upon the glorious kingdom of Carolus
Fürstenberg, to whose threat (that he would "cripple

the weighers of men and worshippers of power")
Stinnes surely never gave a thought.

That he attained this goal later than he had hoped,
and that he was able to retain it contrary to all the
prophecies of famous soothsayers, resulted from the
evil and the blessing of the war. That swept the
merchant into the whirl of German, European, plane-
tary politics, forced the man, tempered in the glowing
current of patriotism, the Nationalist hardened against
all foreign allurements, into physical and psychical
preparedness for far-ranging international enterprises,
and moulded a new Stinnes,—the Stinnes of to-day.

In the myth of the supporter of great parties, the
buyer of fruitful and barren plantations,—Stinnes of
the popular belief,—the never sated busheler-up of
money, the "missing link" between Sforza and Raffke,
—I put no credence. Was not Cecil Rhodes likened to
the East Indian blood-suckers, to John Law the sower
of assignats, to the Turks' Hirsch, to the Strousbergs
and the Ofenheims, and yet was far more and greater
than they? Whether the business of the Mülheimer
flourishes or withers disturbs not me. The "Stinnes
peril," so much groaned over, could rise fiery red out
of the grey clouds to threaten the world—not merely
our German industries,—if Stinnes the merchant had
ceased to be the apostle of the new World-spirit, and
for that very reason he would necessarily remain
smaller than his destiny, which is framed to the scale
of a mighty personality.

"Close to the wall, on a straw-seated low chair,
while nearly all the others are resting in comfortable

maple-wood leather-seated arm-chairs, sits, in his
workday coat, Herr Hugo Stinnes, hardly four and
thirty, and already crowned, beside the sixty-year-old
Herr Thyssen, as mining king, beloved as a hope,
feared as the most dangerous of critics. A head that
would be striking anywhere, the moistly shining eye of
a Nazarene enthusiast, and the mouth of a cold cal-
culator, with lips that do not open readily. Fine
hands, but prematurely aged; the meager loose-hang-
ing frame stiffening at times as if in gloomy fanaticism,
like one who desires not to win money, but to hearken
to the voice that thunders from on high."

So it was I saw the man years ago; as a true son
of the mixed stock in the Rhine dales, where the root-
fibres of the various races are inextricably intertwined.
Something from the Netherlands, such as Fabricius,
Van der Helst, Frans Hals, recorded with masterly art
on a bit of canvas; something which Rembrandt, the
child of genius, while he still utilized the gloriously
supreme gifts left to him by Rubens, might have bidden
stand out from the heads of the artist's mother and
brother, of the man with the gilded helmet, the cloth-
makers or Saul. Yet there was something there, quite
as unmistakable, of Northern France's unadorned
youthfulness, which Ingres could paint even better
than Millet. Only one at a distance, or blind, can
mistake this man for "a wandering bit of coal," or
for a mere secretary of a shipping company, or a coal-
merchant of the type produced by the mingling of
Frankish, Celtic, Frisian, Dutch, or Belgian with Low
German blood; the type so often to be seen between
Luisburg and Brest, Ymuiden and Ostend,—for in this

man's nature elements of the good princes of Orange, of Colbert, the financial seer of Rheims, are also intermingled.

But should he remain a merchant, or become a statesman, with zealous public spirit devote himself to the service of the Polis, the Respublica: "make" money, or hearken to the voice that resounds from the heights? That was the supreme question.

And again, the war seems to have furnished the answer. Its rising roar drove him from the mountain air of Gastein, where he was refreshing himself after arduous labor, back to the Ruhr. It held him, fourteen hours a day, in the telephone booth at Mülheim. Then everything was ready to meet the need.

Wilhelm's theatricals, despite his flattering speeches and gestures, his decorations and other distinctions (at tariff rates), never appealed to the clear brain of the Lower Rhine drinkers of wine (not beer). To Stinnes the merchant he seemed the striding buskined evil genius of Germany. Stinnes had climbed deliberately to the top step of life and felt securely debarred from a political career, indeed desired so to be. He never believed in any conspiracy or unwarranted attack on Germany, never for a day doubted that all the chief errors were made in the Berlin palace and chancellery. Yet, since Germany itself was at stake, he put himself, without reserve or wavering, at the service of what, to him also, seemed "the Cause."

Every week he was at least four nights on the road. In the office from seven in the morning until eleven at night, or when the train started. He provided coal in Italy for the German warships *Goeben* and *Breslau* to make their voyage to the Sea of Marmora. He devised substitutes for lacking raw materials: iron for copper, silk-paper for cotton as it grew scarce in the cannon-foundries (having the paper drenched in a solution of sugar and hardened), for lubricating oil, with which the hope of victory threatened to trickle away, new by-products from mining. At an early date he foresaw the importance of the syntheses which produced fertilizers and poison-gas and promised a practical substitute for rubber. He thought, not too late, about assuring food in adequate amounts, Swedish ore, timber for the trenches.

He heated up, also, again and again, the furnaces of hope in the offices of state, and fanned their zeal as, after a brief flicker, it died down to indolence. He won the labor-leaders Legien and Huë to the use of the comradish watchword "Partnership in labor," which lies like a broad poultice over the cleft in creeds of the class-war.

He was casting out his nets for neutral tonnage. By means of subterranean tubes from cisterns of German sympathy he endeavored to send influence into hostile lands; and he negotiated independently with German and foreign diplomatists, both at once. All this, still, as a merchant!

Under his guidance everything still attainable was manufactured for the army and the people at home. He brought in much also by secret and circuitous routes of international trade. He provided Italy with coal up to the very morning of her decision to enter the war,—and other entire lands as well; but he never hesitated, also, to bring a few tons of salt fish or tubs of butter into our own ports. His inventiveness was constantly hitting upon possible exchanges, whose allurements beguiled even the most reluctant into barter. And always he was firm in his belief that he was obeying no motive save pure patriotism.

With such manifold points of view, mistakes and miscalculations could not always be avoided, the less as private trade pushed more and more into the domain of politics and public business. A man never schooled to political life, ignorant of individual characters and of the barriers and lines drawn by their previous activities, ties and relations, unacquainted with its surface, now slippery as slate, now broken and irregular, he was capable of believing, for instance, in a meek yielding on England's part, merely because, in their last conversation in the fateful year '14, the representative of a great firm had said to him that his house was counting on carrying out an important piece of business in association with Stinnes himself, "after the war."

Longer, indeed, than was to be expected from one of his keen instincts and judgment, he accepted Tirpitz's assurance, and swore by the irresistible power of our naval offensive, the paralyzing force of unrestricted submarine activity. He saw in the sea fight off Skaggerrack not only a proof of extraordinary German efficiency on the sea, but an easement of our politico-strategic position,—which it actually, by rousing England, made more difficult still.

For a time he regarded the incompetent Bethmann as a halfway passable Chancellor. For a longer time he considered the busy ever-ready Erzberger as a

useful specialist fit for political leadership; and he
doubtless held firmly to the bitter end his belief in
the star, the masterly generalship of Ludendorff, who,
indeed, being very tactful, when he chose, in his deal-
ings with men, had understood at their first meeting
how this simply-strong one should be taken.

"With us, in the northeast, a few things have gone
off pretty well; but, take it altogether, believe me,
the war has been so badly carried on that an old
general staff man's eyes are almost shamed out of his
head. And the little bit, too, I myself have been able
to do so far, has been puffed up away beyond its
deserts. Colonel Hoffmann whom you see there, the
one with the skull of a giant, would have done it just
exactly as well,—and he would have had the advantage
of his bigger beak."

This simple frank manner of speech could not but
please Stinnes, the more so as in Ludendorff, the brains
of the east front, he had found a much clearer understanding of industrial problems than in the dull Falkenhayn circle. That he should have taken this unusually
gifted, unceasingly industrious military tactician,—
limited, except in minor matters, to a narrow field of
vision by his own extraordinary short-sightedness,—
for a consummate commander (who, in our time at
least, must, even while destroying, think about creating, and so must have in him some drops of the statesman's blood) was an error made comprehensible by
the desire, the eager longing, of the patriot.

After the first disappointment on the Marne, Admiral Tirpitz returned home sighing, "This time, alas,
the great strategist seems to be on the other side."

Hope continues her quest, and fancies she has found him at Kovno. But was there one of such caliber anywhere to be found? One who would not look for the miracle of victory either from tacticians' tricks nor from ever varied attempts to break through the front, which General Foch called "examples of the buffalo's strategy"? From the foundation stone of the whole doctrine of relativity, also, the judgment of the Mülheimer as to the general, who had not yet come to imagine himself godlike, can be comprehended.

Stinnes, modest in the full sense of self-respecting manliness, never concealed any gap in his own knowledge, any lack of proper training. He learned from his every mistake. He never drank in the war with enjoyment, as Erzberger did on the petty throne of his power, nor ever thought, as did many a barrack hero in his casino, "the war is going all wrong for us again," nor yet did he think of it as a horror soon to grow unendurable. To him it was the final test of the nation's strength and the school that matures the constructive spirit into full mastery. He felt deeply the need of the poor people, all the sufferings of the mothers, wives, sweethearts, children, sisters, who parted at once with their best-beloved and their bread-winners.

These years of unresting labor and gnawing worry left their mark upon him. His body was broader and firmer now than in the autumn of 1914. His forehead higher, lined more heavily by the chisel of Time, his face ploughed deeper with all the pondering and venturing, the lip more ascetic, the dreamer's enthusiasm in his eyes was transformed into brooding seriousness with a sober, often a smouldering glow. Under the rough exterior kindliness nested; and the man, not destitute of humor, in whom, in bright hours, the merry Rhenish nature laughed out, had his especial charm, the magic of personality, which Goethe, all too hastily, called "the highest happiness of earth's children."

The Shakespeares, Dantes, Mozarts, Beethovens, Rembrandts, Velasquez, Vermeers, Buonarottis, Spinozas, Pascals, Kants, Schopenhauers, Nietzsches: these overlords in the realms of art and philosophy did not exist for this man. Did nature in her mighty, wild or gently smiling aspects give him delight? I am not sure. I rather imagine that if a magician's will had borne him to the high plateau of the Himalayas, he, quite unconcerned, would proceed to put to the test the geologico-economic possibilities of the new environment.

Not, however, for the sake of carrying off money from Hinduland to the Ruhr. Of what use would it be, to one who kept his clothing, food, drink, at the low level of what is indispensable, traveled without a servant, carried his own handbag to the station uncomplaining, was housed far more simply than any tolerably prosperous merchant in Berlin, and in his entire manner of living was nearer to the German workingman than to any type of big business man to be seen today? This simplicity did not come, with him, as with other rich men, from any desire to seem an "original," nor from being sated with splendor, nor from the knowledge that only complete abstention from luxurious indulgence would preserve his health. To this man luxury quickly became a burden, the fragrance of culture a wearisome discomfort; the most beautiful unreality remained to him the absolute zero. Of his own innate art of pleasing he was without doubt unconscious.

The construction of great, wide-ranging, not all-too-familiar lines of business delighted him. The money earned therein was simply a means for new possibilities of use and productive power. That allured him.—And it might have proved for him the sovereign's doom.

Three judgments: first Dr. Rathenau's: "You wonder, Maxim, why in my writings I have so often (of course, without naming him), so contrary to my usual habit, urgently assailed your Stinnes. His intellect I rate very high; higher, I am afraid, than I do his ability to steer his course in accordance with his professions. But certainly he is the arch-enemy who daily outwits ten Jews. Essentially a monster. When he says Germany, he means coal. An understanding with Russia is to him petroleum, manganese, mine-timber, cotton, cheap rye-bread. When he, with the patriot's glowing eye, recommends submarine warfare, he thinks that, after the sinking of so many ships, his tonnage will promptly rise in value. He would, like me, whistle (I choose this time the odorless word) for Alsace-Lorraine, if it were not that the Minette allures him more mightily than ever did la Tribade. He is a man with purpose, beyond spirit and divinity; but, if he swallowed all the industries of Germany, he would still bid us adore him as the deliverer of the Fatherland."

And the Bolshevik Radek says:

"He's a bit of real earth. The most decent, least offensive form of capitalism. Crush the villain, just the same! But, of all the big business men that ever I saw at close range, he is the only one that really impresses one of us. No make-up, no humbug. His first word declared that thus far he had had the utmost distrust of the Bolsheviki. 'And Soviet Russia,' I answered, 'has so many worries that it really cannot concern itself with your mistrust!' He with a shrewd smile squared the account. Then our conversation turned serious. But he's a bit of nature, full grown."

Lastly, hear Albert Ballin, the sea-merchant:

"Our Schwerin industrialists of the lower Rhine are mighty big fellows,—and what they do has no warmer admirer than myself. But they have a stiffness in business relations, a raw-boned manner, that irritates anybody who wasn't brought up in Prussia, and to which the world-trade will never submit when it is developed into a regular system. And just because of that they pride themselves on their industrial power. Stinnes is superior to the rest of them in this respect, that he at least feels how disgustingly dangerous that stiffness would get to be. But many a child can let no bit of a tart alone, and many a man, no woman. Just so Stinnes can leave no business to itself. Everything, even if it belongs to some one else, he wants a share in (at the lowest price)."

To Ballin, the ship-man, whom I had introduced to Stinnes, I answered: "You can take your oath on it that wherever he took hold he was sure he would be of service to his country by doing so; also that after the war, with a laughing eye, he will take his place among the ocean ship-men. Your quick retort, that the Hamburg-American line had long had the policy of depending on coalers of their own, he probably did not accept as an extract from your most ancient charter. 'Germany' and 'Stinnes' have become merged in his mind in a single concept; that what profits the merchant could harm Germany is to him unimaginable. Part of his power springs from that very faith. To be sure, it might become megalomania, a danger for land and man."

I did not mean precisely the danger that our bankers call the "Stinnes peril." They fear an all too great tyranny, threatening the general welfare, in his "pyramid" of the various industries, the base resting on Russian mine-floors, the apex scraping the clouds above us.

"In the first place," they say, "you have the most unwelcome watcher in the house, and secondly, the breaking of a single pillar brings down the whole tower of Babel with it. Weak spots there are everywhere; and here, too, 'all that glistens is not'—Siemens-Rhein-Elbe. . . ."

The pyramiding of industries, also the entrance into the Reichstag and the Industrial Council, forced a gradual change in manner of living. The traveling man content with a bedroom only, meeting his visitors in the public rooms of some quiet hotel, had now to have an apartment in the best. It was by Ballin's humorous raillery that he was first persuaded to put on a dinner jacket for the evening meal,—what cultivated

Germans call a *smoking*. He could no longer avoid "Salon" company. He who before had thought out all important problems alone, and generally had discussed them only with her who was dearest to him, required a general staff, a manager, specialists in all departments of industry, trade-diplomats in all the chief lands of our planet, directors of branch offices, and a whole troop of assistants. Out of all this might easily have arisen a court, something quite like courtly conditions. What if his head should have been turned in Cæsar's direction, or toward belief in the high-flying cleverness that would gladly choose him as "folks-kaiser," and in the childishness of its soul crown him, as the hero appointed for the salvation of Germany? But for any such awkwardly Wagnerian mystification he was too sanely low German; in all his ideas and by his will too firmly set on the earth.

In business affairs (all, in Europe at any rate, came to him first or last) he was sometimes a visionary. Why should he not buy the third of the shares of the Berlin Trading Company that was offered to him? The most solid of banks, deeply intrenched in control of funds and profitable industrial contracts, monarchically constitutional, conducted like a mighty private banking house, guided by the financial genius of Fürstenberg: great possibilities showed above the horizon. Forbid a silk-worm to spin?

From early morning till long after midnight negotiations, travail-pains,—birth; out of plans which like the little folk in Faust's Heaven of Women, often hover above the clouds and fly away.

The Stinnes of politics is a son of earth, or was.

"Germany still works too little. On the thirty per cent yet lacking for the complete exploiting of our industrial opportunities depends most of the profit which formerly came in. Reparation? Yes, complete; but the eventually attainable goal must be the liberation of German soil and impartial treatment for German trade."

That the author of the compact formed with the Marquis de Lübersac, President of the Coöperative Company for the Restoration of the Devastated Regions, drawn up in the Rhenish home-castle,—in his heart approved the heroically brilliant Ruhr folly, I cannot believe. On the political path, still unfamiliar to him, he may not have cast his glance far enough ahead. Else he would be the very one to see more clearly what is and what must come to be.

Great industries, from which the exported surplus output, down to 1914, had kept our balance of trade so encouragingly favorable, have since then for the second time been built up in other lands, while at the same time the purchasing power of all countries between the Rhine and the Black Sea, the Lake of Constance and Baikal Lake has fallen to less than half what it was before the war. Whither, then, shall the product of increased German effort be sent on the morrow?

The merchant saw promptly that ore must come to coal. The statesman did not, yet, see that our continent is to sink into helplessness, unless it is forced into economic unity, vertical and horizontal as well? He was learning to see it, learning also that mental adaptability is not weakness, that the strongest can be the most courteous, and that international extension of trade control, untroubled by frontier landmarks, can never be reconciled with nationalistic political action.

VII

KING PETER OF SERBIA

PETER KARAGEORGEVICH, King in the realm of the Serbians, Croatians and Slovenians, died in the third year after the victory, the liberation and union of the South Slavs: a man to whom we all were formerly unjust.

When in 1903 the news came from Belgrade that King Alexander, the last Obrenovich, together with his wife Draga, had been murdered in his Konak by conspirators, and the Serbian crown offered to Prince Peter with the condition that he should let the murderers go unpunished,—a furious outcry echoed around the world. The fellow-conspirator, the arch-plotter and chief beneficiary of the murder, rises, upon a shamelessly scandalous condition, to the rank of monarch? If the kings are not yet such wretched wights, nor their consciences beneath their faded purple not yet so bewildered, as Zarathustra beheld them, then,— shrieked public opinion,—they must ban this interloper!

Between the line of Georg Petrovich, or "Kara" (i.e., Black George), who freed his people from the Turkish yoke (and whose character and deeds are discussed in the first chapter of my book, "War and Peace") and that of Milosh Obrenovich, there had been deadly enmity for a century. The son and the grandson of Black George had a right to call themselves the people's choice, legally crowned Princes. Nevertheless, in the summer of 1903, it was possible for the erroneous belief to spring up that the acceptance of a sceptre from a murderer's hand was an event without precedent in history.

When the Czar Alexander, son of Paul, heard in Paris, after Bonaparte's fall, that King Louis rejected the services of useful people on the ground that in serving under the Corsican they had shared in high treason, he laughed aloud, and exclaimed: "What foolishness! People breakfast with me almost daily who murdered my father." And yet a hundred years later, almost to a day, Chancellor Bethmann-Huckebein groaned in Berlin because he could not comprehend that a Russian czar should oppose the uprooting of a Serbian dynasty: "What do you think, dear Prince, of this Emperor of Russia, who protects the regicides?" All the teachings of history had seeped into the earth parched by the sultry glow of Byzantium's sun.

After the Peace of Lunéville, Bonaparte wished to entertain with a pageant the Italian officials whom he was receiving in Lyons. He summoned Talma and Madame Raucourt from Paris, and Voltaire's *Mérope* was staged for his guests. Loud applause greeted the line:

"A fortunate soldier was the first of kings."

All men's eyes turned to the First Consul, and all hearts cried to him, "You, our most fortunate soldier, we will crown our king!" But the Corsican frowned,

and after the performance said to Count Chaptal:
"*Mérope* is not to be performed again. What sense
is there in the popular saying, 'The first king won
his crown by luck in battle'? He who can make his
way to a throne is the foremost man of his century
and owes his crown to no single lucky chance, but to
his own merit and a nation's gratitude. This piece
is not to be played in France."

Chaptal smiled faintly; such anxiety seemed to him,
a shrewd man, quite too petty: but Bonaparte was
the shrewder. The folk,—so ran his thought,—needs
not to be reminded in the theatre that monarchical
power is based on victorious campaigns and that many
a butcher, by Fortune's caprice, has won a crown.
The people learn enough, too much, without that.

Had it not learned already, in 1801, that kings can
be slain, seized, beaten down like other mortal men,
strangled? In a night in March the officers of the
guard attacked Paul the First in his palace, and
choked him to death. He who yesterday was by God's
grace Gosudar, omnipotent, was today declared an
idiot, a madman, dangerous to the common weal.
That, then, was possible: possible in a land whose
ruler is also the supreme bishop. Even anointed heads
are not safe from murderous hands.

Such progress had the Jacobin spirit made, which
the First Consul considered the deadliest enemy of all
civic order. And was a people in such a mood, bewildered by such terrible news, to be told yet again,
from the stage, how crowns were won and dynasties
arose? No! In the intoxication of his supremacy
Napoleon forgot what Frenchmen had lived through,

in the very last decade, and what a dramatic spectacle his own career was in their eyes. A people that had beheaded a Louis Capet and his Austrian princess, that had huzzaed Robespierre and Marat, could no longer learn any new lesson from Paul's fate.

Whether *Mérope* was played or forbidden, the lucky soldier, Letitia's son, was already clutching at the crown, and every man would soon be forced to realize how an artillery-lieutenant could rise to Emperor. Such an event exerts more influence than any stage-play. Bonaparte forbade Voltaire's tragedy; but Joseph de Maistre, who descried Cæsar's approach, uttered the word of veiled warning: "On the day when Europe's eye beholds a plebeian ascending the throne, a new epoch in the world's history will begin."

Europe remained quiet. It had lived through too much within ten years to excite itself over a Russian revolution. "What has come to pass," said Goethe, "has exercised a resistless influence on the hearts of most men, and that which has seemed impossible takes its place, when once it has occurred, beside the commonplace." A Czar has been slain by the commanders of his own troops. Impossible? It has happened. Ridiculous in his nightgown and nightcap, Paul had jumped out of bed when he heard the conspirators pounding at his door. They found him cowering behind a screen, yelled wildly at him, reviled him, struck him, and finally strangled him with his military sash. The emperor's body was maltreated with fists and feet. Col. Sablukoff records: "I saw Paul on the catafalque. His face, though physicians and painters had done clever work in restoring it, was still black and blue. His hat was so adjusted that his crushed left temple and eye were covered as much as possible."

When the attack had succeeded, all the suspected * officers and officials were slain or put under arrest, and the troops made to swear allegiance in the name of the new emperor. Throughout the land the news was received with loud exultation. Strangers embraced each other on the street. Men, women and children knelt in the churches and thanked the Holy Mother who had let them see this day. The intoxication was as if the millennial reign of peaceful happiness had arrived on Russian soil.

And with the common people, that fancied itself released from heaviest oppression, the nobility, the court-circles, rejoiced no less. Taticheff wrote to Count Voronzoff: "We all feel as if we were born again." And Rogerson: "The event of March 12 (aside from the circumstances, which were perhaps unavoidable, but give a painful impression) has at one stroke revolutionized popular feeling." President Nicolai wrote: "I am overjoyed at this great, this happy event." Admiral Chichagoff said: "The voice of the nation can hardly express the joy which we feel." Count Buturlin said: "We bless Providence!" Count Morkoff: "Since that great event the sun shines on us again at last." Alexei Orloff: "By God's grace a bright star has arisen that announces to us the spring. Even before Easter came the Resurrection. All Russia breathes freer. Even here in Dresden every one, high

* I.e., suspected of devotion to Paul!

and low, rejoices without bounds. Praise we the Lord, that we have not been utterly devoured. Halleluiah, Halleluiah! And yet again Halleluiah!"

Whitworth, who had been England's representative at Paul's court, wrote: "How shall I describe what my feelings were at this stroke delivered by Providence? The more I consider, the more profoundly do I thank Heaven." Smirnoff, the dean of the Russian legation in London, declared: "Now we need no longer start in fright at our own shadows." The good Prince Castelcicada (the ambassador from Naples) wept for joy. The senator and departmental director Veljaminoff's utterance was: "It is impossible to describe the tumult of joy in the capital. At evening there was such a throng in the streets as was never seen before. In the whole city there was soon no champagne left; a single wine-dealer (not the largest one) sold that day sixty thousand rubles' worth. There was an outburst of joy from every alehouse. Petersburg was like a monstrous mad-house."

The Princess Lieven, née Baroness Benckendorf, wrote: "The conspirators did not conceal their action, but boasted loudly of it, and perhaps invented atrocities of which they had not been guilty." Still higher up, the Empress Elizabeth wrote to her mother, the Margravine of Baden: "Now, after four years of oppression, Russia will draw a free breath. The worst impediment is removed. To be sure, it is a terrible thought, that peace is due to a crime. But I must confess, I too breathe freer. Like a mad woman I longed for a revolution. Such an excess of despotic caprice robbed me of all capacity for calm deliberation; my only remaining wish was to see unhappy Russia free;—at any cost."

So spoke Paul's daughter-in-law, his son's wife. And that son himself? The mild Alexander, La Harpe's and Rousseau's soft-hearted pupil, wept, lamented his own sad destiny; and Elizabeth consoled him. Doubtless this wifely duty did not prove an all too heavy burden. From the letter which Nicolai Petrovich Panin wrote to the widowed Czarina, we know that Alexander was aware of the conspirators' plan. His consent, naturally, he did not give, but answered every intimation with: "Of such matters I wish to know nothing." That sufficed. After the deed it was permitted him to act the part of surprise, of horror. The hands that proffered him the cap of the Monomachi had strangled his father. "Painful, but perhaps unavoidable circumstances." After all, it was still the finger of God that had cast Paul down from his throne. Alexander set the cap upon his own head and clasped the hands from which he had received the emblem of hereditary power.

Ought he to have punished the murderers, who had brought his greatest desire to pass, and so to have roused discontent anew in army and court? He was not so stupid. Great lords had arranged the executioners' task: Gen. von Bennigsen, the Counts Pahlen and Panin, Prince Plato Suboff and others in high station. Of such heads not a hair could be touched; and not one ever was. The only one who fell into disfavor was Pahlen, who as stage manager had carefully arranged it all, but did not enter the palace until the deadly work had begun. That, Alexander

did not forgive. So untrustworthy a servant, who had
doubtless counted even on the chance of failure, and,
in case the plan had gone wrong, instead of risking
his life, would have come upon the stage as Paul's
rescuer, and so escaped deadly danger,—for such a
sluggard ("cunctator") Alexander had no use.

Europe remained quiet. The generation that had
seen the descendant of Louis the Pious, and Maria
Theresa's daughter, executed, was henceforth hardened. Paris, that always leads the way, had again
set its heart on Cæsarism already; but elsewhere the
Paris spirit of 1792 still lived on. Men dreamed of
freedom and human rights, and rejoiced when brave
men freed their land of a tyrant.

Is not every king a tyrant? Yes, said Demos, every
one; even the sixteenth and most harmless Louis,
against whom, strictly, no tangible violation of a ruler's
duty could be proven. Bad enough, it seemed, that
in his fourteen years' reign he had squandered 1562
days in hunting and 372 on journeys. The popular
will was uncommonly radical, was minded to disem-
bowel the last priest, to gibbet the last king, and fetch
down from Heaven the eternal rights, "that hang up
yonder inalienable and indestructible as the stars
themselves!" And this world is to feel pity for the
mad despot who was strangled in a silver noose by
those who had cringed to him? He who had raged all
too long thro' Katharina's realm, destroying human
happiness, with gory scythe cutting swaths of human
heads? What had come to him was but his deserts.
Only Bonaparte cursed the evil example: If the court
nobles faced about in such fashion with legitimate

masters out of old and good families, then the *empereur parvenu* might well tremble at the first evening twilight of his fortunes. The Corsican realized the truth of Schiller's words—without knowing them—uttered in his History of the Revolt of the Netherlands: "The misuse of power under which we were born oppresses less than that of power to which we have submitted."

A century and a quarter has elapsed since Paul Petrovich breathed out his life under the hands of his murderers. The youths, like Carlos and Posa, whose cheeks grew fiery hot when Freedom was named, are long since in their graves. Yet the lofty goal of their efforts was attained. All human rights are assured to the citizen, even to the poorest. Gloriously far did we carry it; so far that we no longer need keep our enthusiasm for Freedom aglow. Hence the moral indignation, so early as 1903, at the murder of the Serbian King and his Draga.

Everywhere, even in the Social-Democratic press, the "bestialized Serbian soldatesca" was condemned to Purgatorial flames, and through the bourgeois papers roared the general horror at "the blood-bath in the Konak," "the cowardly doers of murder," "the lamentable apathy of the semi-savage Balkan-horde."

The events of 1801 and 1903 were extremely alike. Paul, also, had at his court a hated woman-favorite; the Princess Gagarin. He, too, wished to force upon his realm an illegitimate successor, the pretty Prince Eugene of Württemberg. There was uproarious rejoicing in Belgrade, even as in Petersburg. Here as there, not a voice was raised for the murdered man.

Everything exactly as then. In form, a military revolt, while in the background waits for success a
claimant to the succession, athirst for the deed: the
victim in his night-gown (the fat paralytic of Serbia
wore red silk in bed); rude maltreatment of the
wounded, the dying, the dead; instead of punishment,
the thanks of the fatherland. Even the truly charming idea of avoiding the hateful words "murder" and
"death blow," and in official or officious announcements to speak simply of "the occurrence" (*l'évène-
ment*)—even that originated from the Neva.

Everything as in that far-away March. Two differ-
ences only: Peter was stronger than Alexander, and—
what, in 1801, was an heroic act of patriotism became
in 1903 a "detestable murder."

Were Marcus Junius Brutus and his associates also
cruel murderers? Their malice smote with sharp dag-
gers three and twenty wounds in Cæsar's body. And
Cromwell, who decapitated his king? Sober-minded
men had no reason to weep a single tear-drop for the
House of Obrenovich. That which was done could
not have been left undone; it could not have been
accomplished more quietly, more quickly, nor with
the shedding of less blood.

Like an evil beast, Alexander had dwelt in the land.
A paralytic, an idiot, an imbecile, no matter how
science names his condition; but no man might say
it aloud. The madness of the great is not easily managed. If a king utters words which would put a private
citizen in a madman's cell, or at least under guardianship, it is called "being elated," "an indication of surprising geniality." If at a banquet he spits in the

central dish on the table, the court-toadies praise the merry whim. So it hath been under every sun. Crowned craziness is recognized only when the official diagnosis is publicly posted; and against such sacrilege enthroned majesty gives protection.

Furthermore, the last Obrenovich had that nimble agility, versatility and loquacity which are not often to be observed in idiots. So long as he wore the crown he was secure. No one could venture to put him under guardianship. So,—what should be done?

Yes, it was said, against deposition no objection would have been made; but so much the more against murder. Very fine, very moral, very sentimental! Only the poor land would in that event never have come to its rest. The banished king would have found friends, won party support, and with the stubborn energy of madness would have moved Heaven and Hell to return to the delights of royal pomp. Such struggles would have cost tenfold, ay, a hundred fold, more human lives than did the palace revolution.

Besides, in the Outland, the pair would have carried out successfully the neat plan which the watchfulness of their enemies in Belgrade had frustrated. Alexander knew that he was incapable of begetting a child, even if he had not taken to wife his father's outworn favorite. Nevertheless, they played before the people the comedy of the expected heir. To every interviewer Sascha sang the same song: "I am only eight-and-twenty, and can experience many a time yet the joys of fatherhood." In exile Draga would soon have come to child-bed (children are to be had cheap anywhere), and so continued the name and lie of the "Obrenoviches" for later mischief.

That the Serbians had had quite enough of this noble family is not a thing to be severely criticized. Milan had plundered the state and, after his banishment, offered his services, against his son, to his deadliest enemies. Madame Natalie was proclaiming her marital unhappiness at every street-corner, and on open postal cards calling her daughter-in-law the vilest of names. The father told everywhere that the son was impotent, and the mother that he was demented. And the dear son barred both from the homeland, praised Milan's banishment, in a solemn proclamation, as a national blessing, and gave orders that papa should be shot down if he crossed the frontier.

It did not come to that; but the king found other victims. Whoever did not bend the knee before Madame Draga was either thrown into prison or quietly expedited to the next world. The officers had to submit passively to insults and blows from the queen's brothers; and the younger of the two rascals was presently to bear the title of crown prince. A family of criminals. Like a poisonous plant it must be rooted out stock and branch.

There should have been gentler measures, the king should have been consigned to the insanity specialist, the slipshod queen tried in the national courts? That would have been long drawn out and would have made great disturbance. Alexander would not have lacked favorable judgments, and the stench of the trial would have infected the whole sty. Draga's brother-in-law with his helpers attended swiftly and slyly to the heavy work. That the beast which is in man should creep forth was to be expected. Before those soldiers who had imbibed courage and activity, the pair whose fists had so long been on their necks cringed in helpless fury.

An execution after due trial and sentence would have been no pleasanter. When Count Pahlen was besought to protect the Czar's body, he responded in untroubled calmness of spirit: "Impossible to make an omelet without breaking the eggs." And one must give the Serbians this much credit: the omelet was quickly prepared.

That merit, to be sure, was acknowledged by the heads of states and national churches, though not until diplomatists and court officials had taught them that the misrule of the mad pair could have been shaken off in no other fashion. Was it not, then, this time also the finger of God? The Metropolitan of Belgrade struck the keynote: "What has occurred was ordained by God's unfathomable determination; and before such Divine decision the people of Serbia must humbly bow." Amen. The Russian Czar was first to congratulate the new king and commend him to heavenly help. Not until long after did that help manifest itself: but always, even in the blackest night, King Peter kept his pious faith in the old Serbian word of consolation which was murmured in his father's ear after his abdication, ,—the ancient prophecy which for all Serbian hearts had come to be a refuge and shelter:

"Years of terror draw nigh, and so cruel shall their ravages become in our land that the living shall envy the dead their happiness in their graves; yet thereafter a time reveals itself which will send into the graves the cry of longing: 'Oh ye dead, why are ye not still alive?'" Peter lived to see both times, that of the blessing, to be sure, only with fast-failing sight.

He was a boy of fourteen when his father, Prince Alexander, was overthrown by the Obrenoviches. The Petrovich family were peasants; Peter's mother, Persida Nenadovich, was also from a humble house. The dethroned pair lived in Hungary, later in Vienna, and sent the son when he grew up to the military Academy of St. Cyr at Paris. At the outbreak of the Franco-German war he did not hesitate to 'fight for France. He was a lieutenant when he was taken prisoner, in the autumn of 1870. In the first hour of the night, before the examination of prisoners, he, with a color sergeant, succeeded in escaping from the German camp. He leaped into the Loire, being obliged to carry the sergeant, who could not swim, on his back, reached the farther shore, and took his place again, under Bourbaki, in the French army.

With such performances the eyes of Balkan princes are not made familiar. The rest of them spend life in wild carousing. If ready money fails, they turn the name, the credit, the hereditary hopes of the family into cash. In time of war, if not safe at home or hiding among the women at Monte Carlo, Cannes or Biarritz, then they seek some post at the most comfortable headquarters.

Peter Karageorgevich never squandered one day of his life. At six-and-twenty he was a knight of the Legion of Honor, and could have made use of his repeated volunteer entrances into the French army in settling the account with Milan Obrenovich, who had usurped the throne of Peter's father. But he did not attempt it; he would not stake the peace of his fatherland on the gambler's chances of a Pretender.

But that fatherland, he saw, was not yet free, not the home of all Serbs. In Bosnia Serbian serfs groan under the Turkish knout. The descendant of that Karageorg Petrovich who still lives in his people's heroic ballads was determined to set them free. He laid aside his name, became a peasant like the rest, gave what he had to arm the insurrection, and led his valiant band against the battalions of the Osmanli— in vain.

Austria, also,—though this very insurrection gave her the excuse for demanding soon afterward the right to occupy Bosnia and Herzegovina,—was still opposed to the man who, if victory had crowned his undertaking, might have overshadowed and pushed from the throne Vienna's obedient parasite, Prince Milan. A price was set on Peter's head, Milan's hireling assassins were at his heels, the Turks beat every bush in the Bosnian forests in quest of him, and Death with swift sickle mowed down his Bosnian band. After twenty months of fierce guerilla warfare, he fled from the spot where no spark of hope for approaching freedom yet glimmered. He slunk, a haggard unnoticed peasant, through Croatia and the Austrian Alps, until he reached Switzerland.

There, from 1877 on, he lived like a hundred other poor devils. Even after his marriage to Zorka, daughter of Nicholas of Montenegro, the sums occasionally advanced him by his father-in-law, himself gasping in eternal money troubles, did not permit any leap to a princely style of living.   In order to make master-pieces of world literature accessible to his fellow-coun-trymen, he translated Milton's "Paradise Lost," German classics, and John Stuart Mill's chief works into Serbian.

His great experience was with Socialism, whose gate was by those banished rebels unbolted to one who lived almost like the proletariat.   At Geneva he is said to have had a seat in that "subterranean assemblage" in which Lenin sketched out what he was going to do when he was "ruler of Russia."   To the average citizen it may well have been the chatter of a madman; yet the speaker did reach the Kremlin,—and the listener the Konak of Belgrade.

In Peter's inward eye a new world arose.   To explore it, and to open it up to his compatriots, became his purpose.   He translated Saint Simon, Proudhon, Bakunin, Marx, wrote articles and expositional book-lets, threw himself into the whirl of Socialist propa-ganda,—until, in June, 1903, the cry resounded, "Thou, Peter, shalt be King of the Servians."

Credible witnesses have testified that Peter was un-aware of the plans of the Belgrade conspirators.   But the democratic Socialist and firm believer in the Greek church was absolutely sure of his hereditary right to the Serbian throne, and felt, in pious humility, that he would be for his tortured and thousand times martyred people a pathfinder of nobler type than Milan's shamelessly drunken brood.   To the question, whether he accepted the crown, he replied: "Only if

I may wear it as the president of a peasant's republic." He returned to his home in plain clothes, was swept into the confusion and noise of a church dedication, and was happy to spend his first hours in the fatherland incognito, among simple folk.

Already nigh to sixty, he had to make haste. Who knew how soon his sun might sink? Louder than the townsman's rose the peasant's cry for aid. King Peter helped on the agrarian reform, and never rested. Each peasant, big or little, became possessor of an unassailable title-deed.

He would fain do more: root deeply in his homeland's life what he had learned in the west. But his neighbors granted him no rest. Austria and Hungary hated the peasant-like stubbornness of the mercenary Obrenoviches' successor, denounced him as the instigator of murder, as the puppet of an assassins' band, and spread caricatures of him the whole world over, in which the long moustache droops dolorously over the distorted face of a born criminal. Serbia might not come to the sea, nor her cattle, almost the only thing she had left for exchange, to any near markets. In her narrow cage she should forget her former greatness, her striving after new national unity. Since the Radical-Nationalists, the champions of the "Pan-Serbian idea" could not withstand this pressure, they stooped to unwise compromises; and thus only provided new grounds for criticism to the enemy in Vienna and Buda-Pesth. There was wearisome strife over Bosnia, ancient Serbian territory, a strife finally decided by the aid Germany accorded to Austro-Hungary. Then came the Balkan Alliance against Turkey,

Bulgaria's withdrawal and the second campaign. The Peace of Bucharest doubled Serbia's territorial extent. The Hapsburg monarchy let its protest fall unheeded, but buried itself so much the deeper in the conviction that this swollen Serbia,—which would inevitably draw to itself the Montenegrins, Bosnians, Herzegovinians, Croats, Slovenians, perhaps even part of the Northern Albanians,—was a deadly peril to the two monarchies on either side of the Leitha mountain-range, a peril, in averting which no available means could be disdained. In the summer of 1913 the blow was to fall. Italy's objection pushed the half-drawn sword of her ally back into the scabbard. A year later, Austrian subjects, of Serbian race, on the anniversary of the Amselfeld fight, killed, on Austro-Hungarian soil, the heir apparent, Francis Ferdinand. Regicide! Most criminal of crimes! Now at last vengeance should come to pass.

So cleverly was the world's opinion created, that at first the complicity of Serbia was everywhere, even in the countries of Western Europe, regarded as unquestionable. But Serbia, since the victory and the extension of her rule over all the ancient realm of King Dushan, had desired only quiet, had postponed her hopes for Bosnia, Croatia, Slovenia, and despite the ugly gesture, after Wilhelm's own fashion, that had been made on St. Vitus' day, she had not the slightest reason to plot against the life of the pro-Slav, anti-Magyar Ferdinand. Peter, whose failing vitality was shaken to its center by the news from Sarajevo, promptly made up his mind to assent to the Vienna ultimatum, although he must have feared that his

house would not long outlast this unheard-of humiliation. By a refusal, Serbia would be left isolated; and
the king longed to secure the benefits of a peaceful
period.

. . . On the 2nd of December (1914) his capital
was taken, but as early as the 15th he was able to
lead his troops, all of whose hardships he has shared,
back into Belgrade. The next autumn brought the
overwhelming offensive of the German, Austro-Hungarian, Bulgarian and Turkish hosts. Before this (the
Seckt-Mackensen) assault the Serbian army had to
give way.

Peter now had the strength of soul voluntarily to
give up his royal power and to have the regency of
his son Alexander declared by the Skuptschina. But
he did not creep away into any comfortable place of
exile. He remained a soldier. His men in the out-
most defensive trench heard him shout, as he dragged
in their ammunition, "Look to your country that needs
you, not to me, grown a useless old man!"   Court,
government, Parliament, were tolerably sheltered;
Peter stayed with the troops. The horrors of the retreat amid snow and ice, through the rude winter
of the Albanian mountain-country, broke him down.
He grew deaf, almost blind, and chilblains cramped his
emaciated bony frame. But he did not waver. With
empty stomach he sat patiently in the ox-cart, went
on, when the beasts had fallen exhausted, afoot,
finally was carried on a rudely fashioned litter.

France and Italy bade him come overseas to rest.

But he would not at eventide, as he had done in the morning of life, part from his beloved Balkan-land. In the Saloniki consulate he was lodged wretchedly, but at least in a circle of Serb warriors.

At last the hour of deliverance struck, and from millions of pious hearts the yearning question went down into the graves, into all the far-flung general graves throughout the land: "Why are ye not still alive, O ye dead?"

All the vigorous youth, a large part of the women, who had shared in the struggle, had sunk into their graves. Bald as winter, bereft of its youthful vigor, stood the Serbian stock. Yet, in the hour of direst need, the roots of Croats and Slovenes had intertwined with its own. Jugoslavia came to be, and could stretch itself far and wide to bays and harbors in warm seas.

In a little park-house the Peasant-king, the soldier-socialist, met his death: in simple silence, even as he had lived, without needs. (His guests were entertained according to their rank and station, but he himself surrendered to no luxury, and never to the devil Alcohol.) Even to enemies of the monarchy the figure of the king was venerable, as he lay begirt with those who gazed as on a tragedy. Even more rapturously than Karageorg will his descendant be praised by Serbian bards in song attuned to the horse-hair strings of the gusla, and upon his monument, by decree of Parliament, is to stand the inscription:

PETER KARAGEORGEVICH,
THE GREAT LIBERATOR.

Was he so, or does he tower so high merely as the type and essence of the strongest of powers, of the manhood, *virtus* of his people, a people that in the World War suffered more than any other, and less than any other complained?

The surviving conspirators of 1903 may rightfully ask, at Peter's grave, whether their act was not a beneficent one, and therefore in the truest sense of the word "patriotic."

VIII

LENIN

THE farmer Ilja Uljanoff gave up agriculture, and in Simbirsk, near Samara, ranking there among the lower nobility, and as imperial state counselor, took charge of the school system. His eldest son, Alexander, while a student and a member of the revolutionary party, Narodnaja Volja (The People's Will), was accused in Petersburg of complicity in a plot against Czar Alexander III, condemned to death and executed. In Ilja's second son, Vladimir Iljevich Uljanoff, born April 10, 1870, there grew with his growth the longing to avenge his brother and the suffering of the beloved mother.

The gloomy, solitary, morose lad, whom his companions accounted haughty, was the best student in the Simbirsk Gymnasium, and was graduated by its Director, Feodor Kerenski (father of a younger boy destined to be Russia's Prime Minister and military dictator), with a most laudatory diploma and the prophecy of a brilliant future in literature. As the brother of a condemned rebel, he found the higher institutions of the capital barred against him. He was enrolled in the University of Kasan, as a student of law, but he was dismissed a month later for "revolutionary intriguing." It was not until after four years of quiet preparation that he was admitted to the State Examination.

He then went to Petersburg, lived the "subterranean" life of a conspirator, attached himself to the fighting group "Osvoboshdenje Truda" (Deliverance of the Fatherland), aided its founders, Plechanoff, Deutsch and Vera Sassulich, in urging the workingmen into a strike, published polemic writings under the pseudonyms "Ylin" and "Tulin" which announced, as the goal of the conflict, the conquest of full political control,—and was banished to Siberia.

There he widened and deepened his knowledge of economics, bored his way into Marx's works, and by his writings on capitalism and socialism aroused regret, among the best minds in Russia, that the path to a teaching chair was not open to him.

Late in the nineties he makes his escape from Siberia. He lives in Zürich, Berne, Geneva, Paris, publishes journals (in collaboration with Nadjeshda Constantinovna Crupskaja, who thereafter remains his associate), and almost every year slips away to Sweden for a few days, to see his mother.

The short-lived uprisings of 1905 allure him home, and he sits in the first Workmen's Soviet at Petersburg. But Czarism is still successful; Uljanoff must flee again, lives at first in Finland, then in Switzerland, later (with Mr. Sinovieff) in Cracow. The opening of the Great War finds him in Galicia, and when he hears that the German Social Democrats have voted for the war-credits he utters the declaration,— modeled after Bonaparte's pronouncement against the House of Braganza: "The Second Internationale has ceased to exist." He is arrested by Austrians on suspicion as a spy, but is soon after set across the border into Switzerland. There from every mountain wall the cry resounds in his ears: "Make thyself what thou art!" He becomes the herald of civil war, whereby, he is convinced, the Proletariat must, can, and will put an end to the imperialistic war.

The short stocky man, with the towering skull above his freckled faun-face, lives in Berne and Zürich like the poorest of the proletariat. He carries his agitation into the workshops. He denounces the German Social Democrats, the Russian Social Revolutionists, even the English Labor party and Independents, as contemptible bourgeois, wretched traitors to the proletariat. With unwearied exertions he strives for a general uprising of the young laboring men. His brain craves the military downfall of Czarism.

Clever folk whisper to the General Staff of Germany that the most effective means to demoralize the military power of Russia and complete her overthrow is for Uljanoff (who for the last ten years has been called Lenin) and his comrades to return home. But England, warned by her ambassador Buchanan, forbids their passage through the lines.

In a March night of 1917 he is received at the Finland station in Petrograd by an exultant crowd, marches through a forest of red flags, through the serried lines of his Bolshevist guards, to the suite once reserved for the Czar's family. The wavering, stammering Cheidse meets him, in the name of the Executive Committee, with the admonition (so surprising at such a moment) to avoid all strife within the party, and to fight in close harmony with the winners of Republican freedom for the ideals of democracy.

Will he answer him? No! Over the head of the bewildered chairman he speaks to the throng: "Soldiers, sailors, workingmen, comrades! In you I see and hail the vanguard of the proletarian world-army. Throughout Europe, after the imperialistic war follows the civil war. In Germany everything is in upheaval. The collapse of the whole national system for exploiting the masses is at hand. We are beholding already the dawn of the world-revolution."

No strife of parties? Be content with what is already attained or attainable? Nonsense! A music-box tune for good children! The Marseillaise, the battle-hymn of the rebel host, roars up. From the front steps of the station, and again from the top of the automobile, the newcomer must stand in the glare of the searchlight and address the people. From that boisterous mob he is taken in an armored car to the quarter of the city on the "Petrograd side," where Bolshevism has its headquarters in the bijou castle of the dancer Kshjesinskaia, formerly under the protection of the Czar and two Grand Dukes. At every corner the car must halt, the returned exile must speak, the searchlight must dance about his head, bathing him in splendor.

He is at once reëlected into the Soviet, speaks in the great hall of the Taurian palace, seizes the editorship of the *Pravda,* to which he had already sent many articles from the outland, and hangs at the corners of his mouth the two pass-words: "Peace at any price!" and "All power to the Soviets!"

The Soviets are in fact growing in the dark, until they overshadow the provisional government, while they demoralize and cripple the armies on the various fronts. The Octobrist, Gutchkoff, and Miljukoff, the leader of the cadets, retire. The lawyer and orator Kerenski proposes to restore the morale of the troops. His alliance with Gen. Korniloff assures a brief continuance in power.

On the 7th of November Kerenski falls overnight. Uljanoff-Lenin is master of all the chief cities, presently also of the provinces. The man who twenty years before laughed to scorn the admonition of Struve: "Go to school to capitalism first, and learn from it the art of statesmanship," is now master of all. Four years later he will himself speak almost like a second Peter Struve. Today he is not for an instant troubled with the thought that the Communist ruler has yet to learn that art from the vanquished capitalist.

He who knows nothing of Lenin's writings, teachings and feuds must, in order to see at least their general outline aright, read the speech which the creator and reformer of the Bolshevistic faith delivered in the spring of 1922 at the eleventh congress of the Communist party of Russia:—the chief statements of which I here repeat in translation:

"We Russians must carry on trade, and so must the rest of mankind. We wish to profit from it, and so do they. This very last year has shown, that the capitalistic powers are forced by their self-interest to trade with us. Our chief difficulty is not at that point, but in the new economic policy.

"First we must revive the spirits of the peasants, the overwhelming majority of whom work little farms in severalty. If we are unable to show that Communism can give prompt aid to the poverty-stricken small farmer, now tortured by hunger, then he will hunt us to all the devils. The credit he has granted us is not an inexhaustible one. We must work nimbly, for at the end of that term the decision will be made as to the permanence of communistic power in Russia. Thus far we have issued programs and scattered promises abroad. That was necessary. Since we counted on a revolution, it was thus that we must begin. Now something else is necessary.

"The simple peasant or laborer, who does not know what Communism is, does know that the capitalist was able to take care of him: that he did it badly, to be sure, exploited, robbed, degraded and insulted his protégé, but after all, did provide for him. Can you do as much?

"The peasant's retort is: 'You are excellent people: but the economic task which you have undertaken you cannot perform. If that is the final answer, then it is a fatal one. The capitalist seeks profit, and is a robber. You seek it. You seek it in another fashion. You paint the most glorious ideal pictures; you yourselves are saints: and ought, in your mortal bodies, to attain to Paradise: only—the capitalist's task, down to the present day, you have not been able to perform.'

"He who so speaks is in the right. We cannot carry on the business. If all those responsible for the communistic undertaking had perceived that we are

incompetent, that we must learn the art from its very
elements, then our game would by this time be already
won. But they do not realize this truth; on the contrary, they believe that this notion is held only by the
'unintelligent folk' who as yet have no understanding
of Communism. No! The time for programs, which
we demand that the peasant shall himself carry out, is
past indeed. Now we must show the peasant and the
laborer that we can give him practical help in his
urgent need; and that we can hold our own in the
competition with Capitalism. The merchant, or his
salesman, goes to the peasant, and instead of chattering to him about Communism, undertakes to construct
or furnish him something. He will make it costly, and
the communist can, perhaps, do it cheaper:—but then
again, it is not certain whether he may not make it
tenfold dearer.

"That in the national trusts and the mixed commissions only the best Communists, those most fully
conscious of their responsibility, have seats, is no consolation, for they have less understanding of industrial work than the average capitalist's clerk, who had
his training under a respectable firm. Our Communists' pride hinders the acquirement of that knowledge. Men who have endured compulsory labor in
Siberia, never feared death, and have brought about
the greatest revolution in the world's history, in which
(not indeed from the summits of the pyramids, but
from the walls of hope and liberation from the capitalistic yoke) forty nations look down,—these same
men are unwilling to realize that they are no business
men, cannot produce goods nor carry on trade: and

from any ordinary clerk, who has run about a store ten years and knows his business, we could not but learn something.

"He who finds himself in a blind alley must turn back: he who has done a thing wrongly must begin it over again. Never pride yourself that you are a Communist, while the other man is of no party, or a White-Guardist,—if he can do the work that must be done, and you cannot. Tho' you had hundreds of offices and titles, you, the tried and true Communist and knight of the Soviet star, must learn from every veteran clerk. This business has to be learned, and not until then shall we endure the test and win out in the race.

"We have no other resource: this time it really is the decisive 'fight to the finish.' Not indeed against international capitalism (with that we shall yet have many a 'finish fight') but against capitalism here in Russia, which rests on the basis of the small farmers' industry. We control all the resources of power, but we lack capacity. Our state has left the track of capitalistic industry and has not yet reached any other. The leadership of the working class, which is called to the great task of reorganization, of reconstruction, has not yet the ability required therefor.

"Pray do not fancy that there is any lack of political power: we already have, doubtless, a bit more than is absolutely necessary: and yet the control of the industrial machine is slipping out of our hands. And why? Because those who aspire to its control have not acquired all the needful flesh and blood.

"For one whole year we had to fall back. That

was hard, doubly hard, after years of constant progress
and immense victories, in which, however, we had
gained so much ground that we must needs go back,—
and might in truth have retired yet farther without
losing our base, the most important of all. Every
retreat causes a depression of spirit. We have poets
who have declared that formerly, in Moscow, despite
hunger and cold, all was lovely, all was pure, but that
now we see again the hateful shapes of the tradesmen and speculators. On the retreat, panic always
threatens, and we cannot, as do the commanders in
the field, post machine-guns behind the van, and open
fire if the orderly retirement seems about to become
frantic flight. Yet we too, at such an instant, must
punish harshly, yes, with merciless cruelty, any such
breach of discipline.

"When the retreat is over comes the necessity for
rearrangement. Trade we have not yet learnt. In a
whole year, with all our boasted energy, we have set up
seventeen commissions, organizations with a few millions of Russian and foreign capital. These have been
authorized by every court of appeal—and our com-
plicated appeal-system is so mad a one that I understand the gaping at this point of my speech! That
so little is done, reveals how heavy, how clumsy, how
deep sunk in Oblomoffism we still are. We shall still
come in for many a thrashing; in our trading-com-
panies the capitalist will give us many a hit behind
the ear according to all the rules of the art. That
doesn't matter so very much. The capitalist would
not have come to us at all if we had not offered him
the easiest conditions for his trade. He still jeers at

us, laughs at our communistic chatterers, but the beginning is made, we have firm ground under our feet, and can now stop the retreat.

"Renounce the ambition to be ingenious people, and to discuss in marvelous language the new industrial policy. Leave poetizing to the poets. Lay off your theatrical costume, the gorgeous festal garb of the Communist; learn to look at realities soberly and mold them practically; prove that you do not manage things worse than the capitalist: then you who hold political control will smite him, and will secure, quicker and more permanently than the private dealer, business relations with the farm-industry.

"There is much that is written here because it is customary so to write in a communistic state, and to write otherwise is forbidden. More useful than these communistic lies (of which I, from my official position, have to read so many that I am often sick to death of them), far more useful, is the harsh truth about our class, which our class foes utter. To that we must give heed. Our ruling communist stratum is as yet destitute of all culture. Look at the horde of bureaucrats in Moscow. Who guides whom? Do the 4,700 responsible communists guide the mass of bureaucrats? To be frank, my belief is that you are guided by them. Just as elsewhere a conquered people is subjected to the higher culture of the victor, so here the 4,700 (almost a division, and all the best of comrades) have been subjected to the higher culture of the vanquished. A poor wretched thing it was, to be sure, but yet a higher culture than that of communistic working men, who had never learned to conduct af-

fairs, and so were easily hoaxed, easily misled. Often
the cleverest poseurs are put in front, because one must
have a proper sign and show windows. Such confes-
sions are not agreeable, but they are not to be evaded.
Only when those in responsible places realize that they
are incompetent executives will they make the due
effort to learn.

"It is quite true, what someone has written: 'It does
not suffice to have conquered the bourgeoisie, to have
thrown them prostrate; we must also compel them to
work for us.' But ninety in a hundred of our responsible men still fancy that with the conquering,
overthrowing and rendering them harmless everything
is accomplished. The Communists are but a drop in
the sea of our people. The delusion that they alone
could complete the Socialistic organization is childish.
If we do not open up the highways of our Russian industrialism in every detail, so correctly that in return
for his grain we can give the farmer the wares he
needs, he will say: 'You are a fine fellow, you have
defended our fatherland, and so I have rendered you
obedience. But take yourself out of the way, if you
can't manage!' Be assured, that is just what the
farmer will say. Only if we learn from the bourgeoisie,
and force them to build up Russian industry along the
lines we point out, shall we attain our goal. Communists fancy they know everything, understand
everything,—and have beaten the shopkeepers: but
the people who were beaten on our fronts were not
the shopkeepers, from whom much is to be learned and
must be learned.

"What the Soviet state has accomplished, no power

on earth, surely, will or can ever nullify. Through long centuries the state of the civic type has been built up. We are the first who have chosen another form. This state may be a poor thing. The first steam engine also was, it is said, a poor one, and we do not know whether it ever worked at all. But the invention had been made: that was the essential thing. Even if that first machine was useless, we owe to it that we now have locomotives. So it is with our state: bad or good, it is created; and the greatest invention in all history is made. Europe may tell, a thousand newspapers may tell, how wretched and disorderly everything appears here; on the laboring class, the world over, the Soviet state exerts an irresistible attraction.

"But for us Communists what we have accomplished is but the unbarring of a door that leads into the open. Now we must lay the foundations of Socialistic industry. That has not yet been done, and it is the worst of all possible errors to believe that it is already accomplished. We have made, for all mankind, a great step forward: the news out of all lands confirms that. But the Russian farmer will not be wholly with us and for us until we have given him practical help.

"In order to be able to do that, we must know what is today the heart of the problem. In 1917 it was to put an end to the war; in 1920 it was defense against the Entente, which sought to strangle us; in 1921 the orderly retreat. We had gone forward so far that we could not hold all our positions, and did not need to hold them all.

"Now it is a question of choice of men. Not so

much of laws and ordinances. For them we were laughed at year after year, and asked if we were really unaware that our laws and ordinances were never carried out. The press of the Whiteguardists always made fresh jests upon them. And yet those ordinances and decrees were necessary: they said to the simple farmer or laborer: 'Thus it is our will that the state be conducted. This is our decree: try it!' So we came to the head of the revolutionary movement, and won the confidence of the masses, the credit which they still give us. But what at the beginning of the Revolution was useful and necessary is so no longer.

"Now the peasant and the workingman laugh if we come to them with decrees and bid them build up, or organize anew, this or that institution. And they have good right to laugh.

"It is now a question of proper distribution of men. Communists, who in the Revolution did creditable work, sit today in industrial and trade commissions, of whose tasks they have no understanding; and behind their backs the rascals hide. In this fashion the truth is made false and the thorough testing of what has been constructed is prevented. The great political overturn is accomplished. Today it is no longer a question of general policy, but of the most prosaic detail.

"Since we must, for a while at least, live in the capitalistic world, the essential thing is to put the right people in the right places, and assure proper oversight, thorough testing of all work done. For that the people will thank us: and the people will permit us to rule only on condition that we recognize their wishes."

The cruelly magnificent frankness of this speech revealed the condition of Russia. Among the poor in spirit, to whom the kingdom of Heaven is promised, Lenin does not wish to be counted. That millions of Russians are starving, prolonging their lives for a few days by cannibalism, he does not mention; but he mentions, because it is universally known, the fact that famine is raging everywhere, not merely in the Volga region, even worse on the farms than in the city.

He speaks like a Czar, the "little father, Batjushka," who disciplines his Russian children with kindly severity; like Peter Alexeivich, when he ordered the Muscovites to cut off their wild beards, lay aside the caftan, and dress in the German fashion. Is the will to obey more effective now than in 1700?

Amid these passivists, empty-heads, garrulous minds, and folk schooled in the lore of Byzantium, the Talmud or Marx, Lenin seemed, even to his last gasp, the one creative force. How much he overtopped even the mightiest in the swarm is shown by a comparison of this speech, at the Congress, with Trotski's book, *The New Haltingplace,* which sees the capitalistic régime decayed, the curve of its development descending, and "establishes" that the ground is shaking under the bourgeoisie.

Lenin never became a bookman, a fanatic with his vision narrowed by blinders to a single direction, nor a journalist, caring more for "success" than for effective results. He alone, with all his learning, retained the instinct, the clear understanding for human nature, and the humor, of the peasant. In him were mingled qualities of the Ukrainian Gogol and of the peasant as drawn to the life by Tolstoy in his middle age. Those unfamiliar with the Russian nature, listening casually, did not hear the undertones of this humor.

And what did he say, in the fifth year of Bolshe-vistic rule? Courts, executive, industry: all beneath criticism. Any ordinary merchant's clerk can do it better. Detestable, laughable confusion in the judi-ciary. The Communist's haughtiness prevents his real-ization that a man at the front and in the Revolution might fight heroically, risking his life on a hair, and yet, in supervision of industry, be a harmful bungler. The same obtuseness blocks the way to the perception that the Communists are but a drop in the sea of the popular masses, and that the mighty current of the peasants' will can sweep the Bolsheviki, in whom it has thus far put faith, into the crater of hell, and will do so, if they do not by tomorrow prove that, in the full possession of political power, they can do at least as much to provide for the farmers' needs as did here-tofore the private trader standing alone. Did any head of a state ever mount to so steep a height of majestically bold acknowledgment? Did one ever have the courage for such a confession?

In the same spring with this "Speech from the throne" (as it may well be called), there followed the news of Lenin's incurable disease, which compelled his withdrawal from the life of his creation.

In a sultry sunless hour, when, just as the canker-worm creeps to his silent murderous work upon the rose leaves, ennui blasted all life and effort, Bonaparte, as Napoleon, Emperor of the French, said: "At the announcement of my death, the world will draw a deep breath, and that 'Ouf!' will be the only utterance it will make on the incident.' He did not dream, even under that chill blast out of the abyss of doubt, that he would die a prisoner, long since stript of power, and that his decease would not be needed to relieve the world from the nightmare incubus of his imperial genius.

Where he, amid eleven thousand burning homes, from the culminating point of a life that to him seemed merely one steeple—and not the highest—climbed, gazed at the white walls, the golden-green, cinnabar-red and blue domes of the Moscow churches, or, idly weary, while round about him in the silent darkness the defensive works of Kutusoff and Rostopchin went on to completion, strode through the ancient spacious halls, wrote the charter of the Comédie Française, read romances in bed, but let two wax-lights burn at his office-window all night, so that the soldiers of the patrol should believe him to be at his sleepless commander's task,—there in the Kremlin, ceased to breathe Vladimir Iljevich Uljanoff, who signed his writings and his decrees "N. Lenin." He too was one who, as it was whispered of Napoleon, forced his way, without the Gosudar's permission, into the Kremlin, and even by that act had turned the Russian world topsy-turvy. In dusty boots, workman's jacket, soft shirt-collar, the little man stepped through the Gate of the Redeemer, bared not his head before the miracle-working figure, and made himself at home, with his official staff, that swelled from moon to moon, in the Pilgrimage-place, the capital of Russian humanity, just as if he were in a business building never pervaded by a holy memory. No reverence for the graves of the Czars, who through three centuries, since Ivan Kalita, have here found rest. No qualm of conscience on the tower of Ivan Veliki, under which the nigh two centuries old Czar-bell (Zar-Kolokol) swings.

There had come to be, on the Moskwa as on the Tiber, a Septimontium. One of those seven hills was built upon by a Golgorouki, Ruric's descendant, in the night after the thousandth year of Christendom; and to it Ivan Danilovich, Prince of Vladimir, transferred his capital in 1327.

Mongols, Lithuanians, Khans of the Crimea and Poles laid the city waste, overran the palisades and the stone walls of the Kremlin. Peter turned his back upon it and led the whole retinue of his court to the Neva: yet Moscow outlived Asia's rage and the disdain of Europe.

And what Peter Alexeivich took away, Vladimir Iljevich restored to the seven-hilled city of his East: the rank of the empire's capital. Petersburg was the child of a whim, created out of a morass, was intended to be "a window toward Europe": and it remained always closed, walled up and boarded up, whenever Russia, in consciousness of her destiny, turned again eastward.

The only strong rulers that it had in its dawning hour, the first Peter and the second Katharina (who rose even above him),—he a man alienated from Russia and she an Anhalt princess from Stettin,—delighted to breathe mists of the Neva, and in their loveliest southern abode always longed for the neighborhood of Europe. But everything that was essentially Russian had a mighty drawing back toward Moscow, to the ancient mother's venerable house.

There Bolshevism first felt itself truly at home. In Petrograd, to which even the Russianized name seemed only to have been elaborately fitted, not to have grown with the city, and in the Smolny Institute, Bolshevism was an interloper, an alien: it seemed to be capable there of living but for a brief span. In Moscow it revealed its true nature as Asiatic Socialism, worked out its theory and practice, as Marxism à la Tartar, yet hardly an alien any longer. Moscow became its source of power: is that city now to prove its grave?

If Lenin dies, the indispensable one, worshipfully beloved by the peasant, by the city workingman, even by the bourgeois bereft of his rights through four long years, as comrade, brother, Father Iljich,—then does all that he, he alone, created and upheld, go down to the dust with him?

In the year 1903, at the London Congress, the Russian Social Democracy had split. The men of the "Jewish Union" had decided to form a separate organization. The majority, the "Hards," followed Lenin: the minority, the "Softs," Martoff. The names of the factions, Bolsheviki (for the majority) and Menscheviki (for the minority) were soon no longer fitting in their original sense, and since then have indicated those who demand most, and least: Maximalists and Minimalists. The Menscheviki wished to work through the national Duma, coöperating with the constitutional National Democratic faction (the Cadets); the Bolsheviki looked for nothing from a Parliament, everything from revolutionary activity; and they stubbornly rejected even so much as a tactical common action with any faction to the right of the "Trudoviki." While the Menscheviki, after the fiascos of 1905, claimed the glory of a pure Proletariat party, drove the Intellectuals out of their ranks, and wished to do away with ("liquidate") leadership altogether, so that simply the mass itself should rule, on the other hand the left wing of the Bolsheviki, with their demand for absolute destruction of private ownership and of all government, was approaching the Anarcho-Socialists, whose most respected leader in the east was Prince Kropotkin. "Maximalists" and "Minimalists" were at that time the usual names for the two wings of the Socialist party, whose proselyting capacity was sinking, ever since the time (1909) when one of their most active members, Azoff,—who had planned the murder of Grand Duke Sergius and of the powerful Minister of Police, Plehve,—was unmasked, by Stolypin's own testimony, as having been for sixteen years the salaried stool-pigeon of the secret police. The Menscheviki lost (because they leaned too far to compromise with the Bourgeois democrats) one leading spirit, Plechanoff, the ablest theorist of Russian Marxism. (Despite his close association with his German brethren in the faith, he was in favor of dragging down the German empire in 1914).

The Bolsheviki in turn divided into Otzovists (opponents of Parliament) and Leninists. In the possession of one of the representatives arrested in 1914, there was found a draught for a party resolution, which took up Lenin's idea, that "the overthrow of Czarism and its army was to be regarded as the lesser of the two evils that might be expected as the result of the war." Against this idea not only the Socialist leader Cheidse had made opposition in the Duma; *Nasche Slovo* (*Our Word*) also, the Paris organ of the Social Democrats, had declared that the Russian workingmen, however far removed from the old-fashioned Chauvinism, would never agree to such a thought. The old warning, "Never say 'never,'" soon proved itself wise once more. In the first year of the war, it is true, Petrograd workingmen, of the reddest dye, were still so desirous to help on the victory of the army that they by unheard-of exertions had ready for delivery, on the thirteenth day, equipment ordered by the military authorities which the manager of the factory believed could at best be delivered in four weeks. In the third year of the war proletariat and bourgeois Democrats dragged Nicholas from the throne: in the fourth the victory of the Leninists became possible.

So early as in May, 1917, in the Taurian Palace, in a public session open to members of all the four national assemblies, Lenin's screed opposing the war was sharply criticized. The National Liberal Chulgin, who in the railway carriage had induced the Czar to abdicate, reproached Lenin (who had returned from exile, across Germany, in a car which was barred and bolted before leaving Geneva) with publishing the doctrine that, because Russia had no army, no bread, and furthermore had only selfishly imperialistic allies, she therefore must have peace, at any price.

"Lenin! That is a signature," he added, "behind

which any bewildered opinion-utterer can hide. And
these fanatics play an easy game, among a people
whose knowledge of politics is so slight as ours."

The Social Democrat Zeretelli replied: "I do not
approve Lenin's agitation. But he fights for ideas
and principles, and only slanderers can accuse him of
having harmed the cause of the revolution. I hope
that his distrust of the bourgeois Democrats is ground-
less. But the opinion is well founded that an attempt
to eradicate militarism in another country by force
of arms is the best way to breed militarism and imperialism in one's own country."

The Menschevik Trotski himself, soon to become
Lenin's chief assistant, did not as yet believe that the
defeat of the national army was essential to the success
of the revolution. In October, 1914, he wrote, that
everybody, from the Parliamentarian Haase (who was
still leader of the majority of the faction) to the German generals at work out there in Poland, were united
under the banner with the inscription, "Down with
Czarism," but that it was only a camouflage. He
added:

"We, who have passed through the school of his-
torical materialism, ought to be ashamed if we can
not,—despite all these phrases, lies, boasts, vulgari-
ties, stupidities, and commonplaces,—clearly recognize
the real interests, the inner connections. To the Germany of the Hohenzollern Czarism is indispensable,
because it weakens Russia industrially, culturally, and
in military strength, and because, without it, German
absolutism would stand out in Europe as the last bul-
wark of feudal barbarism.

"The revolution is not in the least dependent on a foreign war. It needs time to mature, but does not need the lances of the Samurai east of the Elbe,* who, against our will, gave the Czar a welcome opportunity to play a pleasing rôle as the defender of Serbs, Belgians and Frenchmen. Destructive defeats of Russia may hasten the revolution, but must weaken it vitally. And in Germany the tide which turned to ebb when the Proletariat party surrendered to military nationalism, would be hastened the more, the working class would feed on the crusts from the table of victorious Imperialism, even in the realm of ideas,—and the social revolution would be smitten to the heart.† That under such circumstances the momentarily successful Russian revolution would be a false birth, I do not need to argue. The 'liberating' help which German Imperialism, with the pious approval of the German Social Democracy, is bringing us in Krupp's ammunition boxes, we reject with horror. We are not willing to buy Russia's freedom with the destruction of Belgian and French freedom, with the imperialistic poisoning of the German proletariat."

Even in Lenin's Geneva newspaper, it was said: "In Russia a rumor is current that Wilhelm bases his hopes on the outbreak of a Russian revolution. Under the pretext that it is a conflict with the Czar, the German Social Democrats have stooped to an alliance with their Kaiser, and so betrayed the workers' Inter-

---

* I.e., The Prussian junkers, likened by metaphor to the fighting gentry of Japan.

† Trotski could not foresee that America would more than fill the Czar's place, and that Germany's own downfall would leave her no time to exult over Russia's.

nationale. We Russian revolutionists have neither
sought nor desired such aid; and the treachery of our
German associates, whom since that day we despise,
prevented us from making, in the first days of mobiliz-
ing, a strong protest against the war."

So spoke party strategy. But at an early date Lenin
himself wrote that it might, to be sure, be as yet uncertain whether, for the Internationale, the victory of
the one or the other group of Powers would be the
lesser evil. "But we Russians," he said, "are for
Russia's downfall, because it would make easier her
spiritual liberation, her deliverance from the chains of
Czarism."

And in the chief action against eleven Social Democrats accused of high treason, the young advocate
Kerenski, leader of the Trudoviki ("Party of hard-
working men," the Peasant Democracy), emphasized
loudly and repeatedly that the accused were not of
Lenin's following, and were "utterly averse to the plan
for plunging into the fatherland's back the dagger prepared for her destruction." From Kerenski's lips,
again, came the word later so balefully winged, uttered
on February 15 before the Imperial court at Petersburg, "Dagger-thrust into the back of the army in
the field."

Thirty-two months later the army was shattered into
dust, Lenin had taken the young advocate by surprise,
the Constitutional party had been dispersed by the
Red Guards, the minority rule of the Bolsheviki, the
oligarchy of the little Communist group made secure.
It had fought the decisive battle in alliance with the
left wing of the Social Revolutionaries, created with its

aid the constitution of the Soviet republic; then had shaken off the allies and outlawed them in the criminal trial at Moscow, and, finally, had slily bunched them up together with poor rascals and set them in the pillory as a new gang of Azeffs * of worthless villains.

High enthroned sits Bakunin's "Czar of the Revolution," Hertz's "New Attila." And is he who sits on the throne truly, as Frau Luxemburg, in her early feud with Lenin, cried out, "the single-ego of a vain man frantic for power, sitting where only the mass-ego has a right to sit to shape the destiny of the working-class now called to rule"? Could that mass-ego come to expression, or even to self-consciousness, in a land which never had a proletariat, in the European sense of the word, at all, which now, with decaying industries, is farthest from having any, and whose peasant folk insist on being driven, even to their happiness, by the hard fist of a master?

Forty years ago Zola wrote that the Czar who should gather about him a peasantry freed from unendurable pressure of taxation and the yoke of usury would increase his despotic power, but that every revolutionary outbreak, in the cities, of craving for change would issue in a terrible uprising of the peasants, massacre of the bourgeoisie and destruction of the cities—that only the laughter of all competent judges would greet any attempt to transform Russia into a republic.

The world was angrily amazed when an undoubted liberal so expressed himself. And Trotski would dislike to be reminded today of his prophecy: "A revolu-

* For Azeff, stool pigeon of the police, see p. 199.

tion that came on the heels of Russian defeat could only be a miscarriage."

But what did happen? The great Day of Wrath, which John depicts in the Apocalypse, rose out of the gray mist and now waits threateningly, in scarlet veiled. A new Russia was promised: all free, all alike in rights, property, power, dignity: the tiger reposing peacefully beside the roe. From beneath coffin lid and sod uprises the murdered man to embrace his murderer.

Is the assurance fulfilled? Terrifically fierce grew the struggle. No help from without, no creative power within that outlasted the enthusiasm of the coronation day. Russia of the Soviets long resembled a house whose janitor, since he, with his wife and children, was freezing, hewed out first a few beams, then the whole wooden framework of the upper stories, and thrust them in his stove; so that with skull agape and wide open wounds on head and throat it has endured the tempests of the dog days and autumnal rains, and now from afar sees Nekrassoff's "red-nosed Winter" draw nigh in his terrible white array.

All unfree, on the convict's short chain. All, save those in high office or at degrading servile tasks, without rights, poor to beggary, driven by the pangs of frantic hunger even to cannibalism, ay, degraded to the point of feasting on the flesh of children once tenderly loved. The German carpenter, whose daily wage of thirty paper marks does not suffice for a clean comfortable sleeping place and clothes to keep him warm, is a Crœsus or a Morgan beside the Russian owner of a big farm without a cow, seed-corn, farm implements or household furniture. To such a state have things come: and Lenin is ill unto death.

A man whose place cannot be filled. Orthodox Marxists, who swear by the omnipotence of industrial development, but as actual moulders of destiny recognize only the class war, who uphold the cult of personality as a power that determines its environment,— even they (is it not like the grim jest flashing in the heavy air of growing tragedy?) terrified at the ending of this life, banded together, when it seemed to be flickering out, to prevent the tragic message that it was over from reaching the people until they had elaborately prepared the feelings of the masses to receive it. Even those puffed up by the elephantiasis of stupidity feared that the messenger of sorrow suddenly rushing barefoot, with lurid pine torch through the land, springing upon rafts, flashing the light into mines, might, like heaven's fury falling on dead waters, raise up from dull souls a raging flood, to sweep away all their short-lived splendor.

Only a Lenin could venture to give nine-tenths of all property (which was to be, after all, in the approaching Golden Age, a common possession) to the peasants, thus ramming home deeper than ever the idea of private ownership,—and then, in the stress of need, to sacrifice all the external structure and decorations of Communism, to seek relations and a treaty with the thousand-fold accursed capitalistic powers, to take from churches and monasteries the gold and all ornament that could be minted, from the oldest sacred images to strip off their decorations of precious stones, to cast the priests who offered resistance, even the

Patriarch himself, into prison, and hale them before
the judgment seat of godless judges. No one but he
could have perpetuated in undiminished force the af-
flictions which resulted from the war: famine, pesti-
lence, the relapse into bestial ferocity. He, alone,
might have brought about the transformation of dictatorial and cruel clique rule into democracy, into a
union of agricultural states, capable of carrying on
world-trade, a union to which America and Europe
would not long refuse financial credit. "Iljitch commands only what is necessary and beneficial: and if
he will have it so, it goes not otherwise."

Shriller than ever, and with more venomous breath
did the strife for the high places snarl and spit during that spring, through the depths of the Socialist
party. On one side it is declared that the peasantry,
which has already corrupted the Red Guards almost
to the very walls of Moscow, is now disintegrating
the tissues of the party organization, into which it
has forced itself from the national army. On the other
side there is gnashing of teeth to intimate that if the
unruly Sinovieff isn't quickly pulled in, with curb and
bit, to a peaceable canter, then Petrograd will be taking itself out of the empire as an independent republic.

The next year brings fresh strife. Is democracy
(that is the watch-word), is the formation of factions
and groups, within the structure of the Communist
party itself permitted? Trotski, the organizer of
victory over the Czarist forces, steps out of obscurity
to champion the demand of the opposition against the
old high priests, and goes, because no victory beckons
to him from this field, into retirement before the day

of the decision. Karl Radek, who rides comfortably and cleverly in all saddles, loses his seat in the Central Committee, with the control over the press and propaganda. Hot heads, a hailstorm of fiercely accusing epithets, right and left, eyes agleam with hatred. Yet the fiercest feud, tumult to the brink of madness, is controlled by one magic word:—Lenin!

None uttered a word against him. The stubbornest opponents, who regarded his new industrialism as a "weak policy of compromise," clothed their criticism in the garb of pious reverence. To what depths had Russia sunk! Russia, that once extended from the White to the Yellow Sea, from Reval, Riga, Helsingfors, undivided, to Baku, Tiflis, Odessa, that held Poland fast in the eagle's talons, fed a world with her bread, overawed it with her army, whose chief cities, with freshly growing industries, were aglow with prosperity, whose science stood respected beside that of sister nations, and whose art was rising like a new sun upon the outworn Occident! Now torn in fragments, shrunken on both continents, in the East, a republic alienated from Bolshevism; in the South, Ukraine only loosely attached to Moscow; Georgia held only by armed force, Russia herself forced by dire need into an alliance with the Turks, who thus fell heir to the empire of the pseudo-Romanoffs from Holstein-Gottorp stock, which Germany had beaten; without force enough, even, to chasten Poland, her cities falling to ruin, the best farm lands far and wide lying untilled, with millions of starving men instead of the superabundant grain crops, the Intelligentsia struck down, fled into exile, in rags, the lights of science that yet glimmer bereft of oil to feed them, without the tools to make even daily labor possible, the currency of the state a jest for children, only a dim after-glow from the Spring sun of Russian art.

And he who was responsible for this terrific transformation, from the height to the depths, beloved of all! Peasants and city-folk, laborers and soldiers, saw in him the incarnation of the fatherland—the ever-wakeful guardian, never unmanned by drunkenness. He was not merely the banner, the symbol: no, he was the Cause itself.

"Iljitsch will not allow the land to go back from the peasant's hand to the landlord of yesterday. Iljitsch looks out for us, he just loves the bother with the obscure little fellow; very soon he'll make better times for him. No Batjushka (little father, i.e., Czar) was ever so unweariedly busy. He never pushes himself into the spotlight, doesn't woo for applause, slips out of the meeting where he had to make a speech, is satisfied if he can sit quietly at his work sixteen, eighteen hours between sunrise and sunrise, understands and speaks the simple picturesque language of the common man, always goes plainly dressed, with no frock coat and stiff collar, in his dark jacket, a cap on his bald head,—and yet, he's lord of the Kremlin.

"An old stock Russian, with all the marks of the Tartar. The Kalmuck lips under the narrow Mongolian eyes. Twig of the little nobility. Fjodor Romanoff, to be sure, was of a nobler house, but a Lithuanian, or Prussian: foreign-born, like the great Ruric. The new lord of the Kremlin, too, if there were a drop of Bonaparte's blood in him, could have become Czar: all Russia, the whole globe would have recognized him, and from Evan's tower, the emperor's bell 'Zar-Kolokol,' would have rung the knell for the third monomachistic Vladimir."

Let it toll for him, too, though uncrowned. He did not die in the Kremlin. They had taken him out of the Palace city to the manor house in the village of Gorki (i.e., "Bitterness"), which had been equipped as a sanatorium. There, on the 21st of January, 1924, he died. Russia has mourned for this man as for no other since Dostoevski. A pristine Russian. (Trotski, who has in him something of the lyric poet, has written wise words on "Nationality in Lenin.") The undegenerate child of his people. The one man, as Prokosch says of Bismarck, who was providentially

"To cast a nation old
Into another mould."

In him alone, so the myth into which he is already growing will declare, was the proper type of Russian humanity fully formed.

Was the certainty of victory always present in Lenin's mind? Only one filled with that certainty could have ventured on the gruesome frankness which he displayed in his speech at the Eleventh Congress of the Communist party. From the clear air of the glaciers, from a Sinai clad in Polar ice, it seemed to roar down. If it was his last far-echoing speech, he could not have ended more worthily. Just ere the night comes, the sky is once more radiant: and no morning, no noonday dispensed such glorious splendor. . . .

The fall of Bolshevism, had it occurred then, might have brought worse peril for the world than its rise had ever caused. Against any attempt,—with the (indispensable) aid of those Socialists who had been till then under a ban,—to summon a national assembly, to steer into democracy and parliamentarism, in the traditional fashion of western Europe, the true believers in Bolshevism would have made opposition with all the force of their wills and with no anxious scruples against even the most atrocious means.

Twenty millions made bestial by hunger, eighty millions starving, and shuddering at winter's coming and the rock of their trust rent asunder, the shelter it afforded blown down the four winds:—what then?

Military dictatorship, collapse of the empire, separate organisms, rule of princely adventures or of "miracle workers" adored by blind folly, priestly states, pogroms, bloodier than any of the past crusades against the arch-foes of sanctified belief, church robbers, czar-murderers and desecraters of imperial graves, banding together of peasants to sack cities, revolt of demoralized or ill-fed masses of the army, or those allured by masked monarchists:—Chaos! Nothing imaginable would be lacking, which becomes possible in a land of such experiences, of immeasurable suffering, in the cold Orient of Kazamassovian humanity, when the last tie of moral restraint is broken and nowhere round about does any beacon-fire indicate a safer way.

The watchers of the nations were on the watch? Ah, no! Without a pause in the scramble for wealth, without a brake applied to the constant craze for amusement, Europe has let one nation on its eastern edge perish of hunger, typhus, and verminous poison.

Does Europe learn to fear the wrath of the survivors? Or does it hesitate over the little circumstance of the burden of war losses to be borne? Woe to the continent if it had stood by, unprepared, until through the gate of the Redeemer had rung the announcement of the decease of him who, as fearlessly in the Kremlin as in the gipsies' booth at Zürich, had lived his faith, and therefore, in the life task of a giant, never looked a dwarf!

Two years before Russia would not have digested calmly so tremendous a loss. But the strong man rendered the best of all services to the cause that was holy to him as was ever anywhere the divinity to the most pious priest:—his will compelled even Death to be patient.

Lenin died slowly. For twenty months he had withdrawn from state affairs. From time to time, to be sure, there was flashed the world over the report of his near recovery. But that world had fallen out of the habit of counting him among living forces, and no incubus was lifted from its breast, not for the space of an instant did it catch its breath, when his death became an event.

He can never wholly die; never can his nation, not even the class most remotely influenced by his teachings, accustom itself to being the passive creature of an alien will. If the teeming multitude of European humanity fails to uplift itself, to release itself from the meshes (grown thin from eternal chafing and soapy

with the sweat of agonized hands) of trade stagnation
and ever threatening loss, to rise to its higher, its highest duty, to grow at last into consciousness of inevitable
unity,—then it is weaving its own gray shroud, which
will plunge the continent into darkest night. Russia
can live without Europe: Europe cannot live without
Russia.

That land is no longer what it was in 1922. Lenin's
eyes saw the first signs of its reviving health. Industry was rising. England, Italy, lesser powers also,
accorded to the empire of the Soviets (in which the
Soviets no longer ruled) political recognition. That
was not due to Lenin. Any Russia, whether that of
the most worthless Czar or of the most ferocious
rebel, would be girt about by the keen-scented hunts-
men of business as a slaughter-house is by dogs. But
for fifty moons the immense Eurasian land seemed to
hang upon the lips of this one man, and if Peter's
swamp-city does not bear hereafter the name of Lenin,
then perhaps the whole Russian people, just as it has
down to the present day talked of Tartar-China and
Oblomoff-China, may speak of Lenin-China, and dream
of Lenin's time as of a world era.

"He never," murmur his enemies to the left, "was
a Communist, and his writings, strong only contro-
versially, will not last as long as his embalmed body."
It is possible. There would still remain his practical—
tactful genius, his extraordinary personality, which
could attack the problem, be the Paul of Socialism:
there would remain the solitary great man. "Engage
in the battle, then look!" (*S'engager, et puis voir.*)
The titanically insolent motto of Bonaparte was also

Lenin's. To seize the opportunity for swift attack and after that consult the wind and weather, is to mould vision into event.

Chernoff, an honorable foeman seeking for right judgment, describes Lenin as the tight vessel of a short-sighted though keen-scented understanding, served in icy coldness by utmost strength of will—as a fighter and boxer of inexhaustible endurance, skilled in tricks and feinting, whose skin becomes hot in the fight, while his inmost self coolly counts the chances, smiles at kindliness as amusing weakness, whose "good nature" is only the by-product of his consciousness of power, like that of a St. Bernard playing with little poodles.

Cold may prevent decay, but it never creates life. No conscience, no heart? and yet such continuously creative effect? Only because Lenin existed could the Mustapha Kemals, Stambuliskis, Mussolinis, Primo de Riveras, the Ramsay MacDonalds, even the Horthys and Eberts be. The earth did not breathe at his departure as it did before his rise. He who acts is, as Goethe moralizes, always conscienceless. The Lenin of the first epoch uttered horrors, wrote in blood his cruelly harsh decrees, and through his inborn combination of brutal fury and simple comprehension of humanity (all quite lacking in Wilson, his antitype) made his idealism capable of effective action. But has any monarch who waged war with a pious faith in righteousness and duty sowed less suffering over the earth?

From the son of the Tartars, whose favorite companions were children and animals, radiated kindly feeling that warmed even the rudest hut on the remotest steppe. It may be that the goal of his efforts remains for those born yesterday unattainable: but with all the force of his will he strove to lead his people thither, and never trembled at the scorn and hatred which raged shrill about his retreat: he caused the shedding of much—too much—blood, but not a hundredth part as much as that vainly poured out by the gentlest of Czars.

Did it cause him suffering of soul? If so, his smile did not betray it. And, gradually, all learned to love him: even the Bourgeoisie, even the Intelligentsia that were driven into exile by their terrors, and later offered him their loyal coöperation. And why? Because everyone, the mass-ego, came to feel, vaguely or clearly, that this man had not climbed the heights for the sake of tapping the sources of power, to be looked up to timidly as to a divinity, nor to sit at ease enthroned in pomp; but that the aim of all his effort was to lift out of the clouds into the sunshine the folk of Russia, whom he loved as a true man loves.

Never before on our earth have so many millions mourned for one: was it for an ice-cold nature? It was for the man, nor for the organizer of revolution, the peerless party-leader, that Trotski, no weakling, sang a dirge resonant of sobs. Here was a great man, who, devoted with utmost enthusiasm to his task, moulded his doctrine and his life, apparently without effort, as if it could be no otherwise, into complete unity: who with unerring instinct perceived any condition or event which made it necessary to reset the boundary posts and shift the switches on the track.

The popular imagination will weave poetry about Lenin's figure. Out of the Iliad of the Russian revolution Iljitsch will gleam forth as a modern Ilja of Murom, in whom all the natural powers of his homeland, earthly and psychic, were embodied; and who, like the creation of Homer's brain, not as one of woman born, will shine throughout the ages.

IX

SARAH BERNHARDT

WHOEVER in lands of German speech stands and walks on sturdy feet today, be it woman or man, has seen only a fading Sarah Bernhardt and later an aged woman on the stage, has heard only that she was a clever virtuosa, greedy of applause, whose glory had culminated decades ago, who was long since outshone by the splendor of newer stars, and whose later manner of acting impressed one as old-fashioned, *vieux jeu* in the original sense of the phrase.

When I (at least a hundred years ago) was spending a few days in Paris, and was invited by Gaston Paris, the Romance philologist, to tea at the Collège de France, the conversation naturally touched among other subjects on "le Kaiser." He was to many Frenchmen at that time still a Hope, and for almost all continued to be the heroic Modern man who had driven out Bismarck, the ogre in cuirass, had zealously flattered the republic of the Mélines and Waldeck-Rousseaus, the Jules Simons and Meniers. From the same school of wisdom had come Renan's sigh: "May I be permitted to know, before my death, so that the problem may not disturb my repose in the grave,— what is to be the inner development of Wilhelm the Second."

So there arose a more rational discussion of the

question, why one who wooed so eagerly the people's
favor, who everywhere strove to warm the breath of
popular feeling toward himself, was at home generally ridiculed, and, by the wisest especially, looked on
with mistrustful eye.

Then, with a smile, the clever essayist Vicomte de
Vogüé,—he who first taught us to appreciate the rich
nobility of the Russians' style, threw out the remark:
"Doubtless it is much the same with the Kaiser over
there as it is here—our guest will not take the comparison amiss—with Sarah: he, too, has been too often
seen, heard of too often. . . ."

As to the artist (unhappily not in regard to Wilhelm), the judgment is still the same. "Seen too often"
(*Du déjà vu*). Old School. She had her day. And
was, after all, no such lofty spiritual genius as Rachel,
hardly more than the Croizettes, the Bartets, the
Réjanes.

A false judgment, for she was unique: *sui generis*.

But she did live too long, played much too long, and
we were, all of us, too close to her setting sun to find
with ease the right point of view from which to comprehend her artistic personality.

In the Kalver Straat of Amsterdam it was a wreath
of immortelles which hung beneath her portrait by
Joseph Israel, and the cross after her name, that
brought me tidings of her death. The picture may be
a half century old, but it does not portray a young
woman. The Dutch Jew has brought out, so to speak,
in masterly fashion, from the narrow head, the nature
kindred to his own, Semitic and Netherlandish. Noth-

ing there of Rembrandt's Jewish bride or Susannah. More naturally does the memory turn back from this picture to the fascinating ugliness of Jans Vermeer's maidens. The wonderfully soft, delicately gray atmosphere, without which Holland's immortal traditional art of painting would be unimaginable, breathes about the head. A veil, thin as mist, that might have been woven by princesses transformed by witchcraft into spiders, seems to cover that head so that no breath from the outer world may blow upon it. Was this veil really a part of the woman's self? Rhodope, Hebbel's noblest *mimosa pudica*, and the all too public Sarah! The fabled court of Candaules, and the Paris of Gambetta, Zola, Richepin, and of the yet younger Black Cat!

But master your mirth! Signor D'Annunzio in his romance *Il Fuoco* sinned more grievously than Candaules in his bedchamber, baring, not to one man's eyes (and that, one whose Hellenic nobility of soul quelled all sensuous impulse), nay, but to a hundred thousand barbarians, the body of her who had once been dearest to him. And then Sarah, in the shocked pride of womanhood, wrote that she never would play the creation of a poet whose morbid masculinity had stooped to such uncleanness. This despite the fact that she who was so unveiled was Sarah's most dangerous rival, whose performance of *La Dame aux Camélias,* or *Fédora,* was, by the young, unanimously preferred to her own. Yet from Sarah the woman came the horrified cry of outraged femininity. And Sarah the actress (who actually never did play *La Gioconda* nor *Sebastian*) would have been the ideal Rhodope;

not, indeed, with the Frisian chill of the North German woman on which Hebbel's heart was set, but the most womanly and most royal of Rhodopes.*

But France, in the abundance of her own wealth, and in the constant fear (perceptible to this day in her politics) of losing her own identity,—a fear which to the short-sighted view of Björnson and others has seemed a symptom of China-like haughtiness—has always and strenuously set her face against invasion by alien poetry, and, especially by foreign drama, though her actual life has nevertheless received more enrichment from it in form and color than she has given in return.

It is indeed curious! The world-circling glance would hardly light on another land that has yielded so readily to the charm of an alien nature and so eagerly given herself up to it. Clodowech (Clovis), Mazarin, Marie Antoinette, Necker, Kleber, Rapp, Bonaparte, were all strangers. Louis Napoleon was half Netherlander, Eugénie a Spaniard. Victor Hugo had Spanish, Zola and, it is said, Gambetta, had Italian blood in their veins. The Dumas were descended from mulattoes; Rachel Felix, Sarah Bernhardt, M. de Max were importations from the Orient. But as for dramas, only rarely has one born from a stranger's soul been sluiced into the Seine. Is it because men, but not their

---

* The tale of Candaules is told by Herodotus to account for the downfall of his dynasty of early Lydian kings. He forced his chief counselor Gyges to hide in the royal bedchamber to see the full beauty of his queen, Rhodope, unveiled. She silently detected the action, summoned Gyges next morning, and bade him kill himself or his master. Hebbel treats this subject in *Gyges und sein Ring*. The chief characters in *Il Fuoco* have been universally identified as D'Annunzio himself and Duse.

works, could be annexed and Gallicized? Only Wag-
ner, not Goethe, Mozart, Beethoven, Kleist, Hebbel,
Schiller, or Weber has found a permanent place on
the French stage. Shakespeare does not exist for it.
If he is no longer Voltaire's "drunken barbarian," yet
he does remain an "outlander." Just as *Œdipus* was
hunted up as a novelty for Mounet Sully and the
ancient arena at Orange, so is Hamlet unearthed for
the French tragic actor. Directors like Antoine,
Claretie, Gémier, have experimented with *Lear, Macbeth, The Shrew, Sheilock;* * but it all failed to take
root and lasted hardly longer than Ibsen. And the
ghost seer, Ibsen's strongest rival in dramatic power,
of our own days, he who in atmosphere and phantasy,
in colors and tones, is the richest, perhaps indeed the
only one whose world is an immortal creation, Strindberg, is not yet descried from Gallic shores!

So in her youth Sarah never played Juliet, Ophelia,
Desdemona, in maturity never Cleopatra, the yellow
serpent of Old Nile. (She did unfortunately once
assume the rôle of Prince Hamlet.) Nor did she once
play *Salomé,* written for her, in French, by Wilde.
As for Penthesilea, Judith, Rhodope, Marianne, Mary
Queen of Scots, she probably has hardly even thought
of them. Joan of Arc, the most lyrically eloquent of
all the students that Schiller put into petticoats to
portray the soul, the pulse, the sensibilities of womanhood? No, nor that either. Yet the Sarah who, out of
Rostand's delicate literary embroidery, created *La
Princesse Lointaine,* and from his gospel blue-stocking,

* The traditional English spelling is, it seems, like Petruchio,
merely a phonetic device to indicate to the Shakespearean audience
the proper pronunciation.

pervaded with the fragrance of Pinaud's art, molded
the Samaritan Woman—could have accomplished the
miracle for Schiller as well, for femininity was her very
own domain.

A tragedienne? In the necrologies she is listed so.
But she was not, in the meaning of the French tradition, which denies almost invariably to the social
drama the name of tragedy, so does not count as such
creations like Marguerite Gautier, Mrs. Jackson and
Fédora. Nor was she one by the standards of the
mountain-peaks, on which Sophie Schroder (doubtless, for moments, Rachel also) and Charlotte Wolter
stood. Wolter lightened, thundered, snarled and bit
at the air, shrieked her woe heavenward, raved forth
her passion and her fury. Her femininity was aggressive, and in suffering (e.g., Hermione's or Medea's)
it was still by preference on the offensive. Her fierce
glance of sunless gloom devoured the body of the beloved one, singed the eyebrows of him she hated, and
her mouth, a half-blown bud, struck its teeth like a
beast of prey into the foeman's neck or into the flank
of a friend who was deserting her. Her Orsina, Adel-
heid, Messalina, Medea, Lady Macbeth, had their
abode beyond the realm of Sarah's powers.

Bernhardt might indeed have ventured upon the
strand of Tauris and Lesbos, though in her Iphigenia
the austere priestess, the Tantalid, the Atreid, would
have been absent. Nor would she have quivered with
the fevers that distorted Wolter's most feminine shape
into something quite beyond Grillparzer's imagining.
Not only as Phaon's and Malition's friend, the Sappho
to whom the actress (not the author) imparted some-

thing of the lyric poetess' "fine scintillating fire," did
Charlotte Wolter (who in real life is said to have been
tolerably—even intolerably—commonplace) appear of
lofty spiritual stature, a woman to be taken seriously.
Everywhere she seemed queenly, masculine, superior,
in the domain of the will, to all those on whom she
wreaked her feelings, all the various heroes and lovers,
whether it were Weisling, Franz, Marcus Pretus, Jason,
Antonius, Thoas, Phaon, Macbeth,—even those that
were not weakened, unmanned, by the soft Ap-
ponyesque sentimentality of Sonnenthal. It did not
seem at all incredible that from the fury of this sex-
tyrant the Prince of Guatalla fled in exhaustion and
dread to Emilia's budding breast.* That character
of Emilia Galotti, which Lessing left, as he did everything else, in merely theatrical form, Sarah could have
rendered not merely human but all too feminine:
though an elder Charlotte, Frau Ackermann, had said,
most cleverly, that it was "a part one was properly
able to play only when one was too old for the rôle of
a young girl."

Both Wolter and Bernhardt played Phèdre, Marguerite, Fédora, Theodora. But these ribs from the
souls of Racine, Dumas, Sardou, appeared not at all
the same in Vienna as in Paris. Marguerite is not suit-
able for a comparison. This lady of the camelias was
doubtless selected by Frau Wolter only for purposes of
"profitable foreign trade." In the gambling hall, on
the sick bed, brilliant momentary effects were to be

* Charlotte Wolter evidently played *Orsina* (and probably Sonnenthal the Prince) in Lessing's *Emilia Galotti*. Sonnenthal was
the leading actor and later manager of the Hofburg Theater in
Vienna, the scene of Madame Wolter's greatest triumphs.

noted. But still, what sort of Count Giray of Trottel-
hausen would have invited this gloomily majestic Mel-
pomene to a supper where "mad pranks" might be
expected? What Papa Duval would have addressed
her as if she were a hussy available for any one who
had the price? When she tried to appear at least like
a Musette, a grisette of Murger's creation, the actress,
despite the countess' title she had wedded, became a
barmaid.* Justinian's wife she may have uplifted
to the dignity of the Eastern Roman Empire, to the
splendor and the royal purple of a Byzantine Messalina, but she never could have clothed her in the
changeful charms of slender girlhood, out of which
Sarah made the insatiable sex-passion of the magician's
pretty daughter blaze up.

That flame of the princess Fédora, in Vienna, devoured the dandified conspirator Boris Kanoff (who
seemed to have blown into town from the elder Dumas'
Russia of the Boulevards), while in Paris that same
flame only burned away the brush, thorns and tangle
of roots from the path of the humbly beloved one.
Even so Phèdre, here, climbed to the steps of the
thrones from whose supreme eminence Æschylus and
Shakespeare created their words out of Chaos, while
yonder she remained the handiwork of Racine,—finest
of courtier-poets,—even in the whirlwind of her passion still a queen whose soul breathed courtly air.

"They will love each other forevermore!"

Not for the nurse's ear, as she strove to moderate
her queen's fury with the consolatory word, that

* There is a pun in the German text. The lady from Cologne
(Kölnerin) became a barmaid (Kellnerin).

Hippolytus would not see Aricia again! Its thunder-
tone was to reach the very council-hall of the Olympian
gods, startling them from their golden tables with the
news, how great an outrage defiled their earth.

"Always they will love each other."

Madame Bernhardt also uttered it, also, not to the
confidante of her passion and her woe, whose attempt
to calm her she seemed not to have noticed at all.
She uttered it inwardly, in the stormy ground-swell of
passion, to her own soul. Never is the firebrand of
her longing for her husband's son extinguished. The
youth is in love with another, and is by her beloved.*
They are destined to be parted, never mated . . . yet
they will love each other eternally! Can love be enforced like obedience? Like the final link of a chain
forged by the hammering of a brooding brain in the
flame of woman's desire the word of doom fell from
her lips, dully. It was but the breath of a voice stifled,
dying even before the heart ceased to beat; and yet,
melodious!

Can love be compelled? So a Wolter might imagine, as she sprang with teeth and talons to clutch her
man, cursed him when he evaded her, seized like a
vampire, enjoyed like a vampire the even half-willing
victim, cast him aside when he was bled white, and
with dilated nostrils sniffed after fresh prey. Not so
Sarah. She was ready to be captured, to give herself
up, to cast herself beneath the feet of the man she
had made her god, and though he trampled ever so
rudely over her feelings, would bless him tenderly with

* This is of course a close echo from Heine's thrice-familiar:
Ein Jüngling liebt ein Mädchen.

the death-rattle in her throat. Her Marguerite did just that.

Never to be forgotten was her Phèdre, in its mimetic action and utterance, in the spiritualization of her eloquent body, in the visible revelation of thought shaped by heart-throbs.

And no less "a finished performance" was her Lady of the Camelias. At the supper,—not her first, one easily noted,—in the bliss of love suddenly bursting forth, mirroring in a puddle the sunbeam from heaven; in the country, a coquette somewhat *à la Watteau,* striving after the charm of the shepherdess redolent of the meadows; when her gently critical glances, and cleverly adjusting hands, harmonize in glasses and vases the flowers she has herself plucked. No less nobly tactful is her attitude before Armand's father,— never the bearing and step of a lady nor the lisping chirp of a second maidenhood (which any high-priced supper-guest can attain). The woman, purified by the fire of pious devotion to one man, stood as high above the moral sermon as Mary Magdalene, on the birthday of Christianity, stands above the gossip of the street. Under Armand's lashing, welt-raising insults she writhes, groans aloud in hoarse savagery like a perishing animal, regains control of her voice and her hands for a last adjuration, then falls like the lamb under the stroke of the axe. Yet not in swift-releasing death. From the illness which has previously been hinted at with cleverest reticence, she passes uncomplaining, smiling, yet with full realization, to her death, while his misguided jealousy turns to supplication which she rewards not merely with forgiveness, but with her blessing. Whoso believes in the immortality of God's breath in man, in the salvation of sinful women, can dry his tears.

"They will love each other forever." It is said, in his heaven and in his own speech, by Mahadeva,* whose arm of fire drew the Bayadere out from the house of all too earthly love, and uplifted her above the rampart of the clouds.

Sarah's *Lady of the Camelias* was never a thing of beauty. Neither was *With Painted Cheeks* (which in those days were still the privilege, still the stigma, of the Bayadere, but now are the badge of presentability, to be displayed in ambassadors' houses, or at court). "Ghetto air," it was said: "It smells of Galicia." Diplomats' noses, which are always wrong. For Lemberg she was much too thin. Rather from the Joedenbree Street in Amsterdam. Every day the reporters tweaked and poked at her meagerness. Mademoiselle Bernhardt is studying the title-rôle in the new drama *The Skeleton*. She is utilizing her vacation to take an "Anti-fat treatment." An empty carriage drove up. Sarah alighted. "All that never fazes me" (*Cela ne me rate jamais*).

Not beautiful, but a charming riddle. Of alien race, and yet Parisian. Never déclassée, never a lady, not even a bourgeois Madame. A "lost child," that out yonder where the last houses are, attracted the attention of the god who came down to mortal men and again ascended.†

* "The great god," an epithet of the Hindu god Siva, third person of the trinity of chief divinities. The incident is familiar to Germans from the poem *Gott und die Bayadere*, by Goethe.
† The sentence is practically a quotation from Goethe's poem.

A woman. Innermost loyalty to a love that would
not complain, that would not bear resentment, won
forgiveness for Marguerite. Virtuous folk had passed
her by. The priest, even he whose vow was only to
morality, had called her Sinner, Shameless. Now in
his fiery arms the god bore her aloft to his Heaven.
Her eternal femininity. (That it now draws us to itself is the declaration from the Second Heaven of
Faust, the Women's Heaven; but it was denounced in
the First, wherein abode men only, as "Ill tidings,"
and strenuously denied by the angels, winged adju-
tants of the All-Highest Imperial House.) The Inde-
scribable here also came to pass.*

Here, below, however, the eldest carp, and the
youngest scoff.

Those who never saw her as the young Donna Sol,
who never heard her golden voice caressing Hernani,
the beloved lion, know nothing of the fascination of
this woman, have no right to pass judgment on her.

"Even forty years ago her art was decadent."

So a man, not uncritical, whom it entranced in the
year 1900, may not praise it? The Bismarck of
1892 no longer had the vision, the architectural genius,
of the Prussian prime minister who, in 1864, strode
to battle with the un-Roman Empire of the German
nation, and drew breath only at Nikolsburg, after the
victory over his kind—and yet he seems to me nevertheless to have been worthy of serious attention.

"Old stuff": so men in the forties bawl (men who
twitteringly call themselves "we young folks").
"Nothing compared to la Diva Duse; trash beside"—

* Students of Goethe's *Faust* will easily follow the allusions in
this passage.

any Lucie, Helene, Ida, Tilla, Elizabeth, Agnes, etc., honored in these last days upon the banks of Spree.

As for Madame Duse, she remained always, even in Goldoni's *La Locandiera,* an interesting lady. Beneath her supple softness (*morbidezza*) seemed to glimmer a petty marchioness-soul, more profoundly spiritual than sensual. On the stage, only the facial contortions of sensuous feeling, languid, consciously executed,—and for that very reason, like Kainz, the Bassermanns and Moissi, she was the foreordained favorite of an age that 'shrinks from sturdy frankness, and prefers El Greco to Rubens. Even less had she a sense for individual style; she played Sardou just as she did Ibsen, with the affected expression of a morphine-addict and a technique deficient in resource. Her lack both of forceful feeling and of vocal power compelled a frugal rationing of her rôles; for instance, to meet the demands of the final act, she must save herself the previous one.

So it is with players dependent wholly on their nerves, who give themselves only, but cannot bring Art into their service. Their performances, even their single acts, are uneven; and they warn those whose opinion is of weight to them, "Ask me if you had better come that particular evening: else I may play like a pig."

So it was, too, with Kainz. Only Alessandro Moissi, at home in both German lands (though without roots in either), combines so much Italic coolness with Slavic shrewdness that, while still in the lofty pride of youthful and growing energy, he holds his Romeo, Hamlet, Œdipus, in firm control, never demanding of his silver-toned violin voice that which only a fury-driven bow could woo from it.

Madame Eleonora played almost exclusively "good" parts in perishable plays (never, alas, the Princess of Ferrara in Goethe's *Tasso*, a part whose charm, and limitations, are Duse's own). Those rôles were uplifted by her aristocratic personality; but they were not developed out of the progress and action of the play, nor even modified thereby.

Her Lady of the Camelias, who certainly never went out to supper with lecherous counts or giggled with common hussies, remained just the same in the villa as in the cabaret de luxe, lonely of soul, the trace of a tear on her black lashes, hiding a chilly heart behind a heavy veil of melancholy, and could live as like a Florentine lady in the first act as she died in the last. In such a life Armand was merely a chance, not destiny.

What this adept in naturalism attained was within the reach of other interesting ladies, if only by wise training they acquired such self-possession that shame —or at least embarrassment—no longer prevented them from laying themselves bare, with all their nerve-centres, before a thousand eyes; from displaying, to the throng that had paid for it, the saddling-court of practiced impulses, the race-course of vagrant desires.

When she struggled with painful effort for the heights (as Juliet, Cleopatra, even Rebecca), and failed, that was just where Sarah's example, the effect of her art upon the playing of the Italian born two decades after her, was unmistakable. Nor less so in the power of expression imparted by practice to her

whole body, even to the very fingertips; a power that
came near to the genius of a Ristori or a Rossi, sur-
passing Salvini's self-training and the manifold natural talents of Novelli. It was unmistakable, yet
again, in the effort to root as deeply as possible in the
soil of femininity the character to be portrayed, with
its contradictory nature before and during the process
of its development.

Between effort of the will and natural impulse, between intellect and instinct (the names are but empty
sounds!) there is again a real cleavage.

In the richness of her palette, whereon fit colors
were to be found either for Marie Antoinette's Vi-
ennese lightheartedness or for the murderous sleep-
walking ghost of Lady Macbeth, Adelaide Ristori had
outshone Rachel in her own loyal city of Paris. Was
that triumph to be repeated? Madame Duse came to
Paris. She was admired, praised, forgotten. Sane
judgment, freed from the passing cloud of intoxication,
said:

"This interesting lady, who, even beside Madame
Bartet, would adorn our Comédie, is different from
Sarah, the too oft-seen, too long seen; and, primarily
because of that difference, is at first view the favored
one. But she rivals neither the range of capacity nor
the invariable faultlessness of our own Maestra."

After the first performance of La Dame aux Camélias Père Dumas, he of the Three Musketeers, Monte
Cristo—and "the Friends"—finally cried out in witty
anger to his friends, who were absolutely determined
to force him to the confession that the masterpiece was

essentially his rather than the work of his as yet obscure son, "Why! I made the author!" With similar
though not equal right Sarah—who, long after the
younger Dumas' friend Madame Desclée had created
the rôle, conquered the stage of three worlds, even to
the realms of the Maharajahs, despite the hellish-
heavenly competition of Verdi's Violetta,—might have
said of Madame Duse, "Since I am, she could be." To
Duse the woman, she had paid her respects in the
D'Annunzio affair. To her "colleague," her rival, as
a visiting artist Sarah Bernhardt offered the theatre.

Bahr, the patron of art, Duse's own Armand, who
once was as plentifully sprinkled with Corylopsis as
now with holy water, somewhere, sometime, when he
dwelt here among us, a worldling, unregenerate, related that the Italian artist whom (though in truth a
child of the theatre), he "discovered" in St. Petersburg, was once teasingly asked by Frau Wolter (who
was doubtless irritated by the everlasting Duse-craze)
whether she had also played Lady Macbeth. Sarah,
who grew up amid the dismal confusion in Colombier's
time, would never have reminded a guest so rudely of
the limitations of her powers. The courtesy of her
heart was as widely known as her reverence for every
form of honorable art. She was ever ready to ease the
path of young poets toward the light, and even in
budding artistry to point out the value of future results. The literature of France has expressed its gratitude to her by an appreciation such as no theatrical
worker has ever before received.

She acted, apart from the classics and Victor Hugo,
only in poor plays?

Sardou's were good products of theatre-handiwork. Those of the second Dumas were really ingenious, psychologically fine, and *genealogically* he is especially noteworthy, for he marks a new era, and exerted an influence on the work of such men as Ibsen, Lie, Bjornson, Kjelland, Edouard Brandes, and later also on Strindberg's and that of Wedekind and his imitators. Even Nora is half Dumas, and the capital "barker" in *The League of Youth* has unmistakable strokes borrowed from Sardou's lawyer Rabagas. In Scandinavian and German drama who can count Dumas' children? He is the herald of the new stage— psychology ("the ape," now threatened with the death penalty; out of the Land of Nod?). The plays that sprang up in the Scribe-Halévy-Legouré field are of the type which, because it affords for able delineators an opportunity to develop their full powers, seemed to Lessing indispensable for his Hamburgische Dramaturgie.

Sarah could only use pieces that were understood, and felt, in Buenos Aires and Kieff, in Madrid and Chicago, in Moscow and Bombay. Her first choice was Racine (even Corneille seemed to her almost too harshly masculine); but she liked also Rostand and Mirabeau. It was she, if my memory does not fail me, who won a hearing for Musset's *Lorenzaccio*.

As directress she sought the best to stand beside her on the stage,—and not as stars stand about the sun. She engaged Constant Coquelin, Lucien Guitry, Max; she dispensed radiance, and had no desire to receive it as a loan; and she threw out lines toward the favorites Bartet and Sorel. Not every directress is so

good a housekeeper. Not every "star" is aglow with
the desire to shine in the midst of other brilliant con-
stellations. The theatre whose strongest magnet, until
a few years ago, was still Sarah, could have been more
economical.

"But she never comes out right," twittered the spar-
rows on the roof.

What she took in, as, compared with what is now
paid for the hot eyes, the slender body, the delightfully
solid Thusnelda-like weight, is the twelve-fold Du Bar-
ryism of a crank-girl, a mere gingersnap to a Perigord
truffle; but it was more than had ever been received for
drama. All the same, even with bags of gold she would
never have come out better. She gave gladly, and not
to relatives only, and always she was in debt. And
therefore even in old age, after she, in her eighth
decade, had a leg amputated, she must still limp upon
the stage. From the time (which only the oldest Parisians remember) when she ran away from Molière's
theatre, had the doors of the Comédie Française
slammed and locked behind her, she had almost every
evening, and at least twice besides at noon, played a
leading part; and yet had not enough to assure a comfortable decline. The honest rank and file of tragedy,
the operetta players, all who after a lucky début in
melodramas and farces reach the grade of K-actors in
Berlin or Ke- in Prague, shake their sensible bourgeois
heads. "Of course one has one's bank accounts (one
for taxes and one for receipts), and even in the big
rôle itself there is free time enough to ask by telephone
and get the answer about the New York exchange re-

port." In this respect Sarah was not up to the times, nor was she a gypsy,—the more lovable for that!

A singer who was called Diva even before Snob-do-it-all had deified every Lia, Mia, Pia, Ria, Li, Lo, Lu, Muschi and Uschi (without charge?), told me of a call she made on Sarah grown old. A constant coming and going. From time to time the envoy of a great laundry was announced:—he must wait. It was hours before he was admitted. "Oh, dear, about the bill? Twenty thousand francs, was it? But I just haven't it, you see. No, really." (*"Je vous assure, que je ne les ai pas."*) The smile of levity grown grey was divine. The ambassador of the White Kingdom may kiss the traces of the manicurist. Exit ambassador, entranced, by middle door.

"All good advertising." The Berliner would add "Verstehsta?" Yes, I understand that Sarah still rode in a motorless airboat ("glider"), modeled busts, ordered ell-long gloves made for her, that she, a Dutch Jewess, wedded the woe of France, her adoptive father-land, and that from her golden throat little jingoes were born, that she accepted the invitations of Indian princes for private performances, that in the Great War she was god-mother and nurse of many a poilu:—all that, and all the rest, just advertising!

It is almost fifty years ago that Zola defended Madame Bernhardt against the charge of a craze for publicity. "It is not she," he cried, "but you who make the publicity; you, the Public, that can never hear enough about a favorite singer, and you, the Press, who are not ashamed to sate such a longing for tittle-tattle." That was written in the age of innocence before the telephone and noon-day newspaper were naturalized. That press, which tomorrow will drain eagerly to the dregs some little Sadie's morphine-habit, as it did yesterday the great Sarah's "craving for publicity," shrieked even into her grave: "Publicity!" —How the legend arose, let one example show.

In man's costume Madame Bernhardt, early and late, won far-reëchoing theatrical renown, and with no effort on her part. Every public loves to have a "different view, just once," of its favorites. So if the most womanish Donna Sol, Athalie or Phèdre dons doublet and hose after Coppée's, Musset's, even Shakespeare's pattern, then it needs no Richet or Lebon to explain to us why it draws a larger audience than the soubrette who in literary melodrama sobs out her craving for children, or Romeo as Zwirn the tailor. But the victory was not so easy with Rostand's "l'Aiglon," a poem that plays pleasantly with one great shade, and many amusing ghosts. A woman nearer sixty than fifty attempts the part of a boyish prince and officer. (Only the theatre, with its daily discipline of the body and all its combined powers, keeps up the fresh energy of its folk so long that such a venture is imaginable.) The youth's clear tones she still retains. In order to acquire the gait and carriage also, she decides to wear the military tunic and sword of the second Napoleon not only at rehearsals but at home as well, for weeks before the first performance. Most sensible, and an example to be commended to the youngest actresses, who on the stage are to carry a child—an action unfamiliar to them. Only a gar-

ment that he or she has worn thro' the whole day,
with its various requirements, sets at evening as if it
were "moulded on," and only the sword worn at table,
at the fire-side, all but to bed, at the disguised woman's
hip, seems, that eventful evening, a weapon, not an
obstacle that brings mirth even into the gloomiest
tragedy. Sarah's young eagle was, in bearing and gestures, exactly what he purported to be. But as the
word had been passed around that she dined and received her guests in uniform, a swarm of reporters
was presently fluttering about her, and in a little while
the rumor of a fresh bid for publicity was afloat. That
she lived so long and died in a dull theatrical month:
—all for "publicity." And the burial-scene she herself surely had staged. The poor you always put in
the wrong.

As far as Canton, Melbourne, Johannesburg, Sala-
tiga, pictures carried the tidings that all Paris, now
again the capital of a continent, had risen up for this
Farewell: at the departure of one whom Zola in his
day had hailed as the gifted rebel of the stage, and
who at last, because she must play so long, was accounted the representative of what was old-fashioned
and belated.—She never was that. She never had the
heavy rigidity of those women who climb from melodrama, farce, burlesque, operetta up to the heights of
human agony.

Sarah's was not the force of feeling that gushes up
crudely from the heart of the common people, nor the
power of undisciplined action, which perhaps in such
women as Krones and Wildauer, certainly in Hai-
zinger, Galmayer, Helene Hartmann, Formes, Höflich,

Else Lehmann, Roland, Dorsch, and (in plays of Offenbach, Strauss or Anzengruber), Geistinger also, have sometimes produced a stormy elemental effect that was overwhelming. The same may be said as to men of like origin. Mexner, for instance, Martinelli, Thaller, Tyrolt, Girardi, Pallenburg:—and by no means must Chaplin, the revealer of unknown types of humanity, Charlie the unique, be forgotten. Sometimes I said: when they, who gave only out of themselves, who staking only their personal gifts could still win the game, and on the oft-climbed peak "attuned themselves" to harmony—even so their flight to higher spheres was clogged by the earthiness that yet remained. Frau Hartmann in her youth would have had the spiritual force for Gretchen, and in her maturity for Messalina, but she wisely held aloof from both.

From master-spirits of other lands, from Ristori, Rossi, Booth, Salvini, Sarah Bernhardt had learned to see the characters of the "Classic" dramatists (with which she had not grown up, as every Frenchman and Frenchwoman does from childhood), to see them at first hand, unhampered by the tradition of the theatre, which cripples all imaginative power. From those masters, too, she had learned such perfect control over the instrument of her art (her own voice and body), that the most competent critic could hardly be sure at any time whether, during an evening which to him was an epochal event, she remained in her inmost soul calm and cool, or was set aglow through and through by her task.

Her power of delineation was as great as—this side

of Shakespeare's world—it could become. She was for every school the model of perfect recitation: and she could give wings to her utterance, set it sturdily on solid earth, roll it up like a mighty ball, to cast it, high above the dead level of the commonplace, even to the crimsoned peaks of passion; and still, always, the Word, Logos, remained the god of this Jewess.

Old style? Since yesterday it stands newest of all: and its name is Science of Expression.

X

BONAPARTE IN ADVERSITY

"Bonaparte is dead."

Not until two months after the 5th of May, 1821, which heard the dethroned emperor draw his last breath in the British rock-prison, did the report run through Paris. It paced in leisurely wise, without torch or terror-stricken wail, and startled no one out of his every-day calm.

"Like a flash of lightning, it might have been supposed, would the news of this death flame over Europe! Now men heard it unmoved, as it passed on from one indifferent neighbor to the next. Woe to those who can claim no gratitude from the people's memory!"

So it may be read in the papers of the pious royalists; in the liberal ones nothing more cordial. Napoleon's Concordat with the pope, his code of civil law, not including even the penal code, were coldly praised. Nevertheless: an enemy of the church, of freedom, of all civil rights.

The fact that General Rapp, for fifteen years his adjutant, left the king's room at St. Cloud in tears, was only mentioned because to this tale could be attached a pæan of praise to Louis XVIII, whose royal tact censured not the tears but assured the loyal man of double favor.

From the pyramids to the Kremlin, from the Tagus to the Dnieper, Bonaparte had carried the banner of France, carried victoriously the eagles of "Cæsar Au-

gustus by grace of the people," given his commands
to twenty kings trembling with reverence or with fear,
written law for a continent, had been "The Emperor"
as though there were no other,—the Hapsburger (*ce
chétif françois*) a phantom beside him; and had now,
with all the world-wide echoes of his glory, been six
years in oblivion.

Goethe called him "the compendium of the world,"
and "a demi-god"; Hegel, "the world-soul"; this man
under whose foot Fritz's state moaned. His own step-
fatherland did not forget him for long; and never can
mankind forget him who widened the bounds of will
and of possibility. He fancied himself wholly set
apart from all that drew breath about him. "What
are conditions of life for others bind me not at all;"
only from his lips did that not ring like a boast; and
yet it was a sinful struggle to override nature, an
attempt which ordained its own penalty.

In 1795 Europe heard that the Corsican of six-and-
twenty had saved the Convention and thereby won the
command of an army. In 1815 he sat powerless in
Longwood. Between lies an experience beyond compare. Our day does not grant the needful repose of
spirit. For a true synthetic study of him let us, therefore, glance at a few instants during the epoch of his
gradual decline, a period which, more clearly than the
uprising in mist and storm, reveals what was dæmonic,
and at the same time human, in the last of the Im-
perators, the Prometheid.

In 1812, amid the intoxication of the Dresden festival, in the midst of monarchs who adored him, sur-

rounded by toadies and lickspittles, Bonaparte did not learn to enjoy the life. He craved the air of the camp, his will was to be in Russia when the rye was ripe and his cavalry horses could have their fodder from the oat-fields.

"Stir the embers of revolt in Russian Poland. Have the pontoon train waiting at Elbing, which is to set me across the Dnieper ('On that possibility,' he writes to Davout, 'my whole plan of campaign rests'), and organize our advance guard so thoroughly on the Vistula that on the day of my arrival I shall have four hundred thousand men at hand. Rub out of your eyes the last trace of drowsiness from the festival, and—rush!"

Their Majesties the Princes and Princesses begged for the favor of one more farewell audience. "I don't care. At four in the morning. Only, no tiresome whimpering." In a hunting coat which was but a year and a half old, and so had six months' service in it yet, he strode in the grey dawn between the hedge-rows of monarchs. "Quick! I'm in haste. Adieu!" At five he was off, with a rattling and creaking of wheels in his wake. Did he still feel himself wedded indissolubly to Fortune?

When he was hailed in Posen as the deliverer of the Slavs, he detected in the wild huzzas of the Polish people a more forceful vigor than in the hypocritical transports of the cowed Germans; and when above the Jesuit church he saw the flaming leaves of a laurel crown uprise, he followed with stern eye the smoke-wreath blown down the wind—Eastward!

In Thorn he saw again his choicest troops. It was

no time for festivities now. A camp that covered some two hundred square miles, an army of four hundred thousand heads. Whatever munitions could be secured had to be collected there. Still more important for a campaign in a barren region is food. This had to be sufficient for at least three weeks from the day of the first conflict.

"Seize the grain, and waste no time. Let the mill-wheels clatter day and night to grind it. When we are off, the millers may sleep."

East Prussia was green, and the swift-coming Russian spring already dotted the meadows with flowers. An immense host of warriors was armed for attack, and the threatened foe seemed as yet not to dream of the danger close at hand. Every corps had to open up its inmost heart to the commander's eye. Every one was once again examined to the minutest detail. Everything was ready. All burned with desire to show the Emperor what his youths, what his veterans could do.

"With such an army," a battery-commander ventured to say, "Your Majesty can conquer India." A smile rewarded him. Never had the Master been seen so cheerful. Were his powers increased tenfold, or was a new Dæmon subjected to him? At work from early until late at night, then he wandered, almost naked, through the arched chambers and the corridors of the monastery in which he was quartered, thinking out his plans for battle. One night the adjutant heard him sing a verse of the marching song:

"Tremble, ye foemen of France!"

On the night of June 23rd he arrived at the head of the host, in the village Alexota on the Niemen. A few Polish lancers tumbled out, half-drunk with sleep, as the wagon, drawn by six sweating, steaming horses, clattered up. A little man blinking wearily, in dusty clothes, opened the carriage door. The Emperor (with Berthier at his side). *"Vive l'Empereur!"* That sounded as if meant to hide the shame of men caught asleep at the most important outpost. Did the commander hear it? He stood erect, silent, with clear glance, in the stiff posture of one just roused from refreshing sleep. All eye.

Yonder lay Kovno, the objective of the first reconnoissance. He would go himself. But he could not show himself, as a Frenchman, to the Russians, who supposed there were only Poles on Polish ground. To be sure, he was not wont, like Mephisto, to go incognito; but here the conditions ordered it so. In the grey dawn, without having washed or tasted food, he stripped off his guardsman's coat and squeezed himself into the uniform of a Polish colonel. Head-covering? His hat with the tricolor cockade would betray him. The four-cornered Uhlan's czapka was too heavy. A policeman's cap would do. Berthier, too, had to disguise himself.

Forward! The inhabitants of a farmhouse were routed out. From their windows the river was in sight. Beyond it Russia lay silent, without the least suspicion of peril close at hand. For a long time the Emperor stood studying the country, which until this day he had known only from the map.

He came back to his staff in high spirits. "Doesn't the coat fit me perfectly? But one must give back what belongs to others." Clothes changed again. Hasty and scant morning meal. The escort came up with the Emperor's saddle-horse. The generals Caulaincourt, Davout, Duroc, Haxo galloped up. First reconnaissance on horseback. "Just here must, and only here can, the river be crossed." Second ride. "This ravine hides the troops until the pontoon-force has finished its work. Before it is light they must. . . ."

His galloping horse shied, reared, stood stiff and threw the rider, who, absorbed in thought, was holding the bridle loose and did not notice that a hare ran between his horse's legs. This had happened to him several times before, and he had always scolded the grooms violently, or else raged at "the beast, the miserable good-for-nothing jade." Now he was silent, stared at the grey sky, and without a word mounted again. "A bad sign," Berthier whispered in Marshal Caulaincourt's ear. "I could wish we were not going over the Niemen." Did the man who rode silent at their head think as did he who had been his chief of staff ever since the Italian campaign? Did the pallid chieftain still think, today, that he was "irrevocably wedded to Fortune"?

Duty summoned him out of idle introspection. Should a frightened hare, an over-strained horse's nervous scare, embitter his mood? A foppish idler might allow himself such weakness, but not the Master of human destiny. From every side came the tramp of his columns. Before the sun sank, the passage over the river had to be arranged, down to the least detail.

Between the white canvas walls of his tent sat the Emperor with reports and relief charts before him. The most trustworthy he carried beneath his own skull. He dictated: "ORDRE POUR LE PASSAGE DU NIEMEN." Punctually, every possibility foreseen and provided for. . . .

If it only were not so hot!—And if one's head did not ache! Perhaps as a result of the fall? It must have looked funny, too, to see the beast shake me off, funny enough to roar at. The fellows in uniform made uncanny faces; were they stifling their laughter, or did superstition lay an ice-cold hand on their heads? Childish belief in omens!

"Good day, grenadiers! A tiresome march? Over there 'tis better going. Over there, artillerymen! You here too already?"

If there were only an echo, at least, coming from over across there! At most there was only once in a while a patrol of Cossacks that slipped through the brush and the next instant seemed to have vanished without leaving a trace! Was it a land of dead men guarded by phantoms? Ghost-stories, fit for the chimney corner in Ajaccio!

"The rascals have scented something. They know at last that I am close at their throat, and they creep out of sight as far as they can. As soon as we are across, I'll smash them so that the tatters will fly as far as Mamma's wash-house in Moscow! If we were only that far: oh Hell, if we were over!"

At midnight the pontoon columns had finished their work. They had had no light turned upon them, nor had any echoing sound come over to them. From his tent, which had been moved close to the Niemen, Cæsar had looked on, and occasionally had softly hissed his commands. At last! Three bridges led to the land of long desire. Morand's division covered the bridge-heads, Davout's corps took the lead. The dry soldierly good humor revived. Audacious jests fluttered to and fro from the shaking bridges that groaned under the burden of the cannon and horses.

"In five weeks, six at most, we'll be on the Neva and celebrate our Emperor's birthday in Peter's city." Everybody laughed. "Did you hear? In Petersburg. *Vive l'Empereur!* There he is! Where did he ever fail? In the saddle since three. Always at hand where his fighting men are jammed and block the narrow way for those who crowd behind. No ghost ever scared him yet. A running hare today could only make him merrier."

Over! Now with swimming eye from the Russian shore he saw his forces pour their flood into Alexander's empire. Out of the mists of dawn new victory smiled, a greater than was ever won before. His sun was with him; it burned hotly in the sky.

Toward noon it grew gloomy, and soon afterwards the clouds dropped mighty masses of water upon the Lithuanian land. Everything dripped. Everybody shouted joyously. Two hundred thousand men in Russia!

On the 26th of June even Grouchy's dragoons were over. The program had been carried out to the dot.

Bonaparte stood close before the goal of his boldest desire. And Major von der Goltz was already writing his report listing the officers of Friedrich Wilhelm who were ready to fight against Bonaparte. Concerning Hans David Ludwig von York he noted: "Middle-aged, well-informed, ambitious, discontented, hating France; generally recognized as a brave man, quick and far-sighted, more a practical than a theoretical soldier, easily capable of a bold decision; wholly without means." But the *condottiere* from Corsica said: "From Prussia there is nothing to fear," and to Caulaincourt, "I will sign the peace treaty in Moscow if it suits me."

. . . Then he had himself crowned in the Kremlin, that the splendor of his victory might illumine the globe. "Emperor of the West, head of the European union, protector of the Christian faith." So late as June, the handsome Czar Alexander had been in Moscow, amid the noisy enthusiasm of his piously loyal people. Von Stein heard him in the Slovodski palace call upon the nobility to fight the enemy (superior in numbers and arms); and heard the nobles promise to equip out of their own means a large army for home defense.

On the last day of June, Alexander took his departure from the old city of the great prince, all-mother Moskwa, from the Red Place, the bell-tower of Ivan the Great, from the miracle-working holy image at the Gate of the Redeemer. Would he ever see them again? The conqueror drew nigh; already, to be sure, with an army that had grown weaker.

Since the stormy days at Wilna all bonds had been

loosened. There was no well defined route; no reliable
supply of fresh provisions. All granaries, stores, mills
and ovens had been burned. Wilderness, and mud.
The wagon-train was stalled; broken wheels, fallen
horses, crippled men who had sunk down groaning, a
horrible confusion. To demand forced marches of an
army in such a condition, on such a road, seemed,
even to many a commander, madness.

Thousands lingered behind, ran away, dropped
quietly out of the march. Had Germans and Swiss,
Hollanders and Spaniards, Croats and Illyrians to go
hungry and thirsty, to lash their failing bodies forward with the scourge of their will, so that an alien's
craving for sovereignty might attain its goal?

At Witebsk barely two hundred thousand men were
following the colors. Barclay was sure that the enemy
could not long endure the summer heat, the cold nights
after sultry days, the lack of food, the scarcity of
drink that forced them to swallow foul and pesti-
lential water; he evacuated fortified or open places,
carried off the inhabitants and their livestock, beasts
of burden and household goods, avoided every attempt
to surround him, and retired ever deeper and deeper
into the long defile northeastward. Bonaparte must
go on. Only two months more! Then the Russian
winter; then the general call to arms, the Moscow sum-
mons to a Holy War, the tricky guerilla fighting
(which he had learned in Spain), so dangerous to
a European army.

Bonaparte determined that at the Dnieper he would
overtake this Asiatic horde. If even there they would
make no stand, he could at least cut off their lines of

retreat to Petersburg and Moscow. For twenty-four hours before Smolensk, Neveroski delayed Ney (who was to have captured the town by surprise), and so assured the safe retreat of the armies led by Barclay and Bagration. Smolensk was taken; a heap of ruins, a fiery furnace in which dead and wounded were burned. The Russians were not caught, their main body of troops was safe. All the same, they had again lost eleven thousand men, and the road to Moscow, after the hellish massacre at the Borodino, was open at last. Would there be peace? In a letter to the Gosudar Bonaparte intimated the possibility; but he received no reply. . . .

Even from burning Moscow he wrote to Alexander like a friend and well-wisher. Out of consideration for the Czar and to prevent inhumanity, he had occupied the coronation city that the Russian army left deserted. That Rostopechin had had three-quarters of all the houses set on fire was a stupid crime. That the foreign soldiery snatched from the tongues of flame everything of use to them deserved no blame. My people did not find a single fire engine, but sixty thousand muskets, a hundred and fifty field guns, powder, and cartridges, saltpetre and sulphur in immense quantities. Did he behind such senseless confusion feel the awakening of Russia's natural force, and therefore grope for some possibility of an understanding? The armies of Bagration and Barclay de Tolly, on whose permanent separation he had counted, were united and placed under the command of Kutusoff, who knew Russia's Islam even better than he did that of the Mussulmans. It was not for him to devise clever plans for battle. With that amusement Bennigsen, Wolzogen and other German pedants might beguile their leisure. Michael Ilarionovich Kutusoff knew that only the oldest, deepest instinct of the Russian nature could rescue the Fatherland. If he was to have his way, Napoleon would come without a battle from the Niemen to the Moskwa. From the walls of stormed cities glory was to be gathered, but far more essential, not merely brilliant, was the silent demoralization of the enemy.

Between Tatarinovo and Borodino the fat old giant (a native of Smolensk) had knelt on the bare ground among his home guardsmen, he, the commander-in-chief, before the black image of the Virgin, and with eager lip kissed the gold ornaments, the glaze: "Thou alone, O Mother of God, art our refuge and our protection!" Bonaparte would rudely master destiny: Kutusoff humbly submitted to whatsoever was appointed. The contest between these commanders was the battle of the west against the east.

That contest drew close to a decision when the guns of the Peter-Paul Fortress announced the retirement of Napoleon from Moscow. A heap of ruins and a breeder of disease, "a sewer," the Emperor called the city in his "Report of the Grand Army"; the city at which his desire had grasped for so long, and from which his men carried off fifteen thousand wagonloads of plunder!

Again there was a fight at Smolensk, this time under the eye of the Holy Mother; Davout was beaten, Ney's troops scattered. The Grand Army, hungry and cold, had to burn its artillery and baggage. "I cannot let aliens see them in such condition. See to it that I find no representative of the Outland at Vilna."

The living stream that in June seemed impossible to dam had dwindled to a muddy trickle. At Kovno there were missing three hundred and thirty thousand men. Of each corps only the drooping eagles remained. Ney, Marshal of France, fought like a common soldier in the mêlée, threw his musket, for which there was no ammunition, into the Niemen, and wrapped in a cloak slunk through Poland to Königsberg.

Chichagoff's order of the day for October 12 warned all divisions of his troops that the French Emperor was to be taken alive. Description: "Stout and short. Hair short, smooth, and black. Rage or bitterness in his expression. Roman nose, with traces of snuff. Notably projecting chin. Usually wears a plain gray overcoat, and always has a Mameluke with him."

He who is thus described in the warrant for his arrest had once, at the Berezina, taught the hordes of Chichagoff and Wittgenstein to shudder. Soon after he took his farewell of the crumbling army. On a pinewood sledge, in his green fur-coat, he sped like a ghost through Warsaw, his face snow-white with pallor under his fox-skin cap. From Dresden, where he rested five hours, he wrote to Friedrich Wilhelm that he had assigned the supreme command to Murat, was himself hastening to Paris, and that the Prussian corps, with which he was satisfied, should be quickly filled up again to full strength.

Only two moons had waned since Alexander had said: "He or I!" Now Arndt could exult: "The time

has come. The mottled dragon falls!" Stein might
speak: "The great criminal lies in the dust. May all
unite in falling upon the unclean beast that destroys
the repose of Europe!" An old saying came into fresh
honor: "Terrible is the God of Russia!"

"On Elba I was not badly off. I could have artists
come from Italy, had everything needful to stage a
play, and was freer than a German prince. If the King
of France had had good ministers, I should have remained on the island. But the fear of me had so
wholly disappeared that they would not even accredit
a *chargé d'affaires* to me, and they insulted me in every
newspaper. I am but human, after all. I wanted to
show that I was not dead yet. France really must, I
felt, leave me two frigates at least, of which one, for
my own use, should be always lying ready in the
harbor."

This demand (which even at St. Helena, in Longwood, fell from Bonaparte's lips) Louis XVIII and
Talleyrand would have rejected as a proposal for their
self-destruction. They fancied that their deadly
enemy would never find it possible to break out of
his island-cage.

But he had secured for himself the brig *L'Inconstant*. The captain of an English two-master, who
had run into the harbor, smelt the store of bacon, heard
that drinking-water and zwieback had been put aboard,
and asked Chief Marshal Bertrand whether the rumor
that the Emperor was going on a voyage with his
guards had any foundation. "Nonsense. In Porto
Ferraio and in Leghorn such silly stuff is always being

reported. Any one who believes it is being fooled. Are you dining with us, Captain?" The latter was still suspicious, even though Bertrand's manner was a good imitation of cold indifference, and set sail after *L'Inconstant*. He did not notice promptly enough, however, that the Frenchman turned about on the way to Naples; so he did not put in at Porto Ferraio again until after the brig had gone with her most costly cargo.

General Gourgaud describes the hasty departure: "After Bertrand had announced that the wind was fairly favorable, the Emperor had mass said earlier than usual, and the embarkation of the soldiers with their baggage was expedited. The anchor was weighed about ten at night. Early in the morning of February 27, the Englishman hove in sight: 'Danger?' 'No; he's holding his course to Elba.' *'L'Inconstant* steered for the French coast. General exultation.

"A grenadier's sweetheart, who had not been taken along, had gone overnight in a rowboat to Piombino, and it was from there that the news of the flight first reached Leghorn. On Elba, Bonaparte's mother, Letitia, and Bertrand's wife had to undergo an examination.

"Too late! Landing in France March 1, from 5 to 11 bivouac; then 'Forward march.' "

When the news finally leaked through into the Vienna Congress, Wellington immediately declared that the escaped prisoner would hasten straight to power. King Louis also would not be hoodwinked and said to Soult, who wished to console him by a reference to the loyalty of the troops: "Horrible affair! It

all depends on the state of mind of the first regiment
that Bonaparte meets."

He had them fast at once. Had all again who the
spring before were ready to stone him. Marshal Ney,
who had promised to fetch him back in an iron cage,
went over to him with his command. (From ambition, Bonaparte says: "He perceived that folk and
troops were for me, and wanted to warm himself in
my sunshine. Decency must have told him to return
to Paris. The command of his army, which he sent
to me, disgusted me. Ney, who had had crowns at his
disposal! But I had to pretend, and entertain the
orderly officer with the grossest flattery of his Marshal,
whom I even called 'the bravest of the brave.' ")

From Antibes to Fontainebleau was a triumphal pro-
cession. "I returned to France with six hundred men.
My confidence in the people's love and the memory
of my old warriors did not deceive me. The throne
of the Bourbons did not in fact stand on the firm
ground of right. Strangers had built it up for a
family which the people's will had banished, and which
had served the interests only of a little band of greedy
folk. Only the empire can secure the rights and the
glory of the nation."

And now the Constitutional régime, whose morning
glow shone and whose fundamental law Napoleon on
the first of June, in the Champs de Mars, swore to
deserve. Forgotten was the village-mayor who, when
Napoleon landed between Antibes and Cannes,
groaned: "You will destroy the bit of rest and happiness that had at last been granted us!" Forgotten was
the faint-hearted Prince of Monaco, who declared that

with six hundred men the venture could not succeed. His groom understood the popular feeling more clearly. The memory of old grenadiers, and comparison with his likeness on the five-franc pieces carried the cry from farm to farm: " 'Tis he! The Emperor! He that delivered us from the rule of the nobles who wanted to hitch us to the plough! The Bourbon doesn't make us happy. *Vive l'empereur!*" The exultation of the crowd paved the way for him.

"From Cannes to Grenoble I was an adventurer. Not till then did I become again a sovereign. If I had wished it, I could have arrived before Paris with five hundred thousand peasants. I made haste to become master of the capital before the English came into action and occupied Lille."

He did not wish himself back in absolute power? The Chamber, the people, were asked to believe that:

"Permanent institutions, not individual men, can assure the future of countries. The goal of my ambition is to secure all possible liberty to Frenchmen; all that is possible,—for on the heels of Anarchy comes always the Dictator. The immense alliance of armed Powers, whose hosts are threatening our frontiers, counts upon division in our political action, and is striving to weaken us by stirring up civil war. This peril will be overcome by your patriotism, your insight, and your confidence in me. You, Peers and Representatives, will set the people the example of noblest patriotism, and, like the Senate of ancient Rome, will at every hour be resolved to die rather than to live on in a dishonored powerless homeland."

On the 8th of June, 1815, the *Moniteur* thundered this message forth over the land.

Before the Emperor took the field, he dreamed away a half-day at Malmaison. He bathed in the fragrance of the roses, and recalled the hours which he spent in house and Parc caressing Josephine. He sat sobbing on the edge of their bed. Undreamed-of things had happened since the widow of the guillotined General de Beauharnais had sent her pretty boy to Bonaparte to beg for his father's sword. Twice she had sent her card in to him. He could not see her, had sent Lemarrois to make his excuses, and learned,—that she was beautiful, young, amiable, lived in a house of her own. Then he had left his card, had been invited to dinner, had invited her in turn, and had seated Barras, a head of the Directory, and Josephine's friend, at the same table.

"We quickly fell in love with each other. Barras advised me to marry her, because she was on good terms with the ruling classes, both of yesterday and of today, and would bring me strong support; her house, he said, was the finest, and the marriage would make me, a man still called a Corsican, a real Frenchman.

"Josephine's grace made her at that time a charming matron; but in the full sense of the word a matron. I have never loved another woman so much. She liked to lie; but her lies revealed genius. She knew me thoroughly. For her children she never asked anything of me. Nor did she ever ask me for money. Yet her debts ran into the millions. She had poor teeth; but she was so tactful that one hardly noticed it. She should have gone to Elba with me!

"Marie Louise was different from her in every way. She was innocence itself, and never untruthful. She loved me, wished to be always with me, and would have gone with me into exile if she had not had that swine Montebello and the miserable wretch Corvisart close to her. They told her that her aunt had been beheaded, and such horrors might be repeated. Furthermore her father, the foolish Kaiser, had given her the dissolute Neipperg as an attendant.

"Josephine always had intrigues in her head, and often considered the possibility of a Bourbon restoration. While I was still First Consul she said to me, at Malmaison, that Louis XVIII would set up a monument on which I was represented as a guardian angel (Genius) crowning him. I only asked: 'And with my corpse sealed up in the base of it?'

"When I made known to her my intention for our separation, she was dissolved in tears. If the interest of the state demanded of me fifty thousand human lives, I should weep for them, but I should sacrifice them; for the interests of the state must come before all else. To Josephine in tears I cried: 'My decision is fixed. Do you consent? If not, I shall use force.' The next morning she sent me word that she was agreed. But after that, when we came to table, she fell in a faint and had to be carried out and put to bed.

"The Austrian marriage was my misfortune. Could I imagine that Austria would ever treat me so?"

The whole epic of wild and marvelous life-experience

passed before his inward eye in the rose-garden, the dining-hall, the bed-chamber. Here happiness nested! Tranquil, amid the roar of the world-storm.

Almost a hundred suns beheld him now again an Emperor. Was the last of them about to set? All Germany hoped so. "Measureless," von Stein thundered, "was the baseness of this Ney! Eagerly he kissed the King's hand, declared himself ready to die for him, accepted five hundred thousand francs from him to pay off his debts, and declared: 'When I deliver this tiger to you he will wear a muzzle!' When he related that to Napoleon, he added: 'In my heart I was laughing at the fat swine.'

"Levity, greed, stupidity, fickleness, have made France a land of sedition and upheaval. God will bless the arms of the Allies and chasten that debased people.

"The King (of Prussia) is most unfortunately cold. He makes only half-decisions, has no confidence in himself, and none in his people; he believes that Russia is dragging to destruction, and that he will presently see a French army on the Vistula."

And Marwitz: "Again it is to be seen how high our people stands above its government. Despite the latter's irresponsible behavior, there was no reproach, no discouragement to be heard, and all ran to arms again, almost as two years ago. I have lived, and shall live, for the welfare of the fatherland, for justice and truth, and for the secure foundation of our race and its possessions. I wish that my wife may bear me a son, that he may always prefer what is eternal to what is earthly, that my daughter may hand

on virtuous and honorable convictions to other generations, that my fatherland may permanently stand high
above the evil Outland;—and furthermore, if I am to
fall in this war, the passing over will not be hard
for me, as Heaven is better peopled than the earth."

Blücher declared: "Here, on the Rhine, everything
is in glorious bloom, and the weather is splendid. But
the lands are again to be devastated and desolated.
Our enemies will soon see us face to face, and will
realize that we are unchanged. With the hundred and
twenty thousand Prussians that I have in perfect condition at Namur, I would undertake to conquer Tunis,
Tripoli and Algiers, if they were not so far away nor
overseas."

Wellington had posted his army between Oudenarde
and Nivelles, and was himself near Brussels, with his
staff and his reserves.

On the 14th of June Bonaparte's appeal reëchoed
through the lines of his army: "Today is the anniversary of Marengo and of Friedland. Twice has this
day decided the fate of Europe. Then we were all
too magnanimous. We believed the assurances and
oaths of princes, and left them on their thrones. Now
you behold them banded together against Freedom,
against our revered France. Their assault is the most
shameful unrighteousness. Forward! They, and we,
are what we were. The Prussians, who today are so
overweening, were thrice our numbers at Jena, at
Montmirail sixfold superior. Let your companions
who have been in English prisons tell you how they
were maltreated there. Saxons, Belgians, Hanove-
rians, Rhinelanders are forced, to their grief, to fight

for princes who are hostile to all justice, to all popular rights. Can this insatiate Coalition humiliate and destroy the French people? France will be their grave. To every Frenchman who has a heart in his breast this is the hour of fate, which leaves only one choice: Victory or Death!"

He desired to break through at Charleroi, to prevent the English and German troops from uniting. Blücher, informed by Gneisenau of the approach of the French, accepted the gage of battle at once, 'with joy.' Ziethen's corps were to return to Sombreffe, and the Emperor sent the first news of victory to Paris: "Eighteen hours in the saddle. Only three left for rest; but already four Prussian regiments are ground to powder, fifteen hundred men captured, six cannon taken, and our losses are trifling."

Wellington had promised that at ten o'clock on the morning of the 16th twenty thousand British troops should be at Quatrebras:—he could not keep his word. On the 15th he saw his officers dancing in the house of the Duchess of Richmond at Brussels. At dawn of the morrow he mounted his horse and looked down on the French front at Frasnes. At noon he met Blücher on the hill of the Windmill near Bussy, in the rear of the Prussian position, and promised the old man that he would attack at four o'clock. This pledge, again, he could not fulfill. He was himself heavily assailed by the enemy, with superior numbers, at Quatrebras, and brought up reënforcements under great difficulties. He was, indeed, able to beat off the attack but could not frustrate the plan of Bonaparte, who, as the weaker party, did not wish to fight the united

foemen but to meet the several portions on different
fields. The sun burned hot out of storm-clouds. The
fury of battle grew fiercer as it swung backward.
"No quarter! Whoever spares a Prussian's life will
be shot."

A day lost can be regained. Germans and British
were now for the first time striking in soldierly com-
radeship, and before such noble unity the Imperator
must yield. The Duke had already arranged for the
Germans' flank attack; *la belle Alliance* was prac-
ticable.

. . . After the battle, Prince William of Prussia
wrote to his sister: "The glorious though indeed dearly-
bought victory of Blücher came as unexpectedly as
could be. According to today's reports three hundred
cannon and all Napoleon's baggage are taken. He himself rode off in bare shirtsleeves. His coat, hat and
sword were captured. He threw them away so as not
to be recognized, and he was seen with his head
bandaged.

"Six times he attacked the centre. The English
fought wonderfully, but would probably have been
forced back if Blücher had not come up on the French
rear and flank. How extraordinarily our army has be-
haved again! To fight three whole days with only
two corps against the whole French army! They retire seven miles, lose thirteen cannon and fifteen thousand men, then halt, beat the enemy completely, and
capture not only three hundred cannon, but Napoleon's
treasure!"

Four days after the Waterloo *belle Alliance* Bonaparte cried from the Elysée at Paris: "When I began

the war for the independence of France, I had a right
to count on the united action of all the forces, energies
and resources of the nation, and so, despite the fact
that all the Powers turned against us, to hope for
success.   Since conditions seem to have changed, I
offer myself as a sacrifice to the hatred of our enemies.
If, as I hope, their declarations were sincere, their
resentment is centered wholly on me.   My political
life is ended.   I announce the accession to the throne
of my son, who will hereafter, as Napoleon the Second,
be Emperor of the French.   For the present the Ministers will conduct affairs.   As a devoted father I call
upon the Chambers to draw up without delay a
Regency Law.   Unite, Frenchmen, for the protection
of the Commonwealth and of Freedom!"

From the battlefield of Waterloo he hastened back
to Paris, arriving June 20, 1815, in order to rescue
whatever it still seemed possible to preserve.   With
dust-covered coat and skin glistening like bacon he
panted almost breathless into the Elysée.   He desired
to address the Chamber of Deputies, to lash them once
more with stinging words to vigorous resolution.   A
bold decision.   They refused to hear him at all, demanded his abdication.   Fouché, once the head of the
police detectives, now of the provisional government,
and Metternich the Austrian Chancellor, guaranteed
the succession of the little Napoleon.   The deposed
man seemed calm, walked in the garden, answered with
cheerful resignation the citizens who climbed the wall
to urge their Emperor not to retire.   The pressure of
the throng increased.   Jerome, Joseph, Lucien Bonaparte feared that the government, which was already

commanding the people to remain aloof, would take action against their brother's life, or decide to deliver him up to the enemy.

Bonaparte withdrew with Las Cases to Malmaison, where, before his fatal campaign, he had dreamed away a half-day amid melancholy and ill-boding memories of Josephine.* By a resolution of the Chamber, Napoleon II was Emperor of the French; and until he came of age the business of state was entrusted to a Regency.

The enemy advanced to the gate of the capital (where Davout as commander-in-chief still controlled seventy thousand men). In eleven days Blücher's army had come from the Belgian battlefield to Gonesse, close by Paris. If the Emperor should return to head the army? All too loud, on all roads, is still the cry: *Vive l'Empereur!*

The government resolved to have the dangerous man put under the surveillance of Lieut.-General Becker and a troop of gendarmes, and taken out of the zone of disturbance as expeditiously as could be without use of force.

But whither? "In the harbor of Rochefort two frigates are to be made ready to sail; they are to take Napoleon Bonaparte to the United States of America." Next day came a contradictory order: "First to the island of Aix. Becker (whom Fouqué had chosen for the watchman's task because he had a grievance against the Emperor) announced himself at Malmaison as reverentially as if he still stood before the all-powerful

---

* It will be recalled that her life had flickered out during his brief reign in Elba.

ruler. Bonaparte offered, as a simple general, without princely rank, to lead the troops against the enemy. "I shall beat Blücher." As the government declined the offer, he, on the 29th of June, left Malmaison.

The Court Chamberlain, Bertrand, was to take charge of the books. He who may not act, reads. From the library in Paris, Bertrand was to have forwarded works on wars and the art of war, on America and Egypt, a complete file of the *Moniteur de l'Empire*, the best encyclopædia and the most useful dictionaries! Books! He who may not act, reads!

At Saintes the party was assailed by a Jacobin mob, the escort was accused of having brought the state treasure along with them, was locked up in a tavern, but was released by a throng of loyal peasants. Bonaparte himself was not subjected to annoyance.

On the morning of July 3rd, he arrived at Rochefort, where General Gourgaud was expecting him. He put off his uniform, and showed himself in citizen's dress to the crowd from the upper room of the town hall (which, like every house in which the Emperor made a stay, is now called "chateau"). He was quiet, cool; seemed hardly touched by this storm of events. A lieutenant of marines and a naval ensign made an offer to rescue the emperor in a pinnace. A young Frenchman in command of a Danish brig wanted to take him to America. No!

On July 8th, ten minutes after five o'clock, he left the mainland of France. Was the dream of a hundred days, of a hundred nights, dreamed out? From the shore a dense crowd waved farewell to the harbor boat, as it bore their hopes away through the heavy surf. On board the *Saale* Bonaparte was received with the honors befitting his rank. A salute had been expressly forbidden in the instructions to Gourgaud. The general was obliged to remain with the captive, who was now most profoundly shaken, until heavy slumber took pity on him; he was summoned at four to return to Bonaparte's cabin.

Landing on the island of Aix. Rejoicing of the crowd just as at the departure from Rochefort. The fortress and cannon were inspected.

The port commander brought an order of the provisional government. Voyage to be continued within twenty-four hours. Sadness clouded all brows. The Emperor locked himself in his room. Should he stay, arm himself for resistance, flee to Bordeaux, slip away to the United States? Probably it would be most sensible to discover first the intentions of the English. Las Cases climbed on board the English warship in the harbor. What is the ship's name? *Bellerophon.*

A dubious name. It was the name of Sisyphus' descendant who, like Jacob's son Joseph, resisted temptation, and was therefore accused by the disappointed woman of having attacked her, and was sent to her father with a sealed tablet which bore an inscription declaring him deserving of death. The father was more honorable than the amorous queen of Tiryus, and would not murder his guest; but, for the sake of complying in some sense with the dear daughter's demand, sent him on a venturesome quest. Bellerophon tamed Pegasus, killed the fire-breathing Chimæra, and conquered the Amazons. Such a champion the Lycian king determined to retain, despite the passionate

Anteia, and gave him his younger daughter in marriage, and made him his successor. After coming to power he wished to take vengeance on his wicked sister-in-law, pretended love for her, cajoled her to mount his Pegasus, leaped on behind her, and despite her outcries cast her into the sea by Melos. In old age, drunk with success, he was seized by Hybris on the steep way up the ridge of Olympus, and blinded. Hater of men and hated of gods, he wandered through the wilderness to the end of his life. From him the ship had her name. . . .

What was Las Cases thinking? Did he dream that the passport which he wished to bring might prove for his master a Bellerophon-letter? He gave assurance that he understood English, but, with all his cleverness, he could obtain from the stolid Britons nothing anywise favorable. Passports to America the Admiralty never had issued. The parliament flag would not protect a vessel attempting to carry the Emperor to freedom from being fired on; he should go to England, where he would be well treated.

The trap was set. And presently there came from Paris the announcement that the Bourbon king had been enthroned in the Tuileries since the eighth of July. The treacherous Fouché had for the hundredth time broken his word, had come to an understanding with Wellington, nullified the resolution of the Chamber which assured the crown to Bonaparte's son, made his bargain quietly with King Louis, and, after assurance of All-Highest gratitude and favor, had smuggled him into the capital under protection of British bayonets. Second "Restoration" of the hereditary ruling family. And was it really the end of the Bonapartes? *Vive l'Empereur!* It still resounded from the shore of the island and from the frigates, the *Saale* and the *Medusa.* "The enthusiasm of despair," Gourgaud calls it.

The *Bellerophon* was approaching under full sail. Her cannon thundered. Was it to celebrate the entrance of the Allies into Paris? Bonaparte was lodged in the city commandant's house. Should he attempt to escape, or surrender to the British? (That people he did not always hate. Even on St. Helena he said to Montholon: "The English are superior to us. With an English army I would have conquered the world, and their discipline would not have slackened on the long way. After suffering ten defeats like that of Waterloo, not a man, not a voice in Parliament would have deserted me, if I had been the man England trusted, instead of France; and at the last I should have won the game.")

Gourgaud was afraid that every smaller vessel was to be detained, the Emperor taken prisoner and committed to the Tower of London. Savary, Duke of Rovigo, was for flight. So was General Lallemand. On the Danish ship, which had taken on a cargo of brandy, there were only four sailors; the French captain, Besson, had all his papers in order, a valid passport, and could conceal four persons. Agreed. "I am going to America. There I shall live as a plain citizen. To return, as from Elba, is impossible. It will be two months before they get any definite news of me over here. The English would treat me decently. But that very thing will be degrading. I am but human, and cannot endure the thought of living among deadly enemies; and I feel that history will not condemn me because I seek my freedom in the United States. If the ship falls into the hands of the English, I am master of my fate, and can kill myself.

"Yesterday evening I wanted to go aboard the English cruiser and cry: 'Because I will not work for the breaking up of my fatherland, I seek a refuge here, as Themistocles did.' But I did not hold fast to that decision."

Gourgaud caught a little bird that strayed into the room, and called it a lucky sign. "There is suffering enough all about us. Let it go free. But like Roman augurs we will watch the bird closely." The little creature flew to the right. "The direction is toward the English cruiser, Your Majesty." "All in vain. In America, if *ennui* comes sulking in, I can travel a thousand miles away; and I shall never think of returning to France."

A sorrowful supper. The baggage was taken aboard the Danish vessel, but the escort was deluded into believing that the Emperor would go to the British.

In the fourth hour after midnight Las Cases and Lallemand visited the *Bellerophon* again, under the Parliament flag: "In order to save his people from further civil strife, the Emperor is willing to go into banishment. Is not England under obligation to reward such magnanimity, which assures the conclusion of peace, with fitting treatment?" "Yes, and so she will," said Captain Maitland. "England's people will not let themselves be outdone in nobility of feeling, and will gladly give the Emperor what befits him."

Return to shore. Council in the commandant's house. Fifteen hundred marines would be available; the garrisons of Rochefort and Rochelle would be won over; reënforcements from La Vendée might be hoped for. But what could such a handful do against the millions of the Quadruple Alliance? The throne of France was occupied, and the king was united with Bonaparte's enemies. Civil war would be a sanguinary and useless crime. All voices favored England. While still on Aix the Emperor wrote to the Prince Regent:

"Your Royal Highness! As a man assailed by the European powers and by the party fury which is devouring my own land, I am abandoning political life, and seeking, after the example of Themistocles, a refuge at the hearth of the British people. I put myself under the protection of its laws, and beg your Royal Highness, as the stubbornest and noblest of my foes, to afford me protection."

Gourgaud was to take the letter to England, to hire a country place there, and to make it a condition that Bonaparte was not to come to London by day, and was not to be compelled to go to an English colony.

Bonaparte left Aix on the corvette *Stanley;* went to Plymouth, but not to London. He could not speak with Lord Keith, commander of the Channel fleet. No landing. The corvette sailed to Torbay. There the *Bellerophon* lay at anchor. Napoleon Bonaparte on the evening of July 14 went aboard her as a free guest of the British people, he believed, but presently felt that he was a prisoner. Not, as yet, with painful distinctness.

He received Gourgaud at once, and heard that the letter had not been delivered; but still hoped that the promised intercession of Admiral Hotham would bring about a more tolerable state of affairs. The officers were courteous. One only, Captain Gambier, commander of the corvette, was rude, when Bertrand's wife asked him to lend her a newspaper: an evil omen. There was one consolation, the multitude of friendly curious visitors, eager to see the Emperor, whose boats surrounded the ship. Fruits, even, were sent aboard. That did not suit the commander. "No communication with the shore!" Rough words and musket-shots scared off the boats.

July 26. Arrival off Plymouth. What would happen? Bonaparte had been for thirty-five days no longer Emperor, for eleven on the water; and he still did not know what the immediate future was to bring him. Armed boats cut the cruiser off from all intercourse. Lord Keith did not come on board, but ordered Captain Maitland to come ashore to him. The captain returned with clouded brow, was taciturn, and when asked why two frigates had anchored to port and starboard of the cruiser, replied, "Commands of the Admiralty!"

Next morning he went ashore again, and at Bonaparte's desire took the Themistocles letter with him. On his return he brought word that the admiral was coming, but without salute with cannon, so that higher honors might not be paid to him than to His Majesty. That pleased the ear of the powerless one. Yesterday an evil rumor had crept through the cabins, "It is to the Tower!" "No, it is to St. Helena, and the two frigates carry the guards." Even now Bonaparte remained calm. "I am here of my own free will. What conditions I made, my letter to the Regent states. Respond to my confidence with gross treachery? Foolish gossip!"

The sky was bright, the sea covered with pleasure boats. "Thousands,—all England," Las Cases says, "seem to be on a pilgrimage to Plymouth." Music. The exiles lifted their heads. Many men, women and children waved the red carnation, the Emperor's flower. A hundred lips greeted with good wishes the man who appeared on deck at five. Only,—from the papers a different tone emanated; malicious, sinking to gross slander. Finally, on the 28th, Keith came; he was very polite, but stayed only twenty minutes with the Emperor. On the last day of July he brought with him the Secretary of State, Bunbury, who presented a communication from the British government:

"We should neglect our most important duty to our country and to the Allies of our King, if we left to General Bonaparte any possibility of again disturbing the peace of Europe. This consideration must precede all others. The freedom of the general cannot remain unrestrained. As place of residence we have chosen for him the island of St. Helena, where the climate is healthful, and the location makes possible the surveillance of his person without too vexatious precautionary regulations. Three officers of his suite (not Savary nor Lallemand) and the physician Maingaud may accompany the general; but may not

thereafter leave the island without the permission of
the English government.   Rear Admiral Sir George
Cockburn will have charge of the transportation and
will be ready for the outward voyage within a few
days."

The blood of the Latin mountaineer boiled. "Rather
shed the last drop here, on the spot, than go to such
dishonor! Woe to England if it repays in this fashion
the highest honor it was possible to imagine!" The
admiral begged him to give him his refusal in writing,
and received the leaf on which stands, approximately:
"I am a guest, not a prisoner. Rather death than St.
Helena."   Savary and Lallemand also invoked, in
writing, the protection of the British laws (but were
taken to Fort Manuel, at Malta).

After the storm the Corsican was soon quiet again.
On the very first of August he asked Las Cases whether
he might count on him as a companion, and seemed
rejoiced at his assent. On the 2nd he said: "No doubt
I shall have to go. Sometimes, indeed, the desire seizes
me to end it all. Then you could go home to your
families. No forebodings would hinder me; I do not
believe in punishment in the Beyond. The conception
of God's infinite goodness contradicts it, and why
should God punish the desire to come quickly into His
kingdom? But still, a man must not slink away from
his destiny, but must wrestle with it." ("In resistance
to agony of spirit manly courage shows itself as bril-
liantly as under the enemy's fire. He who kills himself, in order no longer to suffer in soul, is like the
coward who before victory runs from the battlefield."
So had the First Consul written in an army order after

the suicide of two grenadiers, in the month Floréal of the year X.) "I will describe my life experiences. Work! Only with the sickle of work are the harvests of time to be gathered. It can be done!"

He was calm, jested at Grand Marshal Bertrand's wife, who heaped dismal reproaches on her husband, General Gourgaud and others, determined (in mockery of the men's ideas on suicide) to throw herself into the water, and was pleased, really delighted, over the quantity of red carnations from the shore and the boats that glimmered in the harbor waters. "Just like hope. Can treason make its home where earnest loyalty watches?"

In the grey of the fourth August dawn the anchors were weighed. English papers had announced that General Bonaparte would be transferred to the *Northumberland*. That ship, it was said, was still being equipped at Portsmouth. Whither, then, the voyage? The Emperor would not see anyone, and would not eat. The rumor was, "He has taken poison." No. Las Cases writes down, in the Channel, the Emperor's protest directed to Keith:

"Before God and Mankind I hereby protest solemnly against the violation of my most sacred rights, and the violence that robs me of my freedom. Of my own free will I came aboard the *Bellerophon*, whose captain had sent word to me that he was directed by his government to bring me to England if it was my wish—as a guest, therefore, not as a prisoner. In good faith I placed myself under the law of England, whose soil I trod when I came aboard this ship. If I have been enticed into a trap by the government which authorized the captain to receive me with that promise, then it has defiled its flag and forfeited its honor. Never again can Britons boast of their integrity, or of the security of justice and freedom in their home. The hospitality of the deck of the *Bellerophon* would bury forever all belief in British good faith. I await with confidence the judgment of history. An enemy, it will say, that had fought England for two decades, came of his own free will, in misfortune, to Britain's hearth. By putting himself under English law, he gave the strongest proof of the respect and confidence which he brought to his old enemy. And how did England requite that high-hearted decision? She made a hypocritical pretence of hospitality to her enemy, offered him her hand, and, when he clasped it, pushed him to destruction!"

He hesitated, then signed: "Napoleon."

On the 6th, after a day of rough weather and general seasickness, the ship came to anchor. Bunbury, Cockburn and Keith came on board. Order of the government: "The Frenchmen are to be deprived of all arms. After the transfer to *H.M.S. Northumberland* Sir George Cockburn is to make a careful examination of General Bonaparte's baggage. Books, wines, furniture are to be passed; also silver, if it is limited to ordinary daily use, and does not appear to be an asset, the sale of which could enrich the possessor. Gold, paper money, diamonds, are to be surrendered. The government of Great Britain does not confiscate them, but takes them into its charge and control. If it should not do so, the escape of the prisoners would be facilitated. Principal or interest will be expended only for the personal needs of the general and those who accompany him, his desire as to the disposition of them carried out as far as possible, the costs of administration borne by the English treasury, and after the death of the general all the provisions of his will to be carried out implicitly to the smallest detail. The Admiral is to take also three officers of the general's suite, who present themselves of their own free will, and are prepared to submit to every measure requisite for security of the prisoner. An attempt of the general to escape would be punished by imprisonment. The same penalty would befall whoever aided him. Letters written by the general and his companions or addressed to them are to be examined by the Admiral or the Governor of the island before delivery. The final appeal on important decisions is to His Majesty's government. Wishes and complaints of the general are to be handed in on unsealed sheets, so that the Admiral or Governor can append to them any remarks that seemed to them necessary." A set of prison regulations.

Wearisome discussion over choice and number of companions. Final decision: Bertrand, Gourgaud, Montholon and Las Cases (as private secretary, so a civilian) go with him. Each officer received a money belt which contained sixteen thousand francs. The Emperor secretly entrusted to Las Cases a leather purse containing the necklace which Queen Hortense had given him before his departure from Malmaison. (This the faithful Las Cases kept on his person, but forgot about it at his departure from Longwood, and it was by the hand of an Englishman that he was able

to restore it to the Emperor.) Las Cases, also, delivered the protest to Keith. The latter ("a handsome
old man with the finest social manners") was extremely
courteous, but avoided all oral communication, and
gave his decisions in writing.

Count Las Cases, himself a marine officer, accordingly laid before him all sorts of grievances: "The
Emperor is furious at the thought of the rummaging
through his baggage; he would rather throw it into
the sea. His legs are swollen, and the sea-voyage may
prove dangerous for him. Captain Maitland has acted
deceitfully." At that for the first time Keith became
excited: "Captain Maitland is no trifler and no villain! What the government has ordered must be done.
Is it not an especial honor that General Bonaparte, as
an unique exception, may keep his sword?"

Cockburn came with a customs official for the examination of the baggage. Eighty thousand francs were
taken in charge. Gourgaud begged that he might retain his servant, and heard out of Cockburn's mouth:
"That's how it is with these famous French officers:
the mere loss of a servant seems to them unbearable!"
Departure of Savary (who was to keep the money in
the belt) and of Lallemand (to whom the Dane's lad-
ing, worth thirty thousand francs, was assigned) from
the *Bellerophon*. Maitland declined the Emperor's
valuable snuff-box, his first and second officers accepted
pistols.

A launch conveyed the little group to the *Northumberland*. All the sailors on deck. Also four members
of Parliament. The Emperor greeted them pleasantly,
remained on deck, talked with the officers and mem-

bers, had dinner with his companions at seven. He learned that a ship's cutter had run down a boatload of inquisitive visitors, and two people were drowned. At eleven he went to bed. The ship sailed, under Cockburn's admiral's flag, for St. Helena.

To prison.

The accommodations on board ship were not bad. Sleeping chamber (with the usual camp-bed), dining room, and chief claim to the use of the ship's salon. But:—"You are a prisoner of war, General!" Not "Emperor." Not one before whom one uncovers and stands at attention. The suite redoubled their evidences of reverence. Cockburn says: "An Englishman will never understand the servile devotion of these people, shall never see it without contempt and disgust."

Bonaparte had intended to be known in America at Col. Duroc or Muiron. "That I am addressed here only as 'General' does not hurt me. I remain none the less what I am." However, it did irritate him, and later he himself acknowledged that it was then that he began in earnest to underscore his imperial title. Had he given up? At the mouth of the Channel, in a tempestuous night, he stormed: "Oh, I ought to have stayed in Egypt! Arabia is waiting for a Man. I would have thrown an army into Judæa and become Lord of the Orient." The days were long. He read much, played chess or "Vingt-et-un"; did not dress fully until dinner. For that the Admiral always appeared with two officers.

In the Tuileries, or in the field, dinner had never

lasted more than fifteen minutes, here, an hour and a half. And music at table. And English cooking. Horrible! Napoleon said little (Las Cases was interpreter). As soon as the coffee was drunk he hurried on deck, and walked there till dark. One day like another.

On the high seas off Lisbon four French ships were sighted. Rescuers?—No!

The only (and curious) August delight:—on his birthday Bonaparte, who almost always lost, won eighty Napoleons at cards.

Over Madeira blew the sirocco. At Funchal cattle and fowls, fruits, wine and water were hastily brought aboard. The heat increased. The General was learning English, played piquet and whist, busied himself with square and cube root, equations of the second and third degree, watched the polisher as he cleaned the rust-spots from the sword of Aboukir, then from that of Maifeld.

Though he had himself passed the equator before, he promised a hundred Napoleons on the day of "crossing the line" to the sailors who were disguised as Neptune, Amphitrite, and the other water-folk:— but he could not get them from Bertrand, his treasurer, nor from the Admiral, who urged that five were enough. Memories and thoughts were dictated, dolphins and sharks watched, questions of belief, history and natural science discussed. "Man is child of the atmosphere and of 'electricity' . . ." "Waterloo? If the battle were to be fought once more!"

On the 14th of October, at seven in the evening, St. Helena came in sight. As if out of dimly glimmer-

ing fire Bonaparte's glance flashed into the distance.
Next noon Colonel Wilkes, representative of the India
Company, came aboard, and stated that the island
(now put in the direct control of the British government) had over two thousand inhabitants, two-thirds
of them slaves. The admiral praised the location of
Longwood village. "You will feel comfortable, General!" Bonaparte observed from the deck the land
now near at hand. Bare rocks. A village closely
hemmed in. "Where am I to live? If I had only
stayed in Egypt! Today the whole Orient would be
subject to me. These English do not know what magnanimity is. Paoli was right, they are shopkeepers!"

After the landing: "My little house, my wretched
hut, clings like a nest to the hot rock-wall. My suite
is far away, and when they come to me they are
escorted by an English soldier. Bread, butter, oil,
coffee: all unappetizing. These villains! Instead of
a bullet the long death-agony! The gang do not even
display the courage needed for open murder. And the
kings of Europe, who called me brother, endure this
outrage against the sacred law of nations! I marched
as victor into their capitals. Did I treat one of them
as England treats me? She recognizes no law of
nations; she is crueler than the savage who kills his
captive. Tenfold better dead than clamped to this
rock. I will be stronger than my fate, uplift myself
on high above it. But the order to shoot me down
would ring in my ears as a blessed message of deliverance at hand. Woe is me, that my blind confidence drove me upon the *Bellerophon,* into the snares
of the faithless British people!"

Prince William of Prussia wrote to Berlin: "Nöppel is to be taken to St. Helena. Another rocky island. When we heard of it, almost all of us said, 'He's sure to come back again.' I too am convinced of it."

He came back no more. Britain's trap held him fast. Bellerophon's curse works even into the age of enlightenment. Suicide? "Only dastards kill themselves." To Gourgaud and Montholon he said that. To the Irish physician O'Meara, "To suffer is harder than to die; and he who kills himself does himself a wrong."

Did any hope remain? To his companions, who were considering whether they should go to Cape Colony, he said: "I shall be in Paris before one of you gets to the Cape." That, after the sinking of the hundred suns that saw him in renewed imperial glory. Above him the sky, and before his eyes, always, the ocean, England's sea. Round about him Britain's guards on guard. If there came an eagle, he would come from Zeus.

So died Bonaparte. So he that was chained to the naked rock lives in the consciousness of mankind.

> "Rejoice, that never soul more proud
> In hateful Golgotha hath bowed.
> Far from his weary ashes, then,
> Be any bitter word of tongue or pen!"

So the aged Goethe wrote, when with chilled brain he translated into (hardly legible) German Manzoni's pompously resonant ode *The Fifth of May*. Over his unwonted and thankless task he no doubt recalled the hour when the Emperor, after a single glance at him, greeted him with the cry, "Voilà un homme!" (*Ecce homo,* that is; though a thousand theologians grunt in horror at the word.)

In that immortal interview, which revealed the Emperor to the poet as a late-born branch from the same stock as Prometheus, Cæsar, Mohammed, there fell from Bonaparte's lip, also, as if to avert the doom of ancient tragedy, the profound word: "The political life is our destiny." Not merely in a dramatic sense was it meant; nor was it simply a reminder that Chance, Fate, and the rest of mythology are dead and that progress, movement of mankind, must be brought about by force in a more modern sense. Rather was it the word of a new Roman, who conceived the State to be the all-moulding world-creator; the word of a man wholly possessed by his thoughts, by the pure Idea within himself, who even on the battlefield, in his gray overcoat and tricorne *sans cocade* (he never wore a general's uniform), on horseback, is always spiritual-minded, abstracted from reality.

As a boy he hardly ever played. He sat in the little attic room of his parents' house in Ajaccio, and read: If he had to come among human beings, to eat, he was speechless; and if he did speak, it did not seem a child's voice. Once at table it was discussed, how the constant ferment in Corsica might be reduced to quiet and repose. "Ten days of Pasha rule would do more for that than ten years of a government like yours." The boy of eleven threw that in the face of M. de Marbeuf, governor of the island (and friend of his mother, the beautiful and gifted Letitia), and then climbed back to his bookworm's retreat.

At Valence the boy-lieutenant of artillery pointed out new possibilities for the improvement of his gun. At Nice he read aloud in a wine shop his plan for a war against Italy, and two years later, according to ,Volney's testimony, carried it out to the minutest detail, just as he had constructed it, in seventeen paragraphs.

A younger brother of Robespierre had introduced Napoleon to him, and after that leader's fall Napoleon was to have been expelled, as "incapable," from the military section of the Committee of Safety. However, he was protected by Carnot; and Josephine's friend Barras raised him to the rank of Commander. When, on the 13th of Vendémiaire he had saved the government, he was named as commander of the army in Italy.

"This meager stripling, this youth of twenty-five, who shows everybody his pretty wife's picture, and surely owes his rank to some perfumed petticoat,— he is to lead us?" So whispered Masséna and other generals. He announced his plan of attack for the next day, and in ten minutes the corps of officers knew. "He has the brains of a leader."

Even in Italy he was planning the descent on the English coast. He went to Egypt as commander-in-chief. When he landed at Fréjus he was borne to Paris on the huzzas of the multitude, whose sole remaining hope he was, and named First Consul. . . . The Pope crowned him. The ruling house of Austria provided him his second wife. He gave his brothers the crowns of Holland, Westphalia, Naples, Spain; in Cairo and in Moscow his will was law; all the kings of the old continent did homage to him, the alien plebeian, who never learned to speak French well, confused such words as "section" and "session," "armistice" and "amnestie,"—but whom the voting power of four million Frenchmen called to an emperor's throne.

His vitality seemed inexhaustible. Fourteen hours in the saddle, five days' fighting (against Alvinczy), a continuous journey from Warsaw to Paris, then a long bath (he often slept an hour in the tub), and immediately thereafter he was fresh and weighty in the council. Whether to bed at eight in the evening or five in the morning did not matter. No consultation could end until he had managed to view the matter clearly from all sides.

A hundred times over, the magical strength of his memory was attested. At a reception of delegates he asked a man from southern France, before whose house he had rested for a minute eleven years before and whom he had never seen since, how his daughters were. During a campaign in Spain he corrected a report as to the number of cannon on the rampart of a west Prussian fortress. 'Twelve hundred rations to provision the corps at Fontenay? It was not there; nonsense! It was on the day at Rochefort. Your records don't agree, Dejean!" Always, for a whole decade, in every case, it proved that he was right.

On the throne he grew stout, and fell into uncouth manners; rose from the table before the soup was served, and the guests quaked in fear of dire disfavor.

He hummed or whistled a tune as he passed between lines of courtesying ladies. He said to old men: "With you 'tis soon over"; to ladies: "Good Lord: I was told you were pretty!" He asked young girls if they had children. He smeared every piece of paper, scratched or cut ruinously all furniture with knives or files, shattered the finest Sèvres china, trampled beds of violets, snapped hothouse flowers off their stems, shot out of the window at rare singing birds.

Honor and virtue? "Abstractions that come to nothing." Women? "Josephine was, Marie Louise is, an angel: but the rest? Merely means for enjoyment." "Duroc, *une femme!*"—That in the midst of the dictation of a decree. He took a sudden whim for one or another, and robbed her husband or lover of her; poured wine on her dress at the court table, and led her into the bedroom to cleanse it.

Chaptal, his Minister of the Interior, was the possessor of Bourgoing, actress at the Comédie. The Emperor desired her. Chaptal must go as ambassador to Vienna, to Madrid, to Constantinople. But he believed he was not fitted for diplomacy. Then he must go—elsewhere! During an evening audience to Chaptal, the court chamberlain announced: "Mademoiselle Bourgoing." "She is to wait." The minister hastily stuffed his papers into his portfolio and left; and while his mistress spent the night with Napoleon he wrote his resignation. It was accepted. Yet his master redoubled his favor and confidence in the retired minister; and the realization that even this earnest statesmanlike spirit soon forgot this gross insult is dainty food for the self-satisfaction of the arch-contemner of mankind.

"What for others are essential conditions of life bind me not at all." Only from his lips does this not have the ring of a comedian's boast. Talma taught him to bear himself like a prince. In the burning Kremlin, amid the smoking ruins of his most cherished plan, he wrote the statutes of the Comédie Française, to this day the model for all theater codes.

But he himself played comedy only when he chose. He could be the soberest statistician, and dig to the very heart of a wholly novel problem in agriculture, manufactures, or trade.

"The English produce more goods than they need to consume, accustom their people to comfort, and, as soon as the export sales fall off, are threatened with uprisings. I have shown the continental states how they can get on without insatiable England, but they will not hearken to me." *

Out of his calm repose comes a sudden roar, his Dæmon rises, and the storm of his breath breaks the delicate machinery of his brain-like rushes.

"Madness, to wed an archduchess, to ally myself by marriage with the old forces! I am the son of the Revolution. Tilsit was worthless rubbish. Only in Constantinople can I dictate my terms of peace: only from the Ganges can I liberate Europe!"

"He was stronger than human society," says Nietzsche. "Ambition served by genius, with three Atlases in his brain," declares Taine. Does it suffice?

---

* Translator's note: This is Mr. Harden's own chief article of economic faith.

An elemental force. A destroyer and a creator. An earthquake, a world-flood, a volcano. His conquests were swept away, crashed down to ruin, sank deep. But the world was a different thing from that into which he came. Tyrant, defiler of justice, mower-down of peoples, he was nevertheless also a sower of justice, a liberator, a doer of deeds, an eternal experience for the spiritual-minded.

An island bore him, on another the eye of his hate was ever fixed, whether from the Tagus, the Nile or the Moskva, an island became his cage and his tomb. It was as if the sea must ever part him, his rise and his fall, from human communion.

In the young general's field library the Bible and the Koran stood in the section labeled "Politics." And politics, remember, he called "our destiny." Jehovah, Jesus, Allah, Mohammed,—means to a political end. Or were they mere steps to the temple of self-deification? The dry island-rock drinks the belated echo of the primeval legend:

"Hybris cast him, drunk with victory and with the delight of action, from the steep summitward path down into the desolate abyss."

THE END